Praise for Abba Hillel Silver's
Where Judaism Differs

"A major literary effort . . . Judaism's case has rarely been more effectively stated." —*American Judaism*

"Dr. Silver's book is written out of a profound conviction that Judaism is intrinsically valuable, and his eloquent arguments can do much to dispel the stereotyped image of Judaism . . ." —*Commentary*

"An important and distinguished book . . . it is magnificent and brilliant . . ." —*The Journal of Bible and Religion*

"Perhaps this book marks a turning point in religious literature. . . . Here, undoubtedly, is one of the great religious scholars of our time." —*Church Management*

WHERE JUDAISM
DIFFERS

*An Inquiry into the Distinctiveness
of Judaism*

Abba Hillel Silver

COLLIER BOOKS
Macmillan Publishing Company
New York
Collier Macmillan Publishers
London

Collier Books
Macmillan Publishing Company
866 Third Avenue, New York, NY 10022
Collier Macmillan Canada, Inc.

Library of Congress Cataloging-in-Publication Data
Silver, Abba Hillel, 1893–1963.
[Where Judaism differed]
Where Judaism differs: an inquiry into the distinctiveness of
Judaism/Abba Hillel Silver.
p.   cm.
Originally published under title: *Where Judaism differed*. New York:
Macmillan, 1956.
Bibliography: p.
Includes index.
ISBN 0-02-037221-3
1. Judaism—Essence, genius, nature. 2. Judaism—Apologetic
works. 3. Judaism—Relations—Christianity. 4. Christianity and
other religions—Judaism. I. Title.
[BM565.S52   1989]
296—dc19   89-30756   CIP

Macmillan books are available at special discounts for bulk purchases
for sales promotions, premiums, fund-raising, or educational use.
For details, contact:

Special Sales Director
Macmillan Publishing Company
866 Third Avenue
New York, NY 10022

Acknowledgment is hereby made to Oxford University Press, Inc.
for permission to quote from *A Study of History*, Volumes IV and V
by Arnold J. Toynbee, copyright 1945 by Oxford University Press.

Originally published in hardcover by The Macmillan Company, 1956

First Collier Books edition 1989

10 9 8 7 6 5 4 3 2 1

Printed in the United States of America

To
Virginia and our beloved sons,
Daniel Jeremy and Raphael David

ACKNOWLEDGMENTS

I wish to express my profound indebtedness to my esteemed friend, the eminent scholar, Professor Solomon Zeitlin of Dropsie College for the many valuable suggestions and comments which he made in the course of a careful reading of the manuscript.

I had frequent occasions to discuss the subject matter of this book with my son, Rabbi Daniel Jeremy Silver, and I profited from his fine insights and his illuminating observations.

I am especially grateful to my young and gifted friend, Harold P. Manson, for the painstaking and meticulous care which he took in preparing the manuscript for publication and for the sound and considerable counsel he gave both as to its content and form.

I also wish to thank Miss Miriam Leikind, Librarian of The Temple, for graciously volunteering to compile the Index.

ABBA HILLEL SILVER

Cleveland, Ohio
September 1956

FOREWORD

My father originally titled his book *Where Judaism Differs*. His publishers put the title in the past tense. The book appeared during the comfortable days of the Eisenhower era, when many people believed, or at least wanted to believe, that the hates and wars of the past could be left behind and that one way to hasten this happy event was to bury, once and for all, old controversies and prejudices.

The editors shared a view, popular at that time, that arguments about religion were feckless, as pointless as the medieval debates about how many angels could dance on the head of a pin. Why so? How could anyone claim title to The Truth in an age which had learned the truth of relativity. Whatever Heaven was, if there was a Heaven, entrance was not restricted to one set of believers. Judaism and Christianity were not distinct religious traditions but variations of a single theme, the so-called Judeo-Christian tradition.

My father had written an essay on the special integrity of Judaism. The book was as its subtitle maintained: "An Inquiry into the Distinctiveness of Judaism." Neither Christianity nor the other religious systems were set up as straw men, foils for self-serving arguments. The editors recognized that *Where Judaism Differed* was not a polemic. They wanted the title changed, not the text. As far as I have ever understood their concern, it was a personal one that no one should be able to charge them with publishing a book which insisted that religious difference still mattered, that there were and are significant differences in the values each religious tradition expresses and the approaches it takes.

Where Judaism Differed spoke to and for a religious community that had only recently faced the fires of hell, the Holocaust,
and not only survived but found the will and the strength to
reestablish their national home. For much of the previous century, Jews, eager to be accepted, had soft-pedalled the distinctiveness of their tradition. No longer. The postwar generation was determined to be itself. Christian civilization had
hardly distinguished itself. Dr. Silver spelled out for that
generation the vitality, usefulness, and importance of their
way—a way, he believed, that had much to offer not only to
Jews but also to the world. Two world wars and a worldwide
depression suggested to him that the atmosphere of pessimism
and the emphasis on other-worldly salvation encouraged by
other traditions not only diverted human energy from crucial
social and political tasks but diminished the spirit and so was
the ultimate cause of those dark emotions that fueled anti-
Semitism, chauvinism, and militarism.

When it was published, some criticized the book on the
grounds that it did not give sufficient attention to the institutions of Jewish life, particularly the role of law. Dr. Silver had
not intended a manual on the Jewish way. He had undertaken
a more difficult task, to search out and express the integrity of
Judaism. Judaism, he felt, had been shaped by a fierce commitment to the oneness of God and the unity of the human
family; a steady faith in God's redemptive grace, coupled with
an uncompromising insistence that humans must do their
part; an affirmation of human capacity and moral freedom;
and a preference for careful reason over impulse, for an active
life over withdrawal, and for moderation over excess, even an
excess of piety and confidence that humans could have a happy
future on earth.

A more substantial criticism was voiced by those who
argued that during its long history Judaism had taken a variety
of shapes and that a book such as this necessarily defined and
defended one set of themes and, therefore, paid too little attention to these variations. The argument has merit, but if followed

strictly any and all discussions of the thematic and attitudinal content of the classic religions would be precluded. Medieval Christianity produced Francis of Assisi and bloodthirsty, loot-seeking Crusaders. Does this mean that we cannot discuss the nature of Christianity?

Dr. Silver set out to paint a picture of Judaism as he perceived it. He knew others had provided, and would provide, other views. Two artists will paint the same scene with quite different results, yet the value of their work is not diminished by the fact that the two pictures are not identical. Dr. Silver knew that serious discussion of basic religious themes must sometimes transcend the logical constraints of academic scholarship, and can do so successfully when informed by broad learning. He also believed such discussion was essential in a world where questions of values remained central. The world needed to rethink its commitments.

The continuing popularity of this book testifies to its success as an art form. It is not an easy book to read. Many have told me that they kept a dictionary at their side, but also that the benefit was worth the effort.

—Daniel Jeremy Silver

CONTENTS

PREFACE

Emil L. Fackenheim

Abba Hillel Silver is remembered most widely as an architect of the State of Israel. Among American Zionists he was a giant. In mid-war, when other American Jewish leaders were still prepared to settle for something less than Jewish statehood in Palestine, he was uncompromising. Once, in 1943, at a gathering of Jewish leaders in New York, he broke a "gentleman's agreement" not to raise controversial issues, and rose to declare:

> We cannot truly rescue the Jews of Europe unless we have free immigration into Palestine. We cannot have free immigration into Palestine unless our political rights are recognized there. Our political rights cannot be recognized unless our historic connection with the country is acknowledged and our right to rebuild our national home is reaffirmed. These are inseparable links in the chain. The whole chain breaks if one of the links is missing.

Silver had not been among the scheduled speakers. Yet when, defiantly, he rose to speak, these words received a thunderous applause. Since 1933 Jews had been homeless, more so than ever before: what they needed in Palestine was not more visas but control of immigration. Since 1939 they were defenseless victims of mass murder, this, too, more so than ever before: what they needed was not only defense by others but also the means of defending themselves, i.e., an army. Both these needs could be filled only by a Jewish state.

As well as a political leader, Silver was a considerable Jewish scholar and an exponent of Judaism. His was a liberal Judaism, and of this *Where Judaism Differs* is the chief statement. When first pub-

lished in 1956, the book bore the title *Where Judaism Differed*. Only
from the foreword to a recent edition, by Daniel Jeremy Silver, did I
learn that this change of tense was made by the editors. Such a
decision, made without an author's explicit consent, is surely aston-
ishing. I wonder whether the younger Silver is not too charitable in
his explanation—that these were the comfortable Eisenhower years
in which everything was relative, in which religious differences no
longer mattered, and in which, if there was a Heaven, the ways into it
were numberless. Would the editors have changed the tense of a book
entitled *Where Christianity Differs?* I think not.

The 1950s *were* comfortable. Will Silver's liberal Judaism still
speak to the 1980s and 1990s, which are comfortable no more? Doubt
may be raised on three scores. First, Silver has "Judaism" teach this
and that: this may jar Jewish readers today as being too easy, taught
as they are by Martin Buber that "-isms" are abstractions, and by
Gershom Scholem, that heterodox kabbalistic mysticism is not to be
ignored. Second, for Silver, religion is "the supreme art of humanity," and therefore Judaism, a human ascent to God; he pays no
attention to those, such as Kierkegaard in Christianity and Buber
and Rosenzweig in Judaism, who have long distrusted so great a trust
in the merely human and have renewed the age-old quest of Revelation, i.e., a descent of God to man. Surely the greatest doubt
concerns yet a third score, and Silver's commitment here may help
explain his stand on the other two. The most terrible war of all times
had ended a decade before. So had the greatest catastrophe of the
Jewish people in its long history. But in the still-comfortable 1950s
Silver had not yet abandoned the nineteenth-century belief in the
steady moral progress of mankind. He wrote:

> Mankind has come a long way, to be sure. It has indeed perceptively
> advanced through the long centuries, but how slowly! And how dark
> and perilous still are our times!

Three decades later a Jew can no longer view the Holocaust as a lapse
that, to be sure, has arrested the march of progress but cannot stop it.

As for the world, it can no longer ignore the threat of nuclear catastrophe.

Written in the comfortable Eisenhower years, then, the book seems to have its own share of comfortableness. Then why, nevertheless, does *Where Judaism Differs* give today's reader so much strength? Because of the book's own strength. The title that the original editors chose to change says it all. Silver does not engage in what he calls "competitive theology": he shows wide knowledge of, and much sympathy with, other religions and various philosophies. If even so he stresses where Judaism differed; if he makes it clear that it continues to differ; if, indeed, he veritably celebrates the difference: all this is because he is filled with love and awe by the "remarkable constancy, unparalleled in all history, of a people to an idea."

To read *Where Judaism Differs* is to be reminded of the fact that there are two kinds of liberalism, and hence of liberal Judaism. Both risk self-exposure to whatever may be the thought, life, and thus challenge of an age, and in this openness lies the quality they share. But whereas the openness of the one is near-empty, so that its eagerness to be up to date makes it easy prey to the latest "life-style," the other, "constant" in convictions already found and tested, tests them yet again in each self-exposure. And while it may emerge with a "yes" to some ideas or life-styles dominant at a given time, it may emerge also with a "no" to others. The liberal Judaism of *Where Judaism Differs* is of the latter kind.

Constancy is not the hallmark of liberalism today, or of its liberal Judaism. The times do not favor it. For liberals of Silver's kind, this is, of course, a paradoxical thing to say, since it is precisely such times that require constancy most of all. Consider how Silver sees Judaism differ in sexual mores in the late Roman Empire, when the writings of Seneca and others

> reveal the moral degeneration of Roman society, in which promiscuity, sodomy and lesbianism were widely practiced. . . . They help us to realize the violent contrast between the standards of this society and the Jewish standards of sexual decency, the sanctity of marriage

and family life. . . . To the Sages of Israel sexual perversion was under the curse of God.

Evidently Silver celebrates how Judaism differed in sexual mores from late Roman society. Evidently his own liberal Judaism persists in this difference in 1956 and would doubtless do so today. More than doubtful, however, is that this particular constancy would have many liberal followers today.

Even so, readers of every kind today might be persuaded by the book that there is something to Jewish constancy; indeed, that they cannot do without it. The oneness of God; the equality of all and equal justice due to all; the love due to the poor; the sanctity of human life; the honor attaching to labor; the view that life is better than death: all these convictions, Silver shows overwhelmingly, originate not in Athens or Rome but in Jerusalem. That was in the distant past. Closer to the present is that, if the Founding Fathers of the American Republic accepted as "self-evident" what is far from so— "that all men are created equal and that they are endowed by their Creator with certain unalienable rights—," it was due to their own "constancy" to an "idea" originating in Jerusalem.

The turbulence of the times is a threat to American as well as Jewish constancy. It is a threat also to Zionist constancy. One is tempted to ask how the man who once called so firmly for Jewish statehood would react to the turbulence surrounding the Jewish state today. Would he have predicted that half a century later the state, then yet unborn, would still be besieged by enemies? Would he have foreseen that the siege would divide Israelis themselves into opposing groups, with the extremists of one calling for maximum concessions to the enemy, the extremists of the other warning against minimum ones, each fearing that the policy advocated by the other might lead to the state's destruction? He could have foreseen none of these things, and any attempt to guess his reaction is inadmissible.

One thing, however, Abba Hillel Silver, a wise man as well as a forthright one, might have foreseen—that too many good people of the world, rather than blame those laying the siege, would blame the besieged. In his *A Study of History*, Arnold Toynbee had castigated the "intransigent" Jews who had fought under Bar Kochba for independence against Roman tyranny, even as elsewhere he had praised British heroism that, in two wars, had fought off Teutonic tyranny. Silver asks:

> Why do theologians and theologic historians become so sanctimoniously international and "spiritual" when it comes to the national interests of the Jewish people, while remaining so patriotically national and "worldly" when it comes to the interests of their own people?

One reads this statement, considers the 1950s and the 1980s, and concludes that the more certain things change the more they remain the same.

INTRODUCTION

There arose among the people of Israel in ancient times a group of men who had a message for their nation and for mankind, which made of Israel a distinct people everywhere for nearly three thousand years. These men were not unaware of the novel and revolutionary nature of their message. They foresaw that they were thrusting a unique mission upon their people, as yet unprepared for it, and the lonely ordeal of a leadership which would set them at war with the world. They had no choice in uttering their message, and they gave their people no choice in accepting it. The burden of spiritual compulsion was theirs, and it came to abide also with their people through the long centuries and amidst many strange vicissitudes of fortune. By it the world came to be profoundly agitated, and the spirit of man was quickened to new adventures in faith and social aspiration.

They were the founders of Judaism, a challenging and differing faith. In later times and in other settings their basic ideas gave impulse and substance to Christianity and to Islam. These prophets and their successors fashioned a way of life for men, which like some strong Gulf Stream flowed for centuries steadily and discernibly through the great waters of humanity.

These men did not carve in marble or cast in bronze, or fashion dramatic art and epic of ageless beauty, or mold the subtle syllogism, or pioneer in the natural sciences, or build large empires or set their victorious triremes sailing the highways of the seas. They developed a clean and noble art of life for men and nations, without which, as we have witnessed in our day, the populous city becomes a heap and man reverts to the jungle.

In subsequent ages gifted sons and daughters of Israel were to achieve distinction in many fields of art and science as well, and in some of them even rare eminence; but in none did the genius of the people of Israel express itself as uniquely, as creatively, and as momentously as in the realm of the moral and the spiritual.

They were not technical theologians, these men who fashioned Judaism, nor did the faith which they founded ever boast of a systematic theology or a science of ethics. There is no attempt to formulate a systematic Jewish theology until the early Middle Ages, almost a thousand years after the final canonization of the Bible, more than two thousand years after Moses. In the Bible and Talmud the doctrines of Judaism are nowhere presented in the unified form of a treatise. They are broadly diffused in prophetic utterances, legal codes, history, poetry, precept, parable, and drama.

There were, of course, many theologians and philosophers among the Jewish people, especially in later times, and some of them were not wanting in great speculative power, but Judaism is not based upon their theology or philosophy. These religious philosophers, in successive generations, employed whatever philosophic thought was current in their day, from Platonism to Existentialism, to defend or to corroborate the basic tenets of their faith, "to prove the ideas of the Torah by correct reasoning." [1] Although metaphysical speculation was not native to Israel, Judaism welcomed the light of reason to elucidate the truths which it proclaimed. It never based itself on any radical skepticism of knowledge, and never urged men to say, "Credo quia absurdum est." It did not restrict itself to rationalism, but it never justified itself by antirationalism. It did not distrust reason in matters of faith, but it never viewed reason as the source of faith or its final arbiter. It revered the human intellect as a divine endowment and taught men to pray daily, "O, favor us with knowledge, understanding and intelligence," [2] but it knew the limits of discursive reasoning. Jewish philosophers like Philo, Maimonides, and Crescas were often profound and original in their metaphysical insights, and they influenced the development of philosophic thought generally. Their conclusions, however, were preordained by the very nature of their self-imposed task. They began with God and the Torah and they never wandered any distance away from them. The author of the *Letter of Aristeas* (2 c. B.C.) noted: "For in their conduct and discourse these men [the Sages who were sent from Palestine to Alexandria to translate the Bible into Greek] were far in advance of the philosophers, for they made *their starting-point* from God." [8]

Men enamored of compact systems will have difficulty in grasping the essence of Judaism, because it is not a tidy and precise arrangement of concepts, any more than history is. But just as history, in spite of its troughs and crests and its patent incongruities, manifests a clear upward movement in human development, so does Judaism reveal in its development the progress and perseverance of a group of cardinal spiritual and ethical ideas. Judaism held high a light in the darkness of the world. Not all the darkness is dispelled, but there is enough light to guide man along his way, and society to a fuller and happier life.

A clear knowledge of God, Judaism maintained, is possible to no one, but an acceptable worship of God is possible to everyone. This profound truth was made known to the foremost among the prophets, Moses, who when seeking to discover the nature of God was told that the face of God was forever hidden from mortal man, but that he might learn much about "all the goodness" of God (Ex. 33:18–23). This was then revealed to him in the thirteen moral attributes (Ex. 34:6–7). In Judaism the true worship of God does not culminate in a mystic ecstasy, or an inner "experience" of God, or in the "identification" of the worshiper with God, but in the good life. "And you shall do what is right and good in the sight of the Lord" (Dt. 6:18).

The accent in Judaism is never on abstract speculation but on an ethical message and a program. Many of the basic theologic and philosophic problems which engaged the minds of men through the ages are propounded in Biblical and Rabbinic literature, and receive various degrees of attention, but the strong emphasis is always on moral action. "The beginning of wisdom is reverence for God" (Pr. 1:7). Reverence for God is made manifest through action. "He judged the poor and needy, then it was well. Is not this to know Me? says the Lord" (Jer. 22:16). It is in this sense that the phrase "to know God," which occurs frequently in the Bible, is to be understood. *Da'at Elohim*—the knowledge of God—means the true worship of God, not a full intellectual fathoming of His nature. "Let him who wishes to glory, glory in this, that he understands and knows Me, that I am the Lord who practices kindness, justice and righteousness in the earth, for in these things do I delight, says the Lord" (Jer. 9:23).

All speculative ways of knowing God lead from one darkness to another. "A man, when he has made an end [of probing the mysteries of God] has hardly begun, and when he ceases, abides in deep confusion" (Ecclus. 18:7). A modern philosopher makes a similar confession for philosophy: "Philosophy begins in wonder. And, at the end, when philosophic thought has done its best, the wonder remains." [4] However profound their insights, men must still resort to human categories to describe God, and they cannot escape the limitations which condition all human knowledge. Judaism has always been aware of this. God does not depend upon His being completely understood, and faith does not wait upon final intellectual sanctions. Judaism is in essence a religion of few subtleties but of majestic range and glowing depths of spiritual consciousness.

No special metaphysics, no unique "knowledge" or secret gnosis which is requisite for salvation, no evangel of a miraculous scheme of redemption are offered by Judaism. It is not a transcendental wisdom so recondite that it can be grasped only by the exemplary few, and by them only after a long and intense psychophysical discipline. Judaism does not attempt to answer unanswerable questions, or to give man what man cannot have.

Judaism is Torah—"teaching." The Aramaic Targum correctly translates it *Oraita*, while the Greek Septuagint ineptly renders it *nomos*—law. Torah is a compendium of moral instructions, a rule of life for all men, a pattern of behavior, a "way" revealed in the life of a people through prophets and sages, which, if faithfully followed, leads to the well-being of the individual and of society. "You shall teach them the statutes and the decisions and make them know the way in which they must walk and what they must do" (Ex. 18:20). "The 'mizvah' [religious commandment] is a lamp, the Torah is a light and the moral instructions are the way of life" (Pr. 6:23). The term Halachah which the Rabbis employed for laws based on the Torah also means the proper *way* in which a man should walk.

Judaism's "way" is designed to sustain and advance life, not to escape or transcend it. Its roots are set deep in the practical needs of man and it is fully responsive both to his instincts and his aspirations. Judaism is a devout morality. The source of its authority is God. The motive force is the love of God and man. Its confidence is derived not alone from revelation, as unaccountably mysterious as the origin of intelligence itself, but also from history and from the empirical experiences of the people of Israel. The reward for man and mankind is now and in the future. To propagate this faith—"to proclaim God's unity in love"—Israel deemed itself chosen as an instrument of leadership. The technique for this leadership is defined: "To learn and to teach, to observe and to practice." [5]

~⊲ I ⊳~

ONE AND THE SAME

When we speak of Judaism, we are dealing with a religion some thirty-five centuries old, covering nearly two-thirds of the recorded history of mankind. Judaism experienced many changes and modifications through its long history—changes induced both from within and from without. Organic evolution accounted for some of them; contact with alien cultures and civilizations accounted for others. Jews found themselves time and time again in new environments, in Palestine and elsewhere, exposed to an almost continuous bombardment of alien ideas and religious cultures, and faced with the necessity of making adjustments to new social, political, and economic conditions. Judaism is no more the product of any one country than it is the product of any one age. Nor is it the precisely formulated creed of a sect or denomination. It is the emergent spiritual way of life of a historic people.

Nevertheless, it possesses organic unity. While numerous inconsistencies may be found in it which should neither be ignored nor exaggerated unduly, there is clearly visible in Judaism a steady and dominant coherence, a self-consistency, which links together all its stages of change and development and gives it structure and unity of tone and character. It possesses the unity not of a system but of a symphony. In their total and continuous integration, the key ideas—unity, freedom, and compassion—

6

came to be sufficiently distinctive and impressive as to be unmistakable.

Judaism, in its long history, was not always spirally ascendant, nor did it always abide on high plateaus. It descended at times into dreary valleys of stagnation. There have been scholars, like Krochmal, who under Hegelian influence detected in the history of Judaism an ordered succession of life cycles—rise, maturation, and decay.[1] Such arrangements of history are as uncertain as they are interesting. The fact of cultural fluctuations, however, even if not of a rhythmic periodicity, is beyond doubt. Judaism definitely experienced such fluctuations. At times its spirit wrote its message firm and clear on a parchment white and clean. At other times it wrote falteringly upon a blurred and worn palimpsest. There are many grades of vision and insight among the seers and teachers of Judaism.

There were many sects in ancient Israel which differed among themselves sharply and at times irreconcilably on what they regarded Judaism to be, both in doctrine and in practice. One of the Rabbis declared: "Israel was not dispersed before it broke up into twenty-four sects of heretics."[2] (One is reminded of the thirty-two heresies which Hippolytus [2 c.] found to exist in the early Christian Church.) Numerous sects flourished during the Second Commonwealth, a period of nearly six hundred years, and in the following generations, both in Palestine and in the far-flung diaspora.

It was a turbulent, culturally agitated, and creative age—next to the prophetic, the most important age in Jewish history. During this period two powerful religious cultures, among others, exercised a strong influence upon Jewish life—the Iranian and the Greek. Many lines of religious cleavage developed among the people, whose resultant conflict contributed to the intense spiritual alertness of that decisive age. A major cleavage developed on the fundamental attitude toward the Written as opposed to the Oral Law. There were many other divisions. Some schools of thought stressed one phase of Judaism and some another. Some were strictly literal in their interpretation of the laws of the Bible; others were more liberal; still others were more mystical. Some unconsciously merged Greek, Buddhist, or Zoroastrian ideas with their own. Some entertained Gnostic views within a Judaic framework. Some emphasized otherworldliness in their religious thought, and austerity in their manner of life. Others were confirmed pacifists. Still others, though laymen, observed priestly prescriptions of ritual cleanliness and kept themselves free from all contacts which they regarded as contaminating. Some lived communally in desert retreats, or in closed covenanted associations in the towns and cities, practicing pious austerities and baptisms, even celibacy, eschewing all private possessions, despising wealth and extolling poverty, and in devout prayer awaited the coming of the messianic age.

The important fact to bear in mind, however, is that numerous and divergent as these sects were, they were at all times minority groups within Jewish life and did not represent the dominant and prevailing views. It is remarkable that in spite of all this great variety, there persisted a Judaism which retained an unmistakable character of its own. Notwithstanding the many byways which frequently led off from it, Judaism's main highway continued clear, steady, and undeflected. Its reverence for the past and for the written Torah ensured for it an essential unity and a historic continuity. The written word proved on occasion to be constrictive, but it had the advantage of steadying the faith and checking extremes and relapses. What was gained was never lost, and the character of the faith was not altered in any of its essentials. Thus, the religious monotheism of the Rabbis of the Talmud and their code of ethics centering in the three constants —unity, freedom, and compassion—differed in no essential regard from those of the prophets who lived nearly a thousand years before them, and they differ in no fundamental respect from those of their successors to the present day. Here and there one finds a difference of emphasis, a weightier or a lighter accent; here and there a nuance, significant but not critical. But there is no transvaluation of values.

One should be especially on guard against the temptation to

exploit a stray quotation which may be found in some corner of Jewish literature and to make it carry more than its weight in order to establish some major deviation from normative Judaism. It should be borne in mind that not every judgment of a Rabbi was law for Israel, and not every personal opinion necessarily reflected the consensus of the Rabbis. One should rather look for the dominant pattern of the whole when considering the importance of any isolated expression, and inquire how far it falls within the authentic Judaic formula. The philosopher Maimonides found it necessary to caution the men of his day against this practice of employing some fugitive phrase or chance expression in the Haggadah, in some Midrash, or in the writings of some Gaon as evidence against a dominant truth of Judaism.[3] To understand Judaism one must avoid forced inferences and one must keep clearly in mind what was requisite in doctrine and what was mandatory in practice—in a word, Judaism's major tenets, its great assumptions, and its accented features. One must see the whole of it before one can properly understand and appraise any part of it.

This is not to suggest that through the ages there were no modulations in the interpretation of the classic Jewish concepts. There were. From time to time, one hears new accents and new intonations, fresh orchestrations on ancient themes.

The prophets sank deep shafts to mine new gold. They redefined for mankind traditional concepts of God, people, temple, sacrifice, kingship, property, slavery, labor, family, stranger, brotherhood, and peace. Rabbinic Judaism continued this process. What was progressive in the contribution of the Rabbis was not the "hedges" or "fences" which they found it necessary to build around the Torah, but the deepening of the essential concepts of Judaism—the disciplines of pious study, Torah for its own sake (*Torah li'shemah*), the hallowing of the Name of God (*kiddush ha-Shem*), suffering inflicted by divine love (*yesurim shel ahabah*), the noble ways of prayer, the higher ranges of charity, the spiritual utilization of the Sabbath, the wider scope and function of the synagogue and how to train oneself for the religious life, how to become "skilled in faith" (*'arum b'yirah*). Medieval Jewish philosophy likewise contributed new insights—the interplay of revelation and reason, the meaning of freedom in man and in God, and how a confident life could be built for man in a world created and governed by the unknowable will of God. A medieval Jewish philosopher, Halevi, gave a profound and new definition to the concept of Jewish nationality, to the autonomy of the Torah and to Israel's unique association with it. Jewish mysticism, likewise, revealed new insights—how to satisfy the hungry soul through devout contemplation of the mysteries of God and His world, how to set pious feet on the road of the eternal quest for the nearness of God, and how to unlock the recondite meaning of the Sacred Text. In a later manifestation, in Ḥasidism, Jewish mysticism refreshed old concepts and introduced new techniques—"Enthusiasm" (*hitlahabut*), "Outpouring of one's soul" (*hishtapchut ha-nefesh*), the sacredness of joy in the practice of faith, and the importance of personality in spiritual leadership. Modern Judaism contributed new and progressive elements, not so much in the abandonment of certain customs and ideas which no longer satisfied the intellectual or aesthetic needs of the new day, but in the substitution of scholarship for scholasticism, of liberty for inflexible authority, and the restatement in modern terms of the basic concept of the mission of Israel.

But in spite of these impressive variations in emphasis which greatly enriched it, the basic theme of Judaism continues throughout, all-dominant and clearly audible. Judaism's spiritual message remained one and the same through the ages.

~⟨ II ⟩~

A PATTERN IN HISTORY

A strong consciousness of history permeates Judaism. The God of Judaism was, of course, the Creator of the world, the God of nature. "In the beginning God created the heavens and the earth." To Abraham God was *El 'Elyon*—"the Lord God Most High, Maker of heaven and earth" (Gen. 14:22). At the time of the making of the covenant, God revealed Himself to Abraham as *El Shaddai*—a term of uncertain etymology, but referring in all probability to some force or phenomenon of nature, the Storm God, perhaps, of the mountains. It was by that covenant, based on election and promise, that *El Shaddai* became the God of the Patriarchs. In the later Sinaitic covenant, which was based no longer on promise but on fulfillment, Yahweh, having redeemed Israel from Egypt, revealed Himself to the people predominantly as the God of their history. "I am the Lord your God Who brought you out of the land of Egypt, out of the house of bondage" (Ex. 20:2). He is no longer *El Shaddai* but Yahweh—"I will be what I will be" (Ex. 3:13-15), another difficult term whose meaning cannot be precisely determined, but one which suggests, among other ideas, that of the eternal God progressively revealing Himself in the processes of history.

Gods of nature, deities of creation, birth and fertility, were worshiped everywhere in the ancient world through rituals which were frequently grossly licentious. No ritual is to be found in Judaism which "symbolizes" anything about the nature of God or His "history." All ritual came to be didactic in purpose, reminding men of their obligations toward God and their fellow men. Judaism, under prophetic guidance, came to subordinate the concept of the Creator God to that of the God of History, of Israel's history and of mankind's. In place of the seasonal drama of death and rebirth and its accompanying orgiastic rituals, Judaism projected a drama of history. Pagan religions were not interested in history, except in the mythological history of their gods, and pagan historians, though often acute in their appraisal of personalities and events, found little of permanent significance to mankind in history and saw no moral pattern in it. The prophets of Israel taught their people to think of God as the wise Ruler of their national destiny. They wished to turn their people away from nature cults, from chthonic or astral ritualism to higher spiritual and ethical forms of worship.

This shift of emphasis from God's theophanies in mighty and overwhelming nature phenomena to His revelation as the "voice of a gentle silence," speaking of duty and mission to the inner spirit, is beautifully dramatized in the account of Elijah's vision of God at Mount Horeb where the Mosaic revelation had formerly taken place amidst thunder and lightning (I K. 19: 11–13).

The mighty drama of human experience, a drama not of sin and redemption, but of building the good society, as well as the millennial struggles and achievements of a unique people, is interpreted by Judaism. Israel was always admonished to recall history, to remember—"consider the days of old"—and on the basis of vital and instructive memories to build its future. Most of the religious festivals of Judaism and even the Sabbath day itself, regardless of their origin, came in time to be principally festivals of remembrance, memorials of the exodus from Egypt— the greatest moment in Jewish history. The seasonal, nature character of these festivals was deliberately subordinated to the historic motif.

Prophets, sages, and mystics alike related their thinking to a

definite pattern of history. The Jews were the first to give mankind a philosophy of History—rather than a philosophy of
Being.[1]

Judaism sees in human history and in the history of Israel no
mere succession of events, but the outline of an unfolding moral
process, the articulation in time of an immanent divine plan,
glimpsed by man in retrospect and then only dimly, but known
to God in its completeness.

There is a pattern in all that transpires, and this pattern is a
spiritual one. The good will triumph, for God has willed it so,
but the triumph can be hastened by humanity's efforts. Coming
as a climax to Trito-Isaiah's superb vision of the New Jerusalem
and the great Restoration, is the verse, "I, the Lord, will hasten
it in its appointed time" (Is. 60:22). There is here an apparent
contradiction. If God has set a fixed time for the redemption,
what is meant by His hastening it? A Rabbi comments: "If Israel
merits it, God will hasten its coming; if not, it will come to pass
in its appointed time." [2] God's ultimate achievement does not
dispense with man's participation in it. This is a basic concept in
Judaism. For Judaism is concerned not alone with the ways of
God in history, but also with man's creative function in it. Basic,
too, is Judaism's view of Israel's unique rôle in history.

Judaism is indigenous to the Jewish people and is inconceivable without it. The Jewish people did not adopt Judaism
as the Romans, for example, adopted Christianity. They created
it. Jews and Judaism entered history simultaneously. Its life and
that of the Jewish people are inseparably intertwined. No other
people, as such, consciously shared in it or helped to mold it, as
was the case, for example, with Islam, which originated with the
Arabs but whose golden age was the achievement largely of
Moslems of non-Arab descent. Judaism exerted its tremendous
influence upon the world from its own base in the Jewish people.
That base, however, was quite extensive. Israel was perhaps the
least parochial of all the peoples of antiquity. "A wandering
Aramean was my father. . . ." From the desert to the sown land

the tribes of Israel moved in the dawn of their history. From their fixed habitation in Palestine many of them were carried away into exile and to distant lands time and again. From the dispersion of the Ten Tribes onward there was not a period when the Jewish people as a whole was concentrated there. Jews were in close contact with many nations and many civilizations, and they were influenced by many cultures. Israel thus acquired a first-hand knowledge of the religions, the modes of worship, and the ways of life of many of the peoples of antiquity. It gained a world outlook. The writings of the prophets reflect the wide horizons of this "cosmopolitan" people. Their prophecies are directed by name to nearly all the nations of the ancient world, and reveal an acquaintance with their traits and their histories.

The faith and ethical insights of Judaism were, however, not monopolized by the Jewish people. They were offered to humanity. Israel's covenant with God was also a covenant with mankind. "I have given you as a covenant to the peoples, as a light to the nations" (Is. 42:6). It was not a solitary and unshared light but a beacon light. The Sages declared that "the Torah was given in public, openly, in a free place. For had the Torah been given in the land of Israel, the Israelites could have said to the nations of the world: You have no share in it. But now that it was given in the wilderness publicly and openly in a place that is free for all, everyone willing to accept it could come and accept it." [8]

The God of Israel was the God of all men, and all men were called to His service. The Jews carried on an active missionary propaganda for their universal spiritual ideas and moral values throughout the world whenever conditions did not prevent them, although they never conceived it as their historic mission to conquer the world, to engage in a Holy War on infidels in order to convert the world and bring it into subjection to the God of Israel. The Rabbis never accepted the principle of forcible conversion. The only instances of such conversion took place under John Hyrcanus and his son Aristobulus, who forcibly Judaized the Edomites and Ituraeans in the second century before the common era. It was never approved by the teachers of Judaism. John Hyrcanus' intolerant religious imperialism extended also to the Samaritans, whose Temple on Mount Gerizim he destroyed. These unprecedented and politically motivated acts contributed to the bitter friction which developed between Hyrcanus and the Pharisees. In Pharisaic law even slaves could not be forcibly converted.[4]

All men, regardless of race or status, were welcomed into the faith. The Jewish people was never a self-enclosed society with an exclusive separatist religion. "Let not the foreigner who joins himself to the Lord say, 'The Lord will surely separate me from His people.' . . . I will bring them to My holy mountain, and make them joyful in My house of prayer . . . for My house shall be called a house of prayer for all peoples" (Is. 56:3, 7). Some of Israel's greatest leaders were descendants of proselytes, including King David, to whom the lineage of the Messiah was traced in later times. A special prayer for "righteous proselytes" is included in the Eighteen Benedictions of the Prayer Book. Hillel (1 c.), the foremost spiritual leader of his day, was especially eager to receive proselytes.[5]

Non-Jews who were not prepared to accept the full obligations of the Jewish discipline, national fellowship, and ceremonial laws were welcomed as Yir'e Shamayim (God-fearers). Some of them were ultimately converted and became Jews, accepting full citizenship in the religious household of Israel. Others accepted monotheism and practiced some, though not all, of the customs of Israel, but remained unconverted. Their spiritual status, however, was in no way regarded as inferior to that of a full-fledged Jew. Judaism never claimed to be the one and only channel through which "salvation" is conveyed to men. It never adopted Cyprian's position: "Extra ecclesiam nulla salus" (No salvation outside the Church). Rather it held to the conviction: "The righteous among the Gentiles will have a portion in the world to come." [6]

The predominant hope of the people of Israel was not to convert the whole world to Judaism but to convert the whole world to God. It did not set as its goal the establishment of one universal Church to which all true believers must belong and wherein alone "salvation" could be found. It looked forward to the day "when God would be One and His name would be One." R. Joḥanan (2–3 c.), founder of the Academy of Tiberias and one of the chief creators of the Palestinian Talmud, declared: "Anyone who repudiates idolatry is called a Jew." [7] Elsewhere it is stated: "He who rejects idolatry acknowledges the whole Torah." [8] R. Joḥanan also shared the conviction of his colleague R. Eleazer, who succeeded him as head of the Academy, that "the Holy One, blessed be He, did not exile Israel among the nations save in order that proselytes might join them." [9] He interpreted the tragic exile as an opportunity for the people of Israel to turn mankind to God, even as Deutero-Isaiah in his day had similarly interpreted the Babylonian exile. In time many of the leaders of Judaism came to realize that there were other ways, perhaps more effective ways, of spreading spiritual truth in the world than proselytism and formal conversion; there was the way of example, and of total dedication to a pattern of life which might inspire others to emulation.

Judaism was, however, fearful of syncretistic tendencies which might do violence to its essential monotheistic faith, and was mindful always of the special covenant and mission which were assigned to Israel. It therefore looked to the people of Israel itself as its enduring sanctuary. The ritual prescriptions which guarded the discipline of its group life did not interfere with its spiritual and ethical universalism.

The spiritual leaders of Judaism of the Second Commonwealth and thereafter, as well as the prophets of pre-exilic times, conceived of Israel not only as a nation, but also as a *ḳehal Adonai* (Dt. 23.4), "a Congregation of God," coextensive with the nation—a covenanted religious community. The congregation or community, however, was never an entity distinct from the nation or the state, as was the case with the Christian Church, nor did it ever displace the concept of nationhood even in periods when the people did not possess an independent political life and its leaders were not kings but high priests. Like king, priest, or prophet, Israel as such had been, as it were, anointed for a divinely commissioned ministry, and by that token had become possessed of a special grace and power, had become a different kind of people. "Touch not Mine anointed and do My prophets no harm" (Ps. 105:15; also Ps. 84:10; 89:39, 52; 132:10; and Hab. 3:13, the latter also in the form of a Psalm. In each case it is the people that is referred to as having been anointed).[10] Israel, as a people and as a community of believers, knew itself to be different. No term defining other nations, races, or religions could ever quite adequately be applied to it. By virtue of the immortal ideals of which it believed itself possessed, it experienced throughout its history a deathless hope, and believed its life to be indestructible. "When you pass through the waters I will be with you; and through the rivers, they shall not overwhelm you; when you walk through fire you shall not be burned, and the flame shall not consume you" (Is. 43.2).

Two world religions kindled their fires at the altars of Judaism. Both Jesus and Mohammed claimed no originality for their message. They did not come, they averred, to found a new religion but to restore the true faith of Abraham. Abraham stands at the headwaters of Judaism, Christianity, and Islam. Jesus worshiped in the Temple of Jerusalem. Mohammed and his followers at first turned their faces in prayer toward Jerusalem. It was only after he despaired of converting the Jews that he ordained that the faithful should pray toward the Ka'aba at Mecca—the Ka'aba of which Abraham was the reputed founder. Both Christianity and Islam turned to the Bible to authenticate their own scriptures. Much skilled typological dialectic was employed by the Apostles and the Church Fathers to prove that everything in their faith was prefigured in the Old Testament.

As part of this effort to establish that the Christians were the true Israelites and their predestined successors, quite a number of attractive philosophies of history were invented to account for the unique story and baffling persistence of the people of Israel. Judaism was by some assigned the role of a historic foil for

Christianity. The argument was popularized that Christianity began where Judaism left off, and that Judaism's creative life ended with—or even before—the advent of Christianity. There are to this day scholars who assign to Israel only a single flowering period, terminating with the last of the Biblical prophets. The many centuries of Jewish history which followed are regarded as a prolonged withering, waste, and fossilization.

The orthodox Christian interpretation of the rôle of Israel, as the star witness for Christian truth, was crystallized for the Christian world by Augustine in his *City of God*. When prophecy ceased in Israel, after the return from the Babylonian captivity, the religious role of Israel came to an end. The Jewish people, thereafter, was afflicted with continual adversity to prove that Haggai's prophecy, "The glory of this latter house shall be greater than that of the former" (Hag. 2:9), applied not to the second Temple which the Jews had built but to the coming of Christ. With his coming, the Jews were "rooted out from their kingdom and were dispersed through the lands . . . and are thus by their own Scriptures, a testimony to us that we have not forged the prophecies about Christ." The Jews were needed by the Church as a living testimony. Hence they were not utterly destroyed. But they had to be dispersed "because if they had only been in their own land with that testimony of the Scriptures and not everywhere, certainly the Church which is everywhere could not have had them as witnesses among all nations." [11] Centuries later, at the time of the Second Crusade (1146–1147), Bernard of Clairvaux, whose eloquence helped set the Crusade in motion, in defending the Jews in the Rhineland against the violent mobs who attacked them, employed the same line of reasoning. The Jews should neither be killed nor expelled because they were needed as a living symbol and a witness to the truths of the Christian faith. Seeing their dispersion and their disabilities, Christians will realize ever anew the truth of the crucifixion and the punishment which overtook those whom they held to be responsible for it.

To serve as a corroborating witness for another faith and to

be superseded has, however, never received the willing cooperation of the Jews and Judaism. They were not impressed by the
premature obsequies which were pronounced over them from
time to time by those who regarded themselves as the lawful
heirs of a faith and a people which, however, refused to die. They
had a strong will to live. The altar of Judaism retained its own
fires undimmed, and amidst the turbulence of wars, invasions,
exiles, and persecutions, the faith was preserved intact. It survived the fallen thrones of its own kingdoms and the ruins of its
own Temples. It wandered with Israel into strange lands and
fearful exiles and often, harried and outlawed, it lived on in the
hearts of the faithful as in an inviolate sanctuary, and remained
in vision and power undiminished.

This has by some been called "narrow," but the "narrowness"
was not of racial pride, or out of lack of love for mankind. It
was a question of technique—how best to transmit the message
unimpaired to the world. Judaism chose one way; Christianity
chose another. As to which was the wiser course, in terms not of
quantitative but of qualitative diffusion, opinions will always differ. The influence of Judaism is not to be measured by the number of its adherents. Judaism never had an Asoka, a Constantine,
or an Omar to hasten its progress; nor was it permitted through
most of the past two thousand years to engage in proselytizing
activities. In the realm of ideas one must be alert to withstand
both the fear of numbers and their prestige. Even in times of apparent neglect and eclipse, Judaism strangely troubled the established orthodoxies of Christendom in the form of a variety of
Judaizing heresies which began almost with the rise of Christianity itself. At other times it upsurged with sharp revolutionary
thrusts in movements such as Humanism, the Reformation and
Puritanism. The very presence of the unassimilated and stubbornly resisting Jew in medieval Europe, daily symbol of a faith
which denied Christianity but in which Christianity sought
authentication, troubled and disturbed the spiritual uniformity
of the Christian world and from time to time forced it to reexamination and revision. The great social and democratic move-

ments of Europe in the last few centuries, which have been re-making our world, turned for their inspiration principally to the Old Testament, to the prophetic message of Judaism—social justice and human equality, brotherhood and universal peace. The dominant apocalyptic elements of Christianity—"My kingdom is not of this world," "It is the last hour," "Resist not evil"—could not well serve as a basis for a program of social reform. The strong emphasis which both Catholic and Protestant Christianity have in the nineteenth and twentieth centuries placed on the social gospel of their religions marks a sharp departure from their traditional positions and a welcome return to the prophetic ethics of Judaism. For while Christian metaphysics was in the main Platonic, and its soteriology an adaptation of a widely diffused Oriental gnosis, its ethical principles, with some notable exceptions, and its cultural-historical background were Jewish. Time and again the social passion of the Hebrew Bible swept in like the reviving sun and rain of a new springtime. How often have socioreligious movements in Christendom, like those of the Puritans and the dissenters, quoted chapter and verse from the Jewish Bible as the all-sufficient justification of their demands for social and economic reform, for free political institutions, and their opposition to the usurpations of tyrants and kings. The violence of the obscurantist attacks in recent years, such as one finds among some Existentialist theologians, upon the humanistic element in Christianity—its Jewish core—is further evidence of the Judaic leaven still powerfully at work. One wonders whether their very violence and dialectic truculence does not betray the throes of a struck and mortally wounded theology. Clearly, there is something unqualified both in the alleged failure of Judaism and in the so-called triumph of Christianity.

The "narrowness" of Judaism had to do not with its God-concept or its world outlook, but with its unique conception of a universalistic faith in the stewardship of a covenanted people. The ideals of universalism and human brotherhood had been part of the essential pattern of Judaism since the days of the prophets. In proclaiming the one and only God, and in denying the very existence of any other god, Judaism created the universal God idea, the universal Fatherhood of God and its logical corollary the universal brotherhood of man. Its "narrowness" was due to its firm determination to retain undiminished its spiritual identity in a world dominated by powerful syncretistic tendencies.

The trend of nearly all the religions of the Greco-Roman world at the beginning of the common era was toward "internationalism." The Greco-Roman world, generally, was "international" in character. The sense of nationhood, peoplehood, and "patriotism" had largely disappeared in the incessant mixing of populations and cultures and in the vast amalgam of races, peoples, and creeds of the far-flung Roman Empire, which was held together by military force and administrative skill. The process had begun centuries before under Alexander, whose dream was of a single world state.

Judaism saw no inconsistency between religious universalism and nationalism. It believed that the independent existence of nations was within the plan of God, and that He assigned to each nation, as to each individual, a distinct task and responsibility. National identities were not, however, irreconcilable, and did not preclude international cooperation and universal brotherhood.

The many cults of the Roman Empire could without much difficulty be contained within the framework of a cosmopolitan, fluid, and tolerant religio-philosophic culture. Neoplatonism provided such a framework from the third through the fifth century, as did Gnosticism in the earlier centuries. Judaism could not and did not fit into any such mosaic.

◄ III ►

ON BEING RECEPTIVE

Jews never sought to isolate themselves intellectually or spiritually behind an iron wall except in periods of persecution, when isolation was forced upon them, or when the surrounding culture was deemed morally noxious and threatened to submerge their own values. In such predicaments the religiously loyal and responsible elements of the people barricaded themselves for a time behind protective ramparts of separatism, and it was at such times that they built "fences around the Torah."[1] They followed a principle of adding safeguard to safeguard.[2] Their reaction was similar to the sharp and instinctive physiological changes which take place in the human body the moment the organism has to mobilize itself to meet sudden danger or to repel attack. Fear and distrust at times prolonged the periods of voluntary sequestration far beyond actual utility, and generations were held spellbound in their isolation. Overconcentration on strategic details and legal minutiae sometimes resulted in a loss of scope and perspective. Thus, the Rabbis continued to discuss and elaborate laws of clean and unclean which were intended to safeguard the holiness of the Temple long after the Temple had been destroyed. Typical of such periods of protectionist fixation were the long retirement following the crushing disaster of the Spanish expulsion at the very time when Europe was experiencing the flowering of the Renaissance and the new Humanism; the earlier voiceless generations which succeeded the age of Ezra and Nehemiah;

the isolationist trends which asserted themselves so sharply following the national disasters of the first and second centuries of the common era; and the inward shrinking and recession of East European Jewry following the Chmielnicki devastations of the seventeenth century.

From earliest times the people had been admonished by their leaders to separate themselves from the morally depraved ways of the heathen peoples about them in order to conserve their own morality and way of life: "You shall not do as they do in the land of Egypt, where you dwelt, and you shall not do as they do in the land of Canaan, to which I am bringing you; you shall not walk in their statutes" (Lev. 18:3). When this failed and the transgressions of the people were many and their apostasies great (Jer. 5:6), the spiritual leaders sometimes undertook to carry out drastic purges and reforms. The thoroughgoing Deuteronomic reformation under King Josiah in 621 B.C. (II Kings 22–23) is the classic example. It was a vast onslaught, under prophetic prompting, on all forms of religious syncretism; and although its success was only partial and in some regards had to be renewed in later times, it was the beginning of the end of idolatry in Israel. Another such purge and withdrawal took place a century after the Jews returned from the Babylonian exile, in the days of Ezra and Nehemiah. The price paid for such drastic religious and social reformations is always high. In this instance not the least of the consequences was the great Samaritan schism, which detached from the Jewish people the descendants of the Jews of the Northern Kingdom who were left after the Assyrian conquest and had later intermingled with imported settlers.

A similar danger arose with the penetration of Hellenism into the social and cultural life of Israel. It ushered in a long and desperate struggle on the part of the faithful which finally culminated in the Maccabean revolt. In spite of the victory of the Maccabees, the relentless tug of war between Hellenistic and Jewish ways of life continued for centuries.

In their violent reaction to the Hellenistic culture of their day, the faithful among Palestine Jewry were demonstrating not against Greek intellectual and artistic excellence, but against the gross moral corruption and decadence which so frequently attended Hellenization. It was not the Academy, the Lyceum, or the Stoa which they feared, but the gymnasium, the stadium, the hippodrome, and the theater, from all of which much profligacy and corruption often flowed, threatening to overwhelm the higher moral standards and religious traditions of the people. (In his *Laws*, I, 636, Plato calls attention to the influence of the gymnasia in encouraging unnatural love among the youth of Greece.)

The Hellenistic civilization which prevailed throughout the Mediterranean world did not derive its major distinguishing characteristics from the great achievements of the Greek mind during its phenomenally creative, but relatively brief, Classical period. There was little of the Socratic spirit in the Hellenism which Antiochus IV sought to impose on Judaea, and little of the lofty spirit of the dramas of Sophocles or Euripides in the entertainments which the Hellenists among the Jews sought to establish.

It was, therefore, not the spread of Greek philosophy which the responsible leaders of Judaism feared—although even some of the highest expressions of the Greek intellect contained ideas which were repugnant to Judaism's standards of humanity and family life. Plato, for example, advocated the community of women and children within the framework of communal possession of property in his ideal state; he also justified infanticide and the killing off of the aged and helpless, and was distrustful of democracy. Plato's philosophic God-concept also fell far short of the Jewish conception of a personal God of justice, mercy, and forgiveness. But it was primarily the licentiousness and depravity of a decadent Epicureanism which the defenders of Judiasm feared. They sought to avert the drainage of sewers of moral corruption into the stream of Jewish life—the moral corruption of which the author of the *Wisdom Of Solomon* (1 c. B.C.) wrote:

For the devising of idols was the beginning of spiritual fornication and the invention of them the corruption of life. . . . They kept neither lives nor marriages any longer undefiled . . . so that there reigned in all men without exception blood, manslaughter, theft, and dissimulation, corruption, unfaithfulness . . . defiling of souls, changing of kind. disorder in marriages, adultery, and shameless uncleanness (14:12f.).

The glamour of Greek civilization caused many Jews to join the heathen and to stand aloof from the sacred law (I Mac. 1:15). Especially did the Jewish youth chafe under the restraints of the strict Jewish code of personal morality and religious discipline. They hankered after the broad-brimmed hat, the high-laced boots, and the graceful dress of the *ephebi* which symbolized for them the fortunate youth of the world who belonged to the dominant civilization and enjoyed a freer and more spacious life.

Some centuries later the teachers of Judaism had to face the challenge of the social and moral corruptions which emanated from Rome, and these lacked even the veil of beauty with which Greek culture was able to cover the ugly features of its vice and cruelty. So widespread were sex perversions in the Roman world that the Rabbis decreed that no one should entrust a child to a heathen to be educated or to be taught a trade, for fear of the child being corrupted by him.[3]

Christianity, too, in the process of defending its faith, was soon forced to become "narrow" and "exclusive." The "narrowness" was here confined not to a people but to a society, a Church. It, too, came to fear heathen contamination. The church manual *Didascalia Apostolorum* (3 c.) follows in many of its prescriptions the disciplines which some of the Rabbis prescribed. The faithful were to avoid the books of the heathen, their festivals, their courts; they were not to enter their temples, their assemblies, their theaters, their fairs, and public baths. They were not to sing the songs of the heathen nor adorn themselves as the heathen did. They were not even to mention the names of the idols. The faithful were to live as a people apart:

The Christian cult was an exclusive cult which required every candidate to break with his past and separate himself from much of the social life because it was tainted with paganism. . . . We may regret this hard intolerance of our primitive faith which sometimes did bare justice to its forerunners and competitors. . . . But we shall less regret this intolerance of primitive Christianity when we reflect upon the nature and necessity of it. . . . Its exclusiveness preserved its integrity.[4]

Under normal conditions the Jews did not isolate themselves but were very responsive to the cultures of the surrounding peoples. The receptive tendency of the Hebrew mind can be observed even in its earliest contacts with the civilization of Canaan. "At the first assault made by the mind superior to itself," writes Goldziher, "it [the Hebrew mind] willingly opened its gates, and even when struggling for its national character and individuality it did not spurn the intellectual property of its antagonists." [5] This was the case also during and following the Babylonian Exile when the Jews came in contact with the rich civilizations of Mesopotamia and Persia. The influence of their ideas and customs is extensively evidenced in the literature of the Second Commonwealth and in the pages of Rabbinic literature. The Jews borrowed copiously and, it may be argued, at times unwisely, from Zoroastrian beliefs and practices, especially in the fields of eschatology and angelology and in sacerdotal matters of ritual purity. Centuries later, Sages like Akiba and Gamaliel expressed their admiration for certain commendable qualities and customs which they found among the Medes and Persians.[6] Egyptian influences, too, were absorbed in the many centuries of political and economic contacts. Jews entertained a high regard for the "wisdom of the people of the East, and all the wisdom of Egypt" (I Kings 5:10). Traces of Egyptian literary influence are to be seen in some of the Psalms; and there are sayings in the Book of Proverbs (chapters 22–24) which closely parallel *The Teaching of Amenemope*. Other Hebrew gnomic sayings point to the reworking of earlier "international" material. Jews freely received and as freely shared insights, learning, and experience.

They thanked God for the wise men among the Gentiles: "On seeing the sages of other nations, one should say: Blessed be God Who hath imparted His wisdom to His creatures."[7] The wisdom of the Gentiles was God's wisdom.

Jews throughout the Hellenistic period in Palestine and in the entire Mediterranean diaspora studied the Greek language with great eagerness and delight. The Rabbis did not forbid its study, although they cautioned against the teaching of Greek philosophy to the young. Prohibitions were especially severe in times of bitter national resentment caused by the loss of political independence, as in the days of the civil war between Hyrcanus II and Aristobulus II (*c.* 67 B.C.): "Cursed be the man who would teach his son Greek Wisdom,"[8] or in the days of the final assault on Jerusalem and the Temple (70 C.E.): "During the war of Titus they forbade the crowns of the brides and that a man should teach his son Greek."[9] Such fierce and dangerous times were always the occasions for withdrawal into a narrowing orbit and for strong introversive tendencies.[10]

Otherwise the study of Greek was not prohibited. Indeed, the Greek language was praised for its beauty. It was the one language other than Hebrew in which the writing of the Books of the Torah was permitted,[11] and was held to be most adaptable for translation from the Hebrew.[12] In the Hellenistic diaspora Greek was, of course, the most common speech of the Jews. "No people in the Hellenistic world adopted the language and customs to such an extent as did the Jews."[13] Many Jews, both inside and outside Palestine, added Greek names to their Hebrew names.

The literature of Judaism, composed in and out of Palestine during the Hellenistic and Hellenistic-Roman periods, extending over eight hundred years, shows a very lively acquaintance with nearly all the major schools of philosophic thought and religious speculation of the pagan world—a much better acquaintance than the classic writers of these centuries evidenced of Jews and Judaism.

While certain schools of Greek philosophy (*Ḥochmah*

Yevanit, "Greek Wisdom") were bitterly opposed by the Rabbis as contributing to heresy and apostasy, philosophic learning as such was not prohibited, and the study of the sciences like mathematics and medicine was never interdicted. The science of astronomy was especially encouraged, for it came to be required for the fixing of the calendar.[14] Some Rabbis were not merely tolerant in their attitude toward Greek philosophy, but seem to have been intimately acquainted with it, and frequently engaged in lively discussion with pagan philosophers. There were of course others, like the Tanna R. Ishmael (1–2 c.), who forbade his nephew to study "Greek Wisdom" altogether.[15] Such fears were to be found in Christian circles as well. Paul alerted the Colossians against those who would make a prey of them "by philosophy and empty deceit" (Col. 2:8). He was as disdainful of the Greeks "who seek wisdom" as he was of the Jews who demand signs (I Cor. 1:22). Tertullian and Tatian of the second century regarded Greek philosophy as an invention of the devil. This was the general attitude toward pagan philosophy. Clement of Alexandria was a notable exception.

A favorite topic of writers and historians since the days of Heinrich Heine and Matthew Arnold has been the contrast between Hellenism and Hebraism, the two main influences in Western civilization. It is doubtful, however, whether any true insights are to be gained from drawing sharp and facile antitheses between cultures which are never really separable.

Some writers have seen a wide chasm between the Greek *Weltanschauung* and the Hebraic *Lebensanschauung*. The Greek mind, it is held, was engrossed in science, art, and philosophy; the Hebraic mind, in religion and morality:

The two interests are different. The one is interested in thought, the other in action. The one proves his point step by step (whether validly or not makes no difference), the other asserts with emphasis, indeed, and deep conviction, the result of insight, but nevertheless, he asserts. On the whole the history of Greek thought is an education of the mind; the history of Hebrew thought is an education of the heart and the spirit.[16]

Other writers, like Canon Oliver Quick and Thorleif Boman, have, on the basis of linguistic and other considerations, catalogued additional contrasts between Greek and Hebrew thought. Hebrew thought, they conclude, is dynamic; Greek thought is static and harmonious. For the Hebrews time is proper to their mode of thought; for the Greeks it is space. For the Hebrew, the decisive reality of experience was the word; for the Greek it was the object. Repose, harmony, composure, and self-control, these were the Greek way; movement, life, passion, and strength mark the Hebrew way.[17]

The versatile scholar Salvador de Madariaga also indulges himself in this selfsame pastime. He discovers the same striking time-space contrast to exist, but in his case it is not between Greek and Hebrew but between the Spaniard and the Jew: "The Spaniard is deeply rooted in space; the Jew in time. . . . The Jews have no roots in space. Their roots are in time; their soil is made of twenty centuries of tradition. They differ from all the peoples of the earth in that their fatherland is history itself."[18] This, according to Madariaga, "is the deepest cause of that urban trend of the Jew which leads him to seek commerce and the liberal professions rather than the land."

To accept these belletristic views, one must overlook a three-thousand-year-old unparalleled attachment of the people of Israel to the land of Israel and the deathless love for it which informs all of Israel's literature, prayers and rituals; one must overlook the indefeasible longing to return to it from exile—surely, the rivers of Babylon were not the only waters by which they sat down and wept when they remembered Zion—and the passion and sacrifices which went into successive restoration movements, culminating in the establishment of the third Commonwealth of Israel after nineteen centuries of national homelessness.

Such contrasts which some detect in world cultures correspond to nothing in reality, and inferences drawn from a scholarship so subjective and so largely dependent on semantic artifices have unfortunately at times fed politically motivated racial mythologies which proved so popular and so disastrous in our times.

There is no unbridgeable gulf between the culture of the Greeks and the culture of the Jews. They are not in polar opposition. Both have antecedents in the Eastern Mediterranean culture which emerged in the second millenium before the common era when both the Greeks and the Hebrews made their appearance on the stage of history.[19] There *is* a marked difference in emphasis. The eagerness with which the Jews of the Hellenistic period absorbed the science, art, and philosophy of the Greeks and, a thousand years later, the equal eagerness with which the foremost among the Jewish philosophers sought to harmonize Judaism with Platonism and Aristotelianism indicate their total unawareness of any insurmountable walls existing between them. The Greeks went far in religion and ethics, but not far enough, not as far as the deep spiritual insights of the Jews; and the Jews fell far short of the Greeks in those areas of art and science where the latter excelled. That is why the peoples of the Western World at the close of the Classical Age turned for their scientific and artistic needs to Greece, and for their spiritual and ethical inspiration to Judea.[20] There is a noticeable emphasis, according to Dr. Joseph Klausner, in Hebrew thought on man rather than on nature, on the group more than on the individual, though not to the exclusion of either. There is also an intensity of feeling, a passionate earnestness, and a prophetic missionary zeal about moral values in Hebraic thought which find slight parallel in Greek thought. Greek religious teachers did not "hunger and thirst after righteousness," though they sought earnestly to understand it and define it.

Plato speculated long about the nature of the Good, but, having found a satisfactory definition in terms of four cardinal virtues whose prototype was a heavenly Form, he did little about it. It remained an abstract intellectual truth. It was not converted into a prophetic compulsion to make the Good triumph in the world.

Plato went so far as to draw up a constitution and laws of an ideal political state in his *Republic* and *Laws*, but history does not record that he spent himself in any way in an effort to bring this ideal state into existence. The very presentation of the idea of his utopia seems to have been sufficient for him. It was part of the basic pattern of his thought that the essence of a thing does not lie in the thing itself but in its ideal form in a supersensible world. Plato did not rush out into the agora, and, lifting his voice like a trumpet, declare unto the Athenians their transgressions and to the House of the Achaeans their sins, summoning them to repentance and reformation. One cannot conceive of Plato, or Aristotle, or Epictetus pleading with the Almighty in the name of Justice to save the wicked city of Sodom, an alien community, for the sake of the few righteous men in it.

Judaism did not speculate much on the nature of the Good, but it taught man what is good and what the Lord requires of him—"to do justly, to love mercy and to walk humbly with God." All who heard Micah knew full well wherein they had individually and collectively failed to measure up to these requirements, and they knew too that what was indicated on their part was not a continuous dialogue concerning these ethical concepts, but repentance and a thoroughgoing amendment of their way of life. Judaism was not primarily interested in the theoretic elaboration of ethical values but in their realization.

The science, wisdom, and skills of the surrounding world were never rejected. Judaism stressed, however, "the end of the matter, all having been heard: revere God, and keep His commandments; for this is the whole duty of man" (Eccl. 12:13). The insistence was always on a code of conduct, "by following which a man shall live" (Lev. 18:5).

The receptivity of the Jewish mind and its responsiveness to alien cultures was especially evident centuries later in Islamic lands where the Jewish people enjoyed long periods free from serious harassment. They drew very close to the culture and civilization of the Moslem world, even closer than they had done to the Hellenistic world. To study the language, literature, science, and philosophy of the Moslem peoples, especially of the Arabs, became part of the curriculum of an educated Jew in Damascus, Baghdad, Cairo, and Cordova. Arabic came to be extensively employed by Jewish authors. While they treasured the Hebrew language and gave it priority in prayer, law, and poetry, they employed Arabic extensively in composing works of philosophy and science and Biblical commentaries. They caught the prevalent Arabic and Persian passion for poetical composition, and under this influence a flowering of Hebrew poetry ensued, and the Hebrew poet soon came to introduce the characteristic linguistic arabesques and erudite allusiveness of Islamic poetry into his own. Jewish scholars turned eagerly to the study of the Arabic versions of the works of Plato and Aristotle. Under Moslem impact a veritable Revival of Learning set in among the Jews; poets, scholars, grammarians, philosophers, and scientists shed luster on the most glorious age in medieval Jewish history. Long pent-up creative forces were released. Jewish philosophy entered its most brilliant and creative period. Saadia, ibn-Daud, ibn-Gabirol, and Maimonides found ways of reconciling Judaism with Neoplatonism, Aristotelianism, and other elements of Greek philosophy which they found congenial even as al-Farabi, Avicenna, and Averroës found a similar reconciliation for Islam, and Albertus Magnus and Aquinas for Christianity. There was far less fear of Greek philosophy than there had been in Talmudic times. Many came to believe that reason and revelation, philosophy and Halachah could well be harmonized.

When, however, the interest in philosophy and secular knowledge came to supplant a primary concern with the Torah and Halachah, resulting in a growing laxity in religious observance and a weakening of the disciplines of Jewish life, frightened voices were raised in warning. In the Provence of the thirteenth century, at the very time and place that Christian orthodoxy was waging war on the theologic heresies of the Cathari and the Albigenses, Maimonides was bitterly attacked for his philosophic rationalism which seemed to endanger the simple faith of the masses. The ban and torch were applied to his books. In Barcelona, Rabbi Solomon ibn-Adret (1235–1310) and his colleagues issued an edict of excommunication against all who studied philosophy and science prior to the age of thirty, excepting those who were preparing themselves for the profession of medicine. Like their Rabbinic counterparts in Hellenistic times, they resolved that their youth should first become thoroughly grounded in the Torah and grow in religious maturity before being exposed to the study of philosophy. The motive behind the ban was not hostility toward philosophy and the sciences as such. (Abba Meir of Montpellier, the prime instigator of ibn-Adret's edict, was himself a man of wide culture and a student of philosophy.) It was a protest against the developing practice of subordinating the study of the Torah to that of philosophy and the secular sciences, and against much unsanctioned allegorizing of sacred texts aimed at bringing the Bible into agreement with the metaphysical theories of alien thinkers.

Maimonides himself reacted similarly, though not as regards the ban. He too insisted that students should first feed upon "the bread and meat" of the Halachah, upon the legal discussions of Abaye and Raba (3–4 c., both heads of important Rabbinic schools) before they began to promenade in the Pardes—the Grove—of speculative thought.[21]

It is of interest to note that it was in the same Provence of the twelfth and thirteenth centuries where the cabalistic movement began its significant career in the West that a ban came to be pronounced also against the study of cabala by immature people. (This followed the example set by the teachers of the Mishnah who had prohibited the discussion of Ma 'aseh Merkabah, the Chariot Vision of Ezekiel, even with one person.) [22] Such bans are to be met with in subsequent centuries as well. The widespread and excessive preoccupation with mysticism—especially after the disasters which befell the Jews of France (1391) and those of the Iberian Peninsula (1492–1496), and in the case of Polish Jewry following the cataclysm of 1648—together with the shift from theosophic and speculative to practical cabala, turned many Jews away from an adequate study of Talmud and Halachah into all sorts of mystic vagaries and occultism which, in time, fed the fires of messianic expectations and adventures.

With the very first printing of a cabalistic book, a sharp controversy developed over whether such books should be printed at all, and whether their dissemination should be permitted. Opposition came not only from those who rejected cabala altogether as spurious, and scoffed at its doctrines, but also from its foremost adherents. They were apprehensive of the evil which might result from the mass dabbling of the young and the unfit in what was after all intended to be an esoteric and recondite science, reserved specifically for the adequately mature and devout scholar and sage, and meant to be transmitted from one initiate to another.[23] The bans were promulgated not against cabala as such, but against an immoderate absorption in it, especially by the unqualified and the very young. What was at best intended to be peripheral and tolerated could not be permitted to become central and dominant in Judaism. The firm foundation and the structure of the faith were Torah and Halachah, not mystic theosophy.

Similar bans were pronounced during the eighteenth century against the pietistic excesses of the Ḥasidim in eastern Europe. Here again, normative Judaism sensed a threat to its way of life which was based on the study and faithful observance of the Torah, and not on unbrided enthusiasm and hero worship. Ḥasidism at times passed far beyond this well defined frontier, and the foremost Rabbinic authority of the day, Elijah, Gaon of Wilna, launched an edict of excommunication against the Ḥasidim in 1772 which was followed by others in rapid succession.

These bans and proscriptions, however, were the exceptions, not the rule, in Jewish life; and the excessive "building of fences" around the Torah, even in threatening times, did not go unchallenged. There were loyal Jews who resisted it. Sometimes the "fence and ramparts" enactments proved to be so extreme that they called forth opposition even from among some Pharisaic Rabbis themselves. These believed that "he who adds too much subtracts." [24] Thus, the Eighteen Measures which were enacted in the turbulent days which preceded the destruction of the Temple were bitterly opposed by the School of

Hillel whose opinions normally prevailed. The School of Shammai, the rigorists and militants, had the majority with them on that occasion. Adherents of these rival trends evidently came to blows over their differences and some were slain.[25] These Rabbinical decrees included far-reaching measures against partaking of the bread, wine, oil, and other foods of the heathen, against contact with their sons and daughters, and against accepting gifts from them for sacrifices in behalf of the health of the Roman emperors.[26] The prohibitions add up to a total separation of Jews from Gentiles. Such extreme measures of isolation had never been taken before, although on several previous occasions, as we have seen, in periods of crisis certain separatistic restrictions had been enacted. Various patriotic factors largely motivated the Eighteen Measures—hatred of the Romans (*the* heathen, par excellence); hope of isolating them economically and socially within the country; and the desire to consolidate the Jews for still fiercer resistance to them.[27]

The most outspoken rebel from within the ranks of the Rabbis themselves against the excessive proliferation of the law was undoubtedly Elisha ben Abuyah (1–2 c.). Among the foremost scholars of his day, he was the teacher of R. Meir, who remained loyal to him until the very end. He challenged the Rabbis not only in debate but in practice as well. He defied their Sabbath regulations by riding a horse on the Sabbath.[28] He probably defied many other Rabbinic enactments. His full story is wrapped in obscurity. He may have been unorthodox also in his theologic views. The Rabbis looked upon him as one "who had trampled the plants in the Garden!" He was ostracized, and his very name was never again mentioned in Rabbinic circles. For them he was just *Aḥer*—"that other one."

To the degree that the decline or absence of a centrally functioning religious authority and a national base where Jewish law could develop organically was felt by the Rabbis, they restricted themselves more closely to legal minutiæ and super-refinements, and bold initiative deserted them. One is at times saddened by the sight of grave scholars gathering faggots in a forest of mighty oaks to prepare a pottage of very thin gruel.

Resistance to the Oral Law as developed by the Rabbis continued all through the centuries of Talmudic consolidation. Our sources, except of course those found in the polemical writings of the New Testament and patristic literature, are meager. It is by indirection that the Talmud reveals such opposition. "Even if a man admits that the whole Torah is from heaven, excepting a single point, a particular *a minori ad majus* deduction, or a certain *gezerah shavah* [verbal analogy], he is still to be included in the category of those who despised the word of the Lord." [29]

The opposition became formidable and threatening with the rise of Islam, and the turbulent religious upheavals, as well as social and political dislocations which ensued—events which had a tremendous impact upon Jewry. The Karaite opposition arose in the eighth century, when Anan ben David began a revolt against Talmudic authority. The House of Israel was for centuries divided against itself by this bitter controversy.

This movement to limit Jewish law exclusively to the Bible could not, however, become an emancipating movement in Jewish life. On the contrary, it spelled petrification. Biblicism is in itself a form of extremism which could not act as an antidote to Rabbinic excesses of which it complained. In time the Karaites accepted some Rabbinic enactments, evolved some of their own by means of an exegesis no less artificial than that of the Rabbis, and produced their own oral tradition. In matters of Sabbath observance, ritual purity, marriage regulations, and dietary laws, the Karaite practice turned out to be far more stringent and constrictive than that of the Rabbis.

It was not until the nineteenth century that a determined effort was made by leaders of both Western and Eastern European Jewry—as a by-product of the Age of Enlightenment—to achieve the twofold objective of adjusting religious laws and customs to the needs of modern life and of reestablishing freer contact with other cultures. They set out to abolish the walls of partition which external intolerance and internal shrinking had erected through the long centuries. They aimed to lift unnecessary burdens, to cast overboard excessive impediments, to apply functional criteria to traditional religious disciplines, to simplify and beautify the worship and ritual, to modernize Jewish religious life which was just then emerging from the shadows of the ghettos of Europe. Above all, they wished to facilitate contacts with the surrounding world, where a new spirit of freedom and tolerance was then making itself manifest. They were guided by the conviction that the validity of Judaism was attested not by how or by whom, but by what it revealed; that its preservation depended not on an unyielding conservationism, but on a progressive unfoldment to meet the changing needs of life—a technique which was not absent from any of the creative periods in Jewish history. This movement to liberalize the disciplines and to reestablish full contact with progressive world cuture, suffering at times from a lack of historic perspective, from excessive "modernism" and rationalism, from a too naïve and impatient faith in a millennium just around the corner, and from an "antinationalism" which is inherently un-Jewish, was nevertheless a vital development definitely within the authentic trends of Jewish history. The ship long becalmed began to move again with the strong currents of wind and tide.

✤(IV)✤

ON BEING DIFFERENT

The ready adaptability of the Jewish people to foreign cultures should not, however, be exaggerated. It had its definite limits. What was clearly repugnant to its way of life was stubbornly resisted. What Israel borrowed, it recast in the crucible of its own spirit and molded into its own image. Out of the universal *Urstoff* of Semitic mythology—the vast primordial mythmass of customs, institutions, and credulities, and the common ways of folk thought and conduct—Israel appropriated much, but it subjected all of it in the course of time to a relentless sifting and screening. What was excluded gives us a better clue to an understanding of Judaism than what was accepted, and the differences are far more striking and important than the resemblances.

The clue to the spirit of any religion is to be found in the points of its strongest emphasis, its highest and most persistent manifestations, its values at their height. No religion, no human culture, and no product of genius can ever be satisfactorily explained by genesis, by parallels or precedents. The Neanderthal man does not explain Shakespeare, nor do Shakespeare's extensive plot borrowings from Plutarch or Holinshed give us any clue to his genius. It is of great historical interest to study Judaism stratigraphically, as it were, and to learn of the many underlying layers of religious cultures which, presumably in its earliest stages, it shared with many other religions of the eastern Mediterranean basin. These earlier deposits, however, did not determine the character of the faith known as historic Judaism which by its revolutionary nature changed the religious face of the world.

The originality of Judaism lies in the new frontiers which it reached and crossed. Its distinctiveness, as well as its importance to mankind, is to be looked for in the decisive break with the common past which other religions failed to make.

From time to time, a precipitate scholarship has discovered the provenance of all Biblical values and institutions in Babylonian, Egyptian, Arabic, and other sources. The Jews, it would appear, were merely passive recipients of alien cultural influences and Judaism was the end product of indiscriminate cross-fertilization. A more deliberate scholarship, reinforced by later insights and archaeologic discoveries, has corrected these notions. Judaism undoubtedly received affluence from many directions, but it was fed preeminently by its own natural springs. Its founders were keenly aware that what they were bringing to mankind was something radically different and new. They were bringing order, clarity, and coherence to the spiritual life of man by banishing the moral chaos of the mythological complex which held the minds of men enthralled. They were bringing moral freedom to men by repudiating the notions of fate and determinism which obsessed them. They taught mankind a new conception of God, a new social sensitiveness as to what was right and wrong, a new awareness as to man's duties toward his fellow men, a new spiritual refinement and delicacy in the relationship between the sexes. They carried on a consistent, and at times violent, opposition to the preponderance of ritualism and eschatology in religion.

A close scrutiny of ancient Near East texts relating to the Old Testament (now conveniently collected in one volume under the editorship of Dr. James B. Pritchard) [1] reveals a host of remarkable parallelisms between Egyptian, Sumerian, Akkadian, Hittite, Canaanite, and Ugaritic myths, laws, customs, ceremonies, and hymns with those of the Old Testament. These extra-Biblical sources, made available by exploration and excavation, help us to a better understanding of the Hebrew Bible. The significant landmarks, however, are the points of departure. A perusal of the texts reveals the long road which Israel traversed away from the spiritual and ethical frontiers of the peoples of antiquity, and the new continent of ideas it discovered and explored. Its key ideas were new ideas, hitherto unknown, and not familiar matter reworked. They were original creations, as original as were the artistic and philosophic ideas and forms of the ancient Greeks, and, like the latter, apparently sprung at a bound.

There was no true monotheism in the ancient world before the age of Moses and the great Prophets of Israel, and none for long centuries thereafter.

How the prophetic monotheistic faith came to Israel is one with the problem of how other distinctions and excellencies of mind and spirit came to other peoples. Much can be explained by tracing back through the mists of the unrolling centuries the lineage of ideas and endowments, but much more always remains unexplained. By sifting and arranging the debris of legends and myths and the broken fragments of prehistoric events, it is possible, to a degree, to trace the stages of mankind's progress through the ages, but the true origin of the new ideas and insights at each culminating stage remains an unsolved mystery.

It was a pleasant fantasy that traced Jewish monotheism back to the bland monotone of desert topography, wherein the early ancestors of the Hebrews lived and moved. Other peoples lived in deserts and produced no monotheistic faith. Geographic determinism has been matched by the equally interesting conceit of materialistic determinism, which sees in monotheism a by-product of a political and economic imperialism that Israel sought to impose upon the world. But unlike Babylon, Assyria, Egypt, Persia, Greece, or Rome, Israel never built an empire. Its national character was never on fire for conquest and victory. At no time did its dominion extend beyond Hamath in Syria to the north and Ezion-geber on the Gulf of Aqabah to the south—a modest empire, indeed.

One does not find a single instance of the rejection of the mythologic concept of deity in the religions of the ancient world. All the gods of lesser or higher degree have their genealogies, their births, their families, their rivalries, and their love affairs, and they are all subject to a power beyond themselves— nature, fate, necessity, destiny. There are realities and existences above and beyond them. The God of Israel is alone *in being alone*, with no power above Him. He is not a personification of any force in nature.

Primitive man looked upon all phenomena of nature as presences possessed of life and power. Nothing was inanimate. It has been correctly noted that early man confronted his world not as "It" but as "Thou." Judaism taught mankind to see the "Thou" only in God.

Native or borrowed myths were either rejected outright by Judaism, or, after having been ethically refined and purged of their polytheism and their sexuality, they remained as mere legends and folklore. All myths and mythical cosmogonies were obliterated in the revolutionary concept of a sole Creator God, Whose will alone determined everything in nature and in life. There is no theogony in the Torah and no theomachy. There are no primordial battles of the gods from which Yahweh emerges sovereign and triumphant. From time to time a seer or psalmist would employ poetically the borrowed imagery of some ancient popular myth to drive home the thought of God's unchallengeable omnipotence. But Rahab and the dragon, who were pierced and cut in pieces by the arm of the Lord (Is. 51:9), or the Leviathan whose heads were crushed by Him (Ps. 74:14), are never assumed to be anything but created beings who were punished for their rebellion against God. Whatever celestial beings, such as angels, were deemed to exist were looked upon not as forces of nature, or as possessed of a will of their own, or as objects of worship, but as messengers of God's will.

On the score of monotheism, Judaism was stubbornly intolerant and uncompromising—God is One and Alone! It did not fuse with other faiths. It did not incorporate indigenous gods. It refused all forms of coalescence and compounding. It did not finally rest content with henotheism—"Chemosh your God . . . Yahweh our God! . . ." (Jud. 11:24) or "Let all peoples walk each in the name of its god, but we will walk in the name of Yahweh our God" (Mic. 4:5). In the end there are no other gods besides Yahweh. What was unique about the God of Judaism was precisely that He was *not* a national God, but the universal God, Who had chosen the people of Israel to proclaim His unity and universality. This was the great continental divide between Judaism and all other religions. "I am the Lord, Who made all things, Who stretched out the heavens above, Who spread out the earth—Who was with me?" (Is. 44:24) And the day was sure to come when all the children of man will acknowledge this truth—when "Yahweh will be One and His name will be One" (Zech. 14:9).

This has led some to speak of Yahweh as a "jealous God," and proof has been adduced from the Second Commandment, where Yahweh is spoken of as *El Kana*. But *Kana* here, as the context clearly shows, means "zealous" and not jealous—quick to reward and punish. Monotheism could not, of course, tolerate polytheism, any more than truth can tolerate falsehood, or freedom slavery. There is nothing "jealous" about such relentless and mutually exclusive intolerances. They simply cannot co-exist.

Frequently mentioned in connection with the development of monotheism in the ancient world are the religious views of Ikhnaton (14 c. B.C.), who sought to carry out a religious revolution in Egypt by instituting the worship of the visible sun disc, the Aton, and whose ideas appear to be an isolated approximation to monotheism in the ancient world. However, the solar monism of Ikhnaton, which hardly survived him, is not yet Hebraic monotheism, any more than was the solar monism of the cult of Helios which spread in the Roman Empire many centuries later. Professor John A. Wilson, in his introduction to *The Hymn to the Aton*, correctly points out:

Because Akh-en-Aton was devoted to this God [Aton] alone, the Amarna religion has been called monotheistic. This is a debatable question, and reserved attitude would note that only Akh-en-Aton and his family worshipped the Aton; Akh-en-Aton courtiers worshipped Akh-en-Aton himself, and the great majority of Egyptians was ignorant of or hostile to the new faith.

Nor does one find a clear-cut rejection of polytheism among the Greeks. Greek philosophic thought was, of course, far in advance of the cult concepts of ancient Greece. With the Sophists in the fourth century B.C. there set in a critical examination of the traditional beliefs of the people. By the beginning of the common era a trend toward monotheism is noticeable among limited circles of devout philosophically-minded pagans. Because they were unable to abandon entirely their mythological and cultic heritage, they made an effort to reinterpret the cults and the myths associated with them in such a way as to raise them to higher levels of moral and spiritual meaning. Nevertheless, the old cults survived, and polytheism, sophisticated or otherwise, remained the public and private religion of the people.

Nowhere outside Judaism was the making or the worshiping of images forbidden. The gods of the ancients were represented either as animals, as in the case of the gods of Egypt, or in human form accompanied by sacred animals or creature emblems, as in the case of the gods of the Near East and of the Greek and Roman pantheons.

Judaism not only prohibited the making of any images, but by every device of metaphor and paraphrase sought to remove from the popular mind all anthropomorphic ideas of God, while retaining the sense of God's nearness and approachability which are so vital to true religion.

The God of Judaism was a Holy God—"holy" no longer in its primitive cult sense of mere "separateness," removedness, and awesomeness, but in an entirely new sense of moral perfection, in the sense in which Isaiah expressed the thought: "The Holy God shows Himself holy in righteousness" (Is. 5:16). He is the ideal and perfect God. He is the source of all moral law and is Himself obligated by the Law which He decreed—so that mortal man may appeal to Him on the basis of that Law. "Shall not the Judge of all the earth do justice?" Abraham remonstrated with God while arguing in behalf of sinful Sodom. "Ḥalilah!—It can not be!" (Gen. 18:25)

There is no arbitrariness or capriciousness in God, such as characterized the conduct of the mythological deities. He is uniquely and preeminently a God of *mishpaṭ*—rectitude and justice (Is. 30:18), even though at times His ways are unfathomable as the great deep (Ps. 36:7). All His ways are *mishpaṭ* (Dt. 32:4). He is bound by no external Power but by His own nature which is *mishpaṭ*, omnipotent but trustworthy. "He judges the world with *mishpaṭ* and peoples with His faithfulness" (Ps. 96:13). Men are summoned to seek *mishpat* (Is. 1:17). God's covenant with Israel is a covenant of *mishpaṭ* (Hosea 1:21). Zion will be redeemed through *mishpaṭ* (Is. 1:27). And the future of mankind, its peace and security, is bound up with *mishpaṭ* (Is. 2:4).

Judaism excised the willful, the erratic, and the amoral from the concept of divinity, and based its theology squarely on moral correspondence and proportion. (See page 149.)

Nowhere in ancient literature is the institution of sacrifices as the essential and supreme form of worship condemned or even questioned, as was the case with the prophets of Israel. One searches in vain for a clear call to distinguish the true worship of God from ritual and sacrifice, and to identify it with ethical conduct.

The God of Judaism was not interested in worshipers trampling His court, in incense and offerings, "in thousand of rams and ten thousand of rivers of oil." His sole requirement was that men should "seek justice, relieve the oppressed, defend the orphan, plead for the widow" (Is. 1:17). Occasionally one catches a fugitive note in the ritual texts of Babylonia and Assyria suggesting a conception of sin as moral offense, as in the Shurpu series of incantations, but little more than that. No line is drawn between taboo sins and moral sins, and there is certainly no attempt, as with Judaism, radically to subordinate one to the other. By making this distinction, Judaism gave new dimensions to man's spiritual world.

Nowhere is there a revulsion against the sex motif which is so central in the mythologies of ancient religions, or against the institution of sacred prostitution, which was connected with their worship, or against the unbridled orgiastic rites of their nature festivals. Judaism alone called these practices and their sex symbolism obscene. "There shall be no cult prostitute of the daughters of Israel, neither shall there be a cult prostitute of the sons of Israel. You shall not bring the hire of a harlot, or the wages of a dog [Sodomite] into the house of the Lord your God . . . for both of these are an abomination to the Lord your God" (Dt. 23:19). Professor Albright states that "it was fortunate for the future of monotheism that the Canaanites, with their orgiastic nature-worship, their cult of fertility in the form of serpent symbols and sensuous nudity and their gross mythology, were replaced by Israel, with its nomadic simplicity and purity of life, its lofty monotheism, and its severe code of ethics." [2]

Along with the banishment of all sexual rites and sacred prostitution, Judaism at the same time refused to sanction vowed chastity as a form of worship—a religious institution which was common in antiquity.

Laxity in sexual matters which characterized so many of the peoples of antiquity and which was sanctioned by the example of their gods was execrated by Judaism in an unparalleled way. Purity of family life, to a degree practically unknown in the ancient world—even among its most advanced circles—became the norm for the Jewish way of life, and it has remained a characteristic of Jewish behavior throughout the ages. To perceive the difference one needs but recall the previously mentioned recommendation of Plato in his *Republic* (Bk. V) and his *Laws* (Bk. V) on the basis of the ancient saying "Friends have all things in common," that women also should be held in common, and children as well—a practice which would destroy family life altogether. The utility of the proposal, in Plato's mind, was beyond question; only the possibility of effectuating it remained in doubt. Lycurgus, the reputed founder of the Constitution of Sparta, decreed for his countrymen the honorable practice of giving "the use of their wives to those whom they should think fit, so that they might have children by them" for purposes of breeding strong men and soldiers, or simply as an accommodation, since the matter was not worth fighting over.[3]

That women are by nature common property was a theory widely held in the ancient world, and Plato therefore did not advance any shocking new proposal when he advocated the community of women for his warrior-saints. This view was also subscribed to by many Stoics. Zeno (4–3 c. B.C.), the founder of the Stoic school at Athens, advocated it, as did the Stoic Chrysippus (3 c. B.C.). So did Diogenes the Cynic, according to the testimony of Diogenes Laërtius.[4] Epictetus, who opposed this view of his fellow Stoics, reports that the idea was very popular among the women of Rome: "At Rome the women have in their hands Plato's 'Republic,' because he insists on community of women."[5]

From the writings of Clement of Alexandria (2–3 c.), it appears that such ideas were entertained even by some of the heretical Christian sects, like the Carpocratians, whose founders derived them from their Hellenistic environment and traced them back to Plato.[6] The orthodox Church denounced and repudiated these sects.

The writings of Seneca, Juvenal, Martial, Tacitus, Suetonius, Dio Cassius all reveal the moral degeneration of Roman society, in which promiscuity, sodomy, and lesbianism were widely practiced. So also do the writings of Paul (Rom. 1:24–27). They help us to realize the violent contrast between the standards of this society and the Jewish standards of sexual decency, the sanctity of marriage and of family life.

Modesty was urged upon men and women by Judaism. The principle laid down was: "Sanctify yourself even in things permitted to you." [7] New concepts were introduced: zni-'ut—modesty, moral delicacy; *boshet*—reticence, sensitiveness to all that is gross. "There is nothing more beloved of God than zni-'ut";[8] and, "He who does not possess the quality of *bushah*, it is certain that his ancestors were not present at Mount Sinai." [9]

This code of *boshet* (Ecclus. 41:16) did not result from any prudery on the part of the people of Israel. It was an expression of reverence for life itself and for the dignity of man. It was the esthetics of morality which Judaism introduced to the ancient world, the "beauty of holiness." Three thousand years of Jewish literature are distinguished by a remarkable freedom from vulgarity and lubricity. "It is a man's duty to keep away from unseemliness, from what resembles unseemliness and from the semblance of a semblance." [10]

Such a concept makes it inconceivable that the obscenities of Attic comedy, for example, which so delighted Athenian audiences, would have been tolerated in any city in Israel. Socrates was a sage of unimpeachable moral character, "the best, wisest and most upright of his age." But what sage in Israel would have boasted, even playfully, of being a lifelong victim of Eros, a "lover" of Alcibiades, and would have spoken of homosexual perversion as complacently as Socrates did? And what was the moral tone of a people that would show no aversion to this?

With the Greeks this phenomenon [*paiderastia*] exhibited all the symptoms of a great national disease, a kind of moral pestilence. . . . In very truth, the whole of society was infected with it, and people inhaled the pestilence with the air they breathed.[11]

It was from the Greeks, according to Herodotus, that the Persians learned this perversion. And as for the Romans—"By the time the last days of the free republic were reached, the vice had attained a fearful degree among the Romans." [12]

To the Sages of Israel sexual perversion was under the curse of God. It was so rare among the people, and regarded with such abhorrence, that "a Jew was not to be suspected either of pederasty or bestiality." [13] Even unclean speech was condemned.

Gehenna is made deep, declared the Rabbis, for the man who speaks lewdly and for him who listens to it and is silent.[14] Throughout they urged men to use the *lashon nekiah*—the clean, chaste speech, the *lishna ma-'alya*—the euphemism, to avoid the coarse, vulgar term.

Many of the Biblical and later Rabbinic injunctions which have been characterized as "particularistic" and "exclusive" were in fact motivated by this overriding concern to keep the life of the individual Jew and the Jewish family clean and uncorrupted.

Man never quite disentangled himself from the dim memories of his subhuman life. Ancient man was aware of a common lineage with the animal, though he was aware also that he was something more than an animal. But no clear boundaries were recognized between man and beast and between man and his gods. In his mythological world there roamed beings who were half man and half beast, and his ancient legends told of cosmic struggles between beasts and gods in human form. His closeness to the life of animals reached even the point of carnal commerce with them. Biblical law punished such perversions with death (Ex. 22:18; Lev. 20:15–16).

The prohibition against partaking of the blood of animals (Dt. 12:16; Lev. 3:17, *et al.*) was in all probability also motivated by the desire to cleanse the nature of man and to remove him from affinity with the beast, for the blood was regarded as the seat of the soul or the life of man and beast. "And you shall not eat the life with the flesh" (Dt. 12:23).

The religious worship of primitive man was largely a matter of magical rites, and few religions emancipated themselves from magic. Rarely does one find in the literature of antiquity any denunciation of witchcraft, sorcery, divination, necromancy, and astrology, such as one finds in the Bible (Lev. 20:6 and 27; Deut. 18:10–12; Is. 65:4; Jer. 10:2).

Magic played a very prominent part in the social and religious life of the Egyptians. Dr. Warren R. Dawson writes:

It affected not only the relations of men with their living fellows but with the dead and with the gods. By the Egyptian, magic was believed to be a sure means of accomplishing all his necessities and desires and of performing, in short, everything that the common procedure of daily life was inadequate to bring about.[15]

Ten measures of magic and witchcraft, declared a Rabbinic Sage, came down to earth. Egypt took nine of them.[16] It is startling to realize how large a place magic held also among the most educated and cultured circles of the Greco-Roman world. "No modern voodoo from the darkest jungle can outbid what magic promised to men in the Hellenistic age, so that the most cultivated and most eminent were prone to resort to magic in moments of strain or danger." [17]

Among Jews, too, certain superstitious beliefs and magical practices persisted. Not all the Jews in any generation were "wise and understanding, and students of the Torah." The vestigial fears and practices of primitive society remained with them also. Charms, amulets, magical rites, incantations, and belief in demons were part of the folk faith of such Jews in almost every generation, from the earliest times through the Middle Ages. But they were never incorporated into Judaism, which endeavored to eradicate them. "He who whispers a charm over a wound will have no portion in the world to come." [18] "He who learns a single thing from a Magian deserves death." [19]

In his recent monumental study of *Jewish Symbols in the Greco-Roman Period*, Professor E. R. Goodenough seems to discover in the persistent subforms of religion which he describes evidence of a definite syncretistic Judaism which existed in the late Roman Empire.[20] The evidence, however, is not conclusive. There is no doubt that after the smelting and refining process was accomplished in Judaism, slag and scoria remained in the folkways of some Jews. But it was not Judaism.

Astrology, which was the most widely accredited "science" in the ancient world, and which from the second century B.C. became "the fashionable creed of the Hellenistic world," [21] found its adherents also among some of the more mystically-minded Rabbis like R. Joshua b. Levi (3 c.) and R. Ḥanina (3 c.). The most authoritative Rabbis, however, like Akiba (2 c.), R. Johanan (2–3 c.), and Rab and Samuel (3 c.), placing themselves squarely on the Bible (Jer. 10:2), flatly rejected it. "Israel," they declared, "is immune from planetary influences." [22] Abraham, who by tradition was a master of astronomical science, wished to entertain a belief in astrology, but this was not permitted him.[23]

Astrology was never allowed a place in authoritative Judaism, although it became very popular among the people, even among some of its leaders and theologians, when it no longer carried with it any polytheistic implications, and when the heavenly bodies came to be regarded not as divine beings but as the obedient instruments of God, predetermined in their nature and possessed neither of judgment nor of free will.[24]

Among the new highways which Judaism built for mankind, its great road toward social justice is of paramount significance in the history of human development. Not only in ethical sweep and outlook, which are normally in advance of law, did Judaism surpass anything which the ancient world attained, but in its legal system as well.

One should be wary of facile and superficial resemblances between Biblical laws and those of other ancient codes. Many parallels and points of contact can easily be drawn between the Covenant Code of Exodus (20:23–23:33 and 34:17–26) and the Code of Hammurabi, for example, which is far more extensive and a thousand years older. The Hebrews upon their entrance into Canaan in the fourteenth century b.c. undoubtedly adopted many of the Hammurabi laws which had long been in operation in one form or another in that part of the world, and which, in turn, were based on still earlier collections of laws. What is significant, however, are not only the laws which the Hebrews did not incorporate into their code, such as the law applicable to a father who devotes his daughter as a sacred prostitute to some god and does not give her a dowry,[25] but the manner in which they revised and recast the laws which they did incorporate and the new laws which they themselves enacted.

The Hammurabi Code recognizes two distinct classes of society, besides slaves, and applies separate standards of legal responsibility toward each. There is one law for the nobility and another for the common people. "If a man knock out a tooth of a man of his own rank, they shall knock out his tooth." [26] "If he knock out the tooth of a common man, he shall pay one-third mina of silver." [27] "If a man strike the cheek of a man who is his *superior,* he shall receive sixty strokes with an oxtail whip in public." [28] "If a common man strike a common man on the cheek, he shall pay ten shekels of silver." [29] In the case where "the son of a gentleman strikes the son of a gentleman of his own rank on the cheek, he shall pay one mina of silver." [30] There is no penalty, apparently, in the case where a man strikes his social *inferior* on the cheek. If a common man strikes the pregnant daughter of a common man and causes her death, his own daughter shall be put to death.[31] But if a nobleman causes such a death he shall pay one-half mina of silver.[32]

The Hebrew Code, which did not originate or develop among a governing caste, makes no such distinctions. No discrimination is made in Hebrew law between a noble and commoner, any more than between the native born and the stranger (Ex. 12:49 *et passim*).

On the treatment of slaves, the Hebrew Code is infinitely more humane. The Covenant Code prescribes punishment for the master who maltreats his slave and causes his death. The slave's death must be avenged as murder (Ex. 21:20). The Code of Hammurabi is silent on this score. The Covenant Code ordains that when a man smites the eye of his slave, male or female, and destroys it, or strikes out a tooth, he must let the slave go free (Ex. 21:26–27). On this, too, the Hammurabi Code is silent. The latter prescribes death to him who helps a slave to escape, or harbors a runaway slave in his house; [33] while the Hebrew law, in sharp contrast, ordains: "You shall not give up to his master a slave who has escaped from his master to you; he shall dwell with you, in your midst, in the place which he shall choose within one of your towns, where it pleases him best; you shall not oppress him" (Dt. 23:16-17).

The Hebrew Code is also far more lenient than the Hammurabi Code to a culprit who commits larceny. If a man steals an ox or an ass or a sheep he must pay double (Ex. 22:3). If he kills what he has stolen, he must pay fivefold for an ox and fourfold for a sheep (Ex. 21:27). The Code of Hammurabi prescribes: "If a man steals an ox or a sheep, ass or pig, or boat, if it belonged to God or palace, he shall pay thirty-fold; if it belonged to a common man, he shall restore ten-fold. If a thief has nothing to pay, he shall be put to death." [34] This Babylonian law may seem less severe when we recall that in England, as late as the eighteenth century, theft was a crime punishable by death, along with 250 other offenses. But in ancient Mosaic and Talmudic law the punishment was by fine only.

As regards the provisions of the Hebrew Code (Ex. 22:21-27; 23:4-6; Lev. 19:9-10) for the care of the stranger, the widow, and the orphan, the mandate to help one's enemy, and the requirement that justice and compassion be shown to the poor—of these there are no glimmerings in the Hammurabi Code, which makes no provision whatsoever for the care of the poor. This also holds true for Egyptian law. Sentiments of compassion and charity were undoubtedly not wanting among individuals; and they find expression in some of the Egyptian mortuary texts, where the deceased make protestations of their virtues and benevolence first by way of a "Negative Confession," listing the sins which they did not commit, and then by way of a positive declaration: "I have given bread to the hungry, water to the thirsty, clothing to the naked, and a ferry-boat to him who was marooned." [35] Neither Egyptian nor Babylonian law, however, makes any formal provision for the care of the needy, such as one finds with the Hebrews—the mandatory sharing in the harvest, the obligatory alms, the tithe (Lev. 19:9-10; 23:22), and the prohibition against exacting interest on money lent to the poor. Nor do they record such thoughtful consideration for the man in distress and such regard for his inviolable human dignity as are contained in the Deuteronomic legislation:

When you make your neighbor a loan of any sort, you shall not go into his house to fetch his pledge. You shall stand outside, and the man to whom you made the loan shall bring the pledge out to you. And if he is a poor man, you shall not sleep in his pledge; when the sun goes down, you shall restore to him the pledge that he may sleep in his cloak and bless you; and it shall be righteousness to you before the Lord your God [Dt. 24:10-13].

In no other regard is the contrast so marked, and it is the very key to an understanding of what was new and different in Hebrew law and ethics.

A large accumulation of evidence supports the considered judgment of Professor J. M. Powis Smith: "When the Covenant Code achieved its present and final form, it was in most of its regulations far ahead of the Code of Hammurabi, so far as religious and humanitarian qualities go." [36]

Reference might well be made in this connection to the *lex talionis* of Ex. 21:23-25—"an eye for an eye." Concerning the *lex talionis*, Dr. Goldin writes:

It substituted for the savage primitive concept of limitless revenge and private resentment a legal punishment as commensurate as possible with the injury inflicted. St. Augustine was one of the first to state that the *lex talionis* was a law of justice, not of hatred; one eye, not two eyes, for an eye; one tooth, not ten teeth, for a tooth; one life, not a whole family, for a life.[37]

Moreover, even in earliest times, this law—in itself a distinct advance over the primitive practice which left the determination of the nature and degree of punishment entirely in the hands of the aggrieved person or his kinsmen since homicide and bodily injuries were not considered crimes against the state—was already superseded. It was abolished in the early days of the Second Commonwealth. In all matters involving bodily injury the compensation was in money.[38]

In the Greek and Roman eras the attitude toward slaves was no less brutal than in earlier times. Both Plato and Aristotle, the two greatest minds of the ancient world, justified human slavery as originating in the very structure of the universe. Plato encouraged a feeling of contempt for slaves as a class. For his ideal Republic he ordained that if a man kills his own slave he shall undergo a formal purification—and nothing more! [39] And Aristotle argued:

Others affirm that the rule of a master over slaves is contrary to nature, and that the distinction between slavery and free men exists by law only, and not by nature; being an interference with nature is, therefore, unjust. . . . There is no difficulty in answering this question, on grounds both of reason and of fact. For that some should rule, and others be ruled is a thing, not only necessary, but expedient; from the hour of their birth, some are marked out for subjection, others for rule. . . . Such a duality exists in living creatures, but not in them only; it originates in the constitution of the universe; even in things which have no life, there is a ruling principle as in musical harmony. . . . It is clear, then, that some men are by nature free, and others slaves, and that for these latter slavery is both expedient and right. . . . The art of war is a natural art of acquisition, for it includes hunting, an art which we ought to practice against wild beasts, and against men who, though intended by nature to be governed, will not submit; for war of such a kind is naturally just.[40]

Roman writers like Juvenal dwell on the cruel and inhuman treatment of slaves, their torture and crucifixion as forms of punishment.

When Rome became a conquering state, the captives in thousands filled the town and the country with slaves and the attitude toward slavery changed. The slave became a mere chattel; in law he had neither wife nor children, and his master had the power of life and death over him.[41]

It was not until the second century of the common era that the law was modified, and an attitude more humane than that which had led in earlier centuries to the frightful rebellions of Eunus, Trypho, and Spartacus came to prevail.

There is, of course, no clear injunction in the Bible against slavery. Judaism did not call for the abolition of the institution of slavery as such, any more than Christianity did many centuries later. It was too indurate a part of the universal social system, too ingrained in the way of life and in the accepted culture of the day. No frontal attack upon the institution was as yet possible. But Judaism never approved of it or justified it or advocated it or proclaimed it as a law of God or of nature, as did Plato and Aristotle. There are no apologetics for slavery in Jewish literature.

Slavery was never extensive in Israel. The incidents of military victories, yielding a large reserve of prisoners of war—the main source of supply for slaves in the ancient world—were too few and far between to fill the cities of Israel with slaves. Nor was the country sufficiently prosperous for any length of time or the number of its rich large enough to result in the acquisition of numerous slaves by purchase. The government seldom had under its control a large class of helots, such as Sparta had, apart from the reigns of David and Solomon when the conquered Canaanites were used as a forced levy of slaves (*mas 'oved*) in the smelter-refineries of Ezion-geber.[42] A small group of Temple servants—the Nethinim—performed the more menial chores in the sanctuary, but they were not slaves. During the Second Commonwealth, Hebrew slavery among Jews rapidly disappeared. No mention is made in the Bible or Talmud of Jewish slave traders, or of slave insurrections, or of female slaves sold for public prostitution—a common practice in the ancient world. Palestine was not built upon a slave economy as was Athens, where the ratio of slave to citizen was at times five to one. Hebrew slaves in Biblical times were actually only defaulting debtors who became indentured servants, or those who were sold into slavery for stealing, or who sold themselves because of poverty, but whose term of servitude could never extend beyond six years (Ex. 21:2). The Jubilee year was intended to terminate such indenture automatically even before the expiration of the six years (Lev. 25:39–43).

The legal attitude of the Bible to slavery is summarized by Mendelsohn: "This denial of the right of possession of man by man in perpetuity is as yet restricted to Hebrews only, but it is a step which no other religion had taken before." [43]

Hebrew slaves lost none of the rights possessed by other members of the community. The master was expected to treat a Hebrew slave with all consideration. "For it was taught: 'He [the Hebrew slave] fares well with you' (Dt. 15:16)—he must be like you in food, in drink, you should not eat fine bread and he coarse bread, you should not drink old wine and he new wine, you should not sleep on a soft bed and he on straw. Hence it is said: whoever buys a Hebrew slave practically buys a master over himself." [44] The Sages also declared that a Hebrew slave must not wash the feet of his master, nor put his shoes on him, nor carry his things before him when going to the bathhouse, nor support him when ascending steps, nor carry him in a litter or a chair or a sedan as slaves do—things which one's son or one's pupil may do. He could not be forced to do anything other than work at his trade. [45] A far-going provision for the protection of the future of the slave who is set free, to enable him to reestablish himself economically, was the Biblical injunction: "And when you let him go free from you, you shall not let him go empty-handed; you shall furnish him liberally out of your flock, out of your threshing floor, and out of your wine press; as the Lord your God has blessed you, you shall give to him" (Dt. 15:13–14).

The spirit of the people did not approve of any one of its members voluntarily choosing to remain a bondman. The law in Exodus provides that "if a slave plainly says, 'I love my master, my wife, and my children; I will not go out free,' then his master shall bring him to God [before the Judges] and he shall bring him to the door or the doorpost; and his master shall bore his ear through with an awl; and he shall serve for life" (Ex. 21:5–6). On this verse the famous R. Johanan b. Zakkai seized "as upon a precious stone," and expounded it to yield an important lesson: "Why was the ear singled out from all other limbs of the body?

The Holy One, blessed be He, said: 'This ear, which heard My voice on Mountain Sinai when I proclaimed "For unto Me the children of Israel are servants; they are My servants" (Lev. 25:55), and not servants of servants, and yet this man went and acquired a master for himself—let his ear be bored!' " [45a]

The heathen slave fared less well. He was a slave in the accepted sense of the term—the property of his master. But Jewish law sought to mitigate the evils of his slavery as well, and to soften its harshness. Judaism required that a heathen slave who suffered injury at the hand of his master must forthwith be set free with compensation.[46] "For the loss of any one of twenty-four tips of limbs, a slave must be set free." [47] This was an amplification of the already noted Biblical law (Ex. 21:26-27): "When a man strikes the eye of his slave, male or female, he shall let the slave go free." A master who kills his slave shall himself be put to death. Heathen slaves, if they were not unwilling, were adopted into the household of their Jewish masters through circumcision and, in the case of female slaves, through baptism, and they shared in the ritual observances and festivals. The non-Jewish slave had his Sabbath day of rest with all the members of the family.

The cruelty of the ancient world to its slaves was matched by its treatment of the poor. Its prosperous and privileged classes were contemptuous of them. "What is the use of being kind to a poor man?" wrote Cicero. Seneca expressed the thought that it was a weakness unworthy of the wise man to feel pain at the misfortunes of others. In Judaism, however, the poor and needy were the special wards of God, and the special responsibility of those who would truly serve God. "For the poor will never cease out of the land; therefore I command you, you shall open wide your hand to your brother, to the needy and to the poor, in the land" (Dt. 15:11). Judaism denounced the oppression and exploitation of the poor, as no religion did before or since. It castigated the rich and powerful for "grinding the faces of the poor" (Is. 3:15), "for joining house to house, and adding field

to field until there is no more room" (Is. 5:8), for "selling the
needy for a pair of shoes" and for "trampling the head of the
poor into the dust of the earth" (Amos 2:6–7). It cried: "Woe to
those who are at ease in Zion . . . to those who lie upon beds of
ivory . . . who drink wine in bowls, and anoint themselves
with the finest oils, but are not grieved over the ruins of Joseph"
(Amos 6:4–6).

Legislation was enacted in ancient Israel to guard the poor
against total and permanent pauperization. No one's land could
be sold in perpetuity and forever alienated. At the time of the
Jubilee year, each man was to be restored to his property (Lev.
25:25–28). Whether the laws of the Jubilee year were ever
applied in practice is a matter of considerable doubt, but the
humane motives of this legislation and its lasting influence on
Jewish social attitudes cannot be questioned.

The same motives informed other Biblical laws: "If your
brother becomes poor, and cannot maintain himself with you,
you shall maintain him. . . . You shall not lend him your money
at interest, nor give him your food for profit" (Lev. 25:35–37).

The care of the poor in Israel was a religious duty. The Biblical
laws which made provision for the poor were greatly elaborated
in subsequent times. Charity came to be regarded as the highest
of all commandments, as in fact equal to all of them combined.
He who did not give charity was likened to one who worshiped
idols.[48]

No literature of mankind abounds in such tender solicitude
for the poor or in so many provisions for their protection as
Biblical and post-Biblical literature. "Draw out your soul to the
hungry and satisfy the afflicted soul" (Is. 58:10). Always one
human soul reaching out to another; always one heart beating
in sympathy with another.

No community in history organized itself so early to provide
adequate relief for the needy as the Jewish community. Every
Jew was taxed for the maintenance of charitable agencies. Col-
lectors and overseers were appointed for their administration.
Every community had its central food depot (*Tamḥui*) from

which food was distributed daily to all who applied, and its charity fund (*Kupah*) from which moneys were distributed every Friday to the poor of the city.[49] "We have never seen nor heard of any Jewish community," writes Maimonides in his Code, "which did not have its charity fund." [50] Door-to-door begging was discouraged, for the poor must not be put to shame when forced to seek help.[51] Hospices were established for the poor traveler. Special funds were raised as dowries for poor brides. Provision was made for the decent burial of the indigent poor and for the redemption of captives. The orphan and the widow were the especial concern of the community, for the God whom Jews worshiped was the "Father of the fatherless and the Protector of widows" (Ps. 68:5). Charity took priority over the building of the Temple. King Solomon was not permitted to make use of the silver and gold which David, his father, had accumulated for the building of the Temple (I K. 7:51), because that wealth should have been used during the three years of famine in King David's reign to feed the poor and to save lives.[52]

There are eight ascendant degrees in charity, and the highest of these is that charity which helps a poor man to a trade or occupation wherewith he is able to support himself.[53] There are many ways of giving charity, but "The man who gives charity in secret is greater than Moses our teacher." [54]

The basic humanity of Judaism is seen also in its attitude towards labor. Physical labor was held in disdain in the ancient world. Because of the nigh universal institution of slavery, the labor even of the free citizen suffered the contempt felt for the work of the slave.

Leading Greek philosophers despised labor and looked upon it as degrading. These aristocrats of the mind were also disdainful of the trader and the merchant. Among the intellectual and upper classes of society, almost everywhere in the ancient world, the earning of a livelihood by manual labor was contemned. The attitude of Egyptians, Greeks, and barbarians toward work and trade is given by Herodotus:

I have remarked that the Thracians, the Scyths, and the Persians, the Lydians, and almost all other barbarians hold the citizens who practice trades, and their children in less repute than the rest while they esteem as noble those who keep aloof from handicrafts, and especially honor such as are given wholly to war. These ideas prevail throughout the whole of Greece, particularly among the Lacedaemonians. Corinth is the place where mechanics are least despised.[55]

Aristotle was of the opinion that laborers, artisans, and merchants were unfit for the exercise of virtue and for citizenship. In the eyes of the Romans, too, labor and trade were in disrepute. Unbecoming to a gentleman, according to Cicero, and vulgar are the means of livelihood of all hired workmen, who are paid for their manual labor, and all mechanics, and all small tradesmen.[56]

Except for rare periods in the economic history of the world, when, as a result of war or plagues or other disasters, the demand for labor greatly exceeded the supply and forced higher compensations and fairer treatment, this attitude persisted down to the twentieth century, even among some of the most civilized peoples of Europe.

The Bible regards a man fortunate and blessed who is privileged to eat of the fruit of the labor of his own hands. "You shall be happy, and it shall be well with you" (Ps. 128:2). The wisdom literature of Israel is replete with passages extolling labor, industry and the honest craftsman.

The Rabbis also stressed the importance of men working with their own hands. "Blessing does not rest except on a man's handiwork." [57] "A man must work with his two hands before God will bestow blessing upon him." [58] R. Joshua b. Levi (3 c.) said: "When the Holy One, blessed be He, said to Adam, 'Thorns and thistles shall it bring forth to you' (Gen. 3:18), tears flowed from his eyes, and he pleaded before Him, 'Sovereign of the Universe! Shall I and my ass eat out of the same crib!' But as soon as God said to Him, 'In the sweat of your face shall you eat bread' (Gen. 3:19), his mind was set to rest." [59]

The ennobling powers of labor were also stressed by the great Rab. He said to R. Kahana: "Flay a carcass in the street and earn a wage and say not, 'I am a great man and such work is degrading to me.' " [60] "Let not a man say, 'I come from a noble and distinguished family and I cannot stoop to work and degrade myself.' Fool, your Creator, God Himself, performed work before you were born!" [61] Famous Rabbis like Hillel, Akiba, Ḥanina, Jose b. Ḥalafta, Joshua, and many others were artisans, cobblers, blacksmiths, tailors, bakers, potters, charcoal burners, and of numerous other occupations. In no way was the social status of the wage earner and the artisan of Talmudic times affected by their means of earning a livelihood. On the contrary, it was held that work honors those who perform it.[62]

The Rabbis, who valued study so highly, nevertheless were opposed to scholarship without physical labor, and advised their disciples to combine study with some worldly occupation. Rabbi Gamaliel, the son of the compiler of the Mishnah, declared: "Excellent is the study of the Torah together with a worldly occupation, for toil in them both puts sin out of mind. But all study of the Torah without physical labor comes to naught in the end and drags sin in its train." [63]

Israel had itself experienced brutal exploitation and unrequited labor in Egypt. Into its social code, accordingly, there were early written admonitions to lighten the burden of labor, to reward labor promptly and adequately, and to respect the dignity of the workingman. They are the first definite provisions on record for the protection of the workingman.

The problems of a highly industrialized society and of a large proletariat obviously did not exist in the predominantly agricultural and rural society of ancient Israel, but legislation is nevertheless recorded which aimed at the protection of the rights of the workingman. A just wage should be paid, and paid promptly (Dt. 24:14–15; Lev. 19:13). A day of rest every week—the Sabbath—was ordained for the worker and the servant as well as for the master. The exploiter of labor was the particular object of bitter denunciation: "Woe to him . . . who makes his neighbor serve him for nothing and does not give him wages. . . . You have eyes and heart only for your dishonest gains, for shedding innocent blood, and for practicing oppression and violence" (Jer. 22:13–17). "Then I will draw near to you for judgment: I will be a swift witness against . . . those who oppress the hired worker in his wages" (Mal. 3:5). "He that takes away his neighbor's living slays him," declared Ben Sira, "and he that defrauds the labourer of his hire is a shedder of blood" (Ecclus. 34:22).

The same reverence for human life is again in evidence in Judaism's opposition to the abandonment of the aged and the exposure of infants, practices which were all too common in the ancient world. "There was, owing to the chronic warfare of the time, usually a dearth of men and superfluity of women among the early Indo-European peoples. Hence girl infants, as not needed, were often exposed. Old people, too, were frequently put out of the way especially in time of need." [64]

Plato's already noted approval of infanticide was unequivocal: "The offspring of the inferior, or of the better when they chance to be deformed, will be put away in some mysterious, unknown place, as they should be." [65]

Justin Martyr (2 c.) denounced this shameful practice, widespread in the Greco-Roman world of his day. The exposed infants, if they did not perish, were picked up and brought up for prostitution and sodomy.[66] Centuries later Mohammed had to forbid the practice of infant exposure to his followers.[67]

To leave the aged to die of hunger and to expose them to wild beasts was also far from rare among the Hindus, Persians, Greeks, and Romans.

Jewish law forbade the murder or the exposure of infants. It was practically unknown in Israel. "It is a crime among them to kill any newly born infant," writes Tacitus, who is not otherwise distinguished for his admiration of the Jewish people.[68]

Old age was revered in Israel. "You shall rise up before the hoary head, and honor the face of an old man," we read in the Holiness Code (Lev. 19:32). "Despise not your mother when she is old" (Pr. 23:22). Men were advised to turn to the aged for guidance: "With the aged there is wisdom and in length of days there is understanding" (Job 12:12). Old age is noble: "A hoary head is a crown" (Pr. 16:31). "As the clear light is upon the holy candlestick, so is the beauty of the face in ripe old age" (Ecclus. 26:17). The aged should be cared for, sheltered, and honored. Children are charged with the duty of looking after and providing for their parents even when it involves the greatest of sacrifices on their part, even when, as R. Simeon b. Yoḥai puts it, it involves the necessity of begging for them.[69]

Thus, in a world of cruelty and inhumanity, where life was cheap, Judaism taught men to open the wells of pity in the human heart. It condemned all callousness. It taught men to rise to higher levels of sensibility and sympathy, and to move away from the old savageries and primitive animality. Mercy and compassion were forever to be the distinguishing marks of a true Israelite. "Whoever is merciful to his fellow-men is certainly of the children of our father Abraham, and whosoever is not merciful to his fellow-men is certainly not of the children of our father Abraham." [70]

More than social justice, more than personal rectitude were taught by Judaism. It called for a quality of humaneness, tenderness, and magnanimity, a sensitiveness to the hurt, physical or mental, of one's fellow men. It extolled the "understanding heart" that "knows the heart of the stranger" (Ex. 23:9). Basing itself on the Biblical injunction "And a stranger you shall not wrong, nor oppress him" (Ex. 22:20), the Mishnah taught that the wrong includes also the wrong done by words. "If a man was a repentant sinner, one must not say to him, 'Remember your former deeds.' If he was the son of a proselyte one must not taunt him, 'Remember the deeds of your ancestors.' " [71] One must not say to a man who is visited by suffering, afflicted with disease, or who has buried his children what the companions said to Job, "Who ever perished being innocent?" Another Tanna declared: "He who publicly shames his neighbor is as though he shed blood." [72]

Judaism's universal rule of kindness extended also to animals. "Until the nineteenth century, cruelty to animals was nowhere illegal, except in Jewish law." [73] Animals, too, must rest on the

Sabbath (Ex. 20:10). "The duty of relieving the suffering of beasts is a Biblical law." [74] "A righteous man has regard for the soul of his beast" (Pr. 12:10). The Deuteronomic law ordains: "You shall not muzzle an ox when it treads the grain" (Dt. 25:4). "You shall not plow with an ox and an ass together" (Dt. 22:10), for the strength of the ass is less than that of the ox and he would be overtaxed if forced to keep up with the ox. [75] A man is forbidden to eat before he gives food to his beast, declared R. Judah in the name of Rab. [76] It is strictly forbidden to cut off a limb while the animal is still alive (Dt. 12:23). The young of an animal must not be taken from its mother for the first seven days after birth, even for a sacrifice. The mother and her young must not be killed on the same day (Lev. 22:27–28).

The story told in the Talmud of the Patriarch Rabbi Judah I (2 c.) dramatizes this attitude of kindness toward animals. A calf was being taken to slaughter when it broke away, hid its head under the Rabbi's cloak, and lowed in terror. "Go," said he, "for this wast thou created." Thereupon, they said (in Heaven), "Since he has no pity, let us bring suffering upon him," and Rabbi suffered for thirteen years. Then, one day Rabbi's maidservant was sweeping the house and, seeing some newborn kittens lying there, she made to sweep them away. "Let them be," he said. "It is written 'and His tender mercies are over all His works'" (Ps. 145:9). Whereupon they (in Heaven) said: "Since he is compassionate, let us be compassionate towards him." [77]

The humanity of Jewish law is most clearly revealed in its attitude toward capital punishment. While accepting it in principle as prescribed in the Mosaic law, the Rabbis nevertheless hedged it about with so many strict laws of evidence as to make its application well nigh impossible. A Sanhedrin which imposed capital punishment once in seven years was considered tyrannical. Eleazer b. Azariah (2 c.) added, "even once in seventy years." [78] R. Ṭarfon and R. Akiba declared, "If we had been members of the Sanhedrin, no man would ever have been put to death." [79] The strong tendency of Pharisaic legislation was to do away with capital punishment altogether, and there was a marked trend to mitigate all forms of judicial punishment. The moderation of the Pharisees in these matters was noted by Josephus. It was one of the issues which brought them into conflict with the Sadducees, who were rigorous in the application of the Biblical penal code.[80]

No circumstantial evidence was admissible in capital cases. The evidence of at least two reputable eyewitnesses was required. No man could incriminate himself—a principle not found in Roman law. Thus torture was ruled out.

Writing of law enforcement in ancient Egypt, at the time of the New Kingdom (16–8 c. B.C.), Erwin Seidl states:

Criminal law and criminal procedure were inhuman. In contrast to the Jewish law which limited corporal punishment to forty strokes, one hundred strokes was the ordinary punishment in Egypt. Torture was often used, not only upon the accused but also upon independent witnesses. Strange forms of capital punishment seem to have been practiced, such as leaving the prisoner to be eaten by crocodiles. It was a special favor to allow a convicted criminal to commit suicide. Numbers of criminals, with their ears and noses cut off, were condemned to forced labor in concentration colonies on the frontiers of the country.[81]

Athens and Rome also permitted the torture not only of slaves but of others to obtain evidence. Roman judicial procedure developed a very elaborate system of torture of the accused (*quaestio*) and of reluctant witnesses. The Fourth Book of Maccabees (1 c.) enumerates a list of the horrible instruments of torture—wheels, joint screws, dislocators, rocks, and bone-crushers, catapults, caldrons, braziers, thumbscrews, iron claws, wedges, and branding irons (8:13). From Rome, the institution of torture passed over to medieval Europe and was standard practice in England, Scotland, France, Italy, Spain, Germany, and elsewhere until the eighteenth century. The Church itself, through the Inquisition, employed torture to extort confessions. Heretics were often tortured by the civil power at the direction of the religious authorities. In Asiatic countries, torture as part of the legal system was well nigh universal. Modern totalitarian régimes have added psychological forms of torture to the already crowded chamber of human horrors.

Judaism forbade torture. There is no mention of it in the Bible and no reference to it in the Talmud except as employed by the Romans or by King Herod, who in many other cruel respects copied the ways of the Romans.[82]

No kinsmen, paternal or maternal relatives, or relatives by marriage were eligible to act as witnesses. If the accused had not been first warned by the witnesses of the consequence of his contemplated crime, he could not be found guilty.

The court sitting in a capital case was composed of twenty-three judges, and the trial was held in the court of the Hewn Stone in the Temple at Jerusalem. A simple majority was sufficient for acquittal, while a majority of two was required for conviction. All, including the disciples of the Sages who were not among the judges, might argue in favor of acquittal, but not all in favor of conviction. There had to be a dissenting voice raised in favor of the accused. Unlike non-capital cases, one who had argued in favor of acquittal could not afterward change his mind and argue in favor of conviction, but he was always free to alter his position in favor of acquittal. A verdict of acquittal could be reached on the same day of the trial, but not a verdict of conviction. A verdict of conviction could be reversed, but not a verdict of acquittal.

The judges declared their opinion in order, beginning with the youngest who sat at the sides of the benches which were arranged like the half of a round threshing floor. This was done so that the younger judges might not be influenced by the opinion of their elders. Witnesses were thoroughly examined in inquest and cross-examination. "The more a judge tests the evidence, the more is he deserving of praise." The witnesses were most solemnly admonished:

Perchance ye will say what is but supposition and hearsay or at second hand, or (ye may say to yourselves), we heard it from a man that was trustworthy. Or perchance ye do not know that we shall prove you by examination and inquiry? Know ye, moreover, that capital cases are not like non-capital cases: in non-capital cases a man may pay money and so make atonement, but in capital cases the witness is answerable for the blood of him (that is wrongfully condemned) and the blood of his posterity (that should have been born to him) to the end of the world. . . . It was for this reason that but one single man was created in the world (Adam), to teach that if any man has caused a single soul to perish from Israel, Scripture imputes it to him as though he had caused the whole world to perish.

If the accused was finally found guilty and sentence was pronounced, every precaution was taken to the very last moment of the actual execution, to reconsider the verdict in case any new evidence were forthcoming. The court appeared to be hoping against hope to the very end that some new evidence would turn up to clear the man, or that some technicality would be pointed out to force an acquittal. As the condemned man was being led away to the place of execution, a man stood at the door of the court with a flag in his hand, and another, mounted on a horse, at a distance. If in the court someone said, "I have something new to argue in favor of acquittal," then the man waved the flag and the horseman hastened and stopped the condemned who was being led to execution. Even if the doomed man himself said, "I have something new to argue in favor of my acquittal," they must bring him back, be it four or five times, provided that there is anything of substance in his words. . . . A herald went before him calling out: "If any man knows anything in favor of his acquittal, let him come and plead it."

When everything failed, the condemned man was urged to make confession, "for everyone that makes confession has a share in the world to come." He was given a strong drugged wine to drink to benumb his senses.[83] If his punishment was hanging, his body was let down immediately after the hanging, and was never allowed to remain on the scaffold overnight (Dt. 21:23). That would have been a needless indignity inflicted on a human being.

"And God Himself is sore troubled at the blood even of the ungodly when it is shed." [84]

At every stage of the trial, sentence, and execution, one is made aware of the scrupulous care which Jewish law took to protect the accused—a care scarcely paralleled anywhere in the ancient world, and not everywhere in the modern world. Judaism's deep regard for the sanctity of human life, its vast compassion for the erring and the sinner, its profound humanity and its instinctive abhorrence of the shedding of blood—even the blood of the guilty—are everywhere in evidence.

There were other regards in which Judaism differed from the beliefs and practices of the ancient world. Nowhere else was there a conception of prophecy which went beyond fortunetelling and divination. "For these nations which you are about to dispossess give heed to soothsayers and to diviners; but as for you, the Lord your God has not allowed you so to do" (Dt. 18:14). That this admonition often went unheeded has already been noted. There were soothsayers and diviners in ancient Israel too, like the bacchantic *Nebïim* whom Saul met "coming down from the high places with harp, tambourine, flute and lyre before them," prophesying and whipping themselves into a sacred madness so that "they stripped off their clothes and lay naked all the day and all the night" (I Sam. 10:5; 19:18f.). Many forms of divination were practiced. Even in the central sanctuary in Israel, before the Babylonian exile, there was an official apparatus for ascertaining the will of God, the Urim and Tummim. Dreams, too, possessed for a long time a semiofficial status as a channel for divine revelation, though the prophet Jeremiah bitterly assailed this (Jer. 23:28).

But prophecy in Israel went far beyond all that. Mantic gifts and traditional forms of divination were placed at the service of a God of justice and love. Hebraic prophecy rose to the highest level of spiritual revelation, and the prophet became a consecrated messenger and spokesman of God's moral demands upon men and nations—the Reprover (Mochiah), the moral censor, the people's conscience. This above all else distinguishes the literary prophets from the seers and soothsayers of the ancient world, and from the guild of diviners among their own people whom they denounced as "false prophets." It also distinguishes prophetic Judaism from all the religions of antiquity.

The deep religious earnestness of Judaism and its indomitable loyalty and dedication to God are best reflected in the life, labor, struggles, and sufferings of these amazing spiritual pioneers of mankind—"eagles soaring above the tombs" of the ancient faiths —who gave the basic stamp to Judaism for all times. Here, as in so many other cultural experiences of the human race, the peaks thrust up suddenly and sharply, at the very beginning, and were never thereafter surmounted.

The prophets began their work with an assault upon the Baal-Yahweh syncretism which developed following Israel's settlement in Canaan. They summoned their people to return to the simpler faith of their nomadic ancestors in the wilderness which had been the cradle of their race, where in the dawn of their national life the prophets believed Israel had worshiped only Yahweh and "there was no strange God beside Him."

The struggle of the prophets to eradicate polytheism and syncretism from among the people was often heartbreaking, and many of them were destroyed in the process. The hold of nature worship was powerful upon popular imagination. But the fearful national catastrophes which came upon the people in 722 and 586 B.C., which the prophets were quick to interpret as proof of Yahweh's displeasure, greatly strengthened the cause of monotheism in Israel. By the sixth century the last traces of conscious hybridism disappear from the official religion of the people.

These prophets were the inspired architects of the faith of Israel. They were followed centuries later by competent builders and skillful craftsmen who completed the edifice. While historic Judaism is by no means the exclusive achievement of the prophets from Moses to Malachi, theirs was the transcendent vision which forever after guided the labors of Scribe, Sage, and Rabbi. The message of these trumpeters of a new dawn for mankind remained forever the constantly developing theme of Judaism: "Thus says the Lord: 'Stand by the roads, and look, and ask for the ancient paths where the good way is; and walk in it, and find rest for your souls' " (Jer. 6:16). In the concord of their many voices one strong dominant note is unmistakable—The good way! And the good way is not to throng the courts of a Temple and bring vain offerings to God. It leads directly and humbly to where men penitently and prayerfully wash the blood of sin, cruelty, and oppression from their hands, search their hearts and make themselves inwardly clean, cease to do evil and learn to do good (Is. 1:12f.). At the heart of the message of Hebraic prophecy, and subsequently of Judaism itself, is a summons to men not to rest content with the evils of society or with their own personal shortcomings, but to correct them. There was great and urgent work to be done in the world—"for violence and destruction are heard within" (Jer. 6:7), for "justice is turned back . . . truth is lacking" (Is. 59:14–15). To accomplish this work the prophet set out to alert and mobilize his people. The prophet's insistence on action, his driving compulsion to translate rapidly the ideal into the real, has remained the dynamic, always glorious, often imperilling, heritage of the people throughout their long history.

The life of the prophet was a life of swords. These were men of strife and contention. They did not welcome the ordeal of prophecy. They knew the frightful tension of the unuttered burden of the spirit, and the hand of God placed that heavy burden upon their hearts. They did not see themselves in the rôle of saviours or redeemers of mankind, possessed of some privileged grace. "I am a herdsman and a dresser of sycamore trees, and the Lord took me from following the flock, and the Lord said to me, Go prophesy to my people Israel!" (Amos 7:14–15). Their speech was at times very bitter, and their invective like scorpion whips. They were not given "to praise the Athenians among the Athenians." They spared no one, except those whom God would spare—the weak, the poor, the denied, the broken.

The spirit of Israel at times resented the unbridled severity of their speech even though it acknowledged and bowed before the truth of their indictments. Some Rabbis declared that Moses, Elijah and Isaiah were punished by God because they condemned their people too severely.[85] But it was not out of any lack of love for their people that even the sternest among them spoke as they did, but rather out of great anxiety and solicitude.

The prophets of Israel were strong "nationalists"—if such a modern term can properly be applied to these ancient spiritual leaders. It is used here to correct the impression which both Jewish and non-Jewish "universalists" have attempted to create: that the prophets of Israel were "nonpolitical" and supranational seers, even "unpatriotic," not at all interested in the survival of the Jewish state, or the Jewish nation, but wrapped up wholly in faith and morals—as if religion is any less universal when it embraces the love of one's country, or the pride of one's own people. There is no evidence for such strange notions anywhere in the writings of the prophets. Within their ample world outlook the prophets found room for man, nation, and humanity. The prophets of Israel loved their people with a surpassing love, loved them even when they castigated them, fearing that their sins would bring disaster upon them. "All the prophets begin with denunciation and conclude with consolation." [86] They agonized over their people's misfortunes. They wept over the destruction of their country. They ached for their ruined city of Jerusalem, "the perfection of beauty, the joy of all the earth." They prayed for its restoration. They comforted their people in their exile. What superb prophecies of consolation and restoration are those tender and compassionate utterances of Jeremiah, Ezekiel, and of that prophet-laureate of Israel's rebirth, Deutero-Isaiah! These men who could smite so fiercely with the tempest of their rebuke—how lovingly they soothed with the balm of their sympathy and the shared sorrow of their hearts. They were proud of their people. "You only have I singled out of all the families of the earth" (Amos 3:2). Their world outlook was inextricably bound up with the political rehabilitation of Israel and the upbuilding of Zion and its recognized rôle of leadership among the nations of the earth. Their vision was not limited to Israel. The whole world, they hoped, would some day come to learn and follow in the ways of God; but their proud conviction never failed them "that out of Zion would go forth the law, and the word of the Lord from Jerusalem" (Is. 2:3). The prophets did not wish their people to cease to be a nation. "Thus says the Lord, Who gives sun for light by day and the fixed order of the moon and the stars for light by night; . . . if this fixed order departs from before Me, says the Lord, then shall the descendants of Israel cease from being a nation before Me forever" (Jer. 31: 35–36). They wanted their people to be *more* than a nation, to be a holy nation, bound by a historic covenant and dedicated to a heroic mission to mankind.

The prophets of Israel were interested primarily in the moral tone of their nation and of society generally, in social righteousness, human brotherhood, and peace. Their spiritual kinsmen, the Psalmists, were interested primarily in personal piety and in the individual's quest for the light and nearness of God. They supplemented one another. In neither respect did the ancient world approximate their vision, their passion, or their piety.

Few indeed in the ancient texts and vague are the traces of a personal religion of spiritual quest and inwardness wherein the human soul "thirsts for God, for the living God" (Ps. 42:4), and finds supreme joy in communion with Him. To know that there is a God and that righteousness is the proper way of life acceptable to Him is one thing, and a great thing. To hunger and thirst for God—"O God, Thou art my God, I seek Thee, my soul thirsts for Thee, my flesh faints for Thee, as in a dry and weary land, where no water is" (Ps. 63:1)—that summit of spiritual pathos and quest was not scaled in the ancient world by any but the devout seers of Israel.

The ancients revered their gods, feared them, and worshiped them. They did not love them. One misses in ancient and classical literature any outpouring of love, any deep-stirring affection for any of their gods—even though their pantheons enshrined many gods and goddesses of Love. To love God with all one's heart, with all one's soul, and with all one's might (Dt. 6:5) must have been a strange sentiment to the peoples of antiquity. It appears to be uniquely Jewish. There must be a personal God as the object of one's love, one sole God to whom the worshiper can completely surrender himself. Only a monotheistic faith can give rise to such a disposition of devoted love. All polytheistic nature-religions were devoid of it, and so were all pantheistic faiths. (In Hinduism the *bhaktimarga*—the way to gain salvation from the round of rebirths through love and devotion of the "Adorable One"—received its full expression only in the Middle Ages in the strong reaction led by Ramanuja [11 c.] against Shankara's [9 c.] monist teachings of an absolutely impersonal God and of existence as *māyā*—illusion. The concept of *bhakti* is traceable earlier in Hinduism, but only in such monotheistic trends as are discernible in parts of the *Bhagavad-Gita* [200 B.C–200 C.E.]. Here the love of God is strongly stressed.)

Abraham, the founder of the faith, is called the Lover of God (Is. 41:8; II Ch. 20:7). All the truly righteous are called lovers of God (Ps. 5:12; 31:23). The people of Israel knew that their God in His anger could be stern and smite with fury the wicked and the faithless, but they were nevertheless drawn to Him with bands of love. "I love the Lord," sings the Psalmist (Ps. 116:1); "I love Thee, O Lord, my strength" (Ps. 18:1). They were confident also that God loved them with an everlasting love (Jer. 31:3), even when He chastised them.

When Israel was a child, I loved him, and out of Egypt I called my son. . . . How can I give you up, O Ephraim, how can I hand you over, O Israel! . . . I will heal their faithlessness; I will love them freely, for my anger is turned away from them. I will be as the dew to Israel . . . they shall flourish as a garden, they shall blossom as the vine, their fragrance shall be like the wine of Lebanon [Hos. 11:1,8; 14:4-5,7].

Israel had entered a covenant of love with God: "I will betroth you to Me forever; I will betroth you to Me in righteousness and in justice, in steadfast love and in compassion" (Hos. 2:21). The feeling that the covenant was one of love (Dt. 7:12) was not limited to prophet, Psalmist, or mystic. In later ages even the "legalistic" Rabbis found the most perfect expression of the intense reciprocal love which they felt to exist between God and Israel in the passionate rhapsody of the Song of Songs!

Nowhere in the ancient world was there the glimmer of a concept that a whole people might wish to become "a kingdom of priests and a holy nation" and dedicate itself to the establishment on earth of a universal brotherhood under God, even at the price of martyrdom. No people in antiquity longed to become a servant of mankind. They all aspired to be its master.

Nowhere is there a vision of a world welded in a universal brotherhood of men and nations, reconciled in the love of the one God, beating their swords into ploughshares and learning war no more (Is. 2:4); and of a social order when men would sit "each under his vine and fig-tree with none to make them afraid" (Mic. 4:3-4). Judaism gave mankind the concept of Humanity, and the vision of Universal Peace.

All these ideas, from monotheism to human brotherhood and peace, all the flowering concepts of unity, freedom, and compassion were fundamentally alien to the ancient world. They were new insights of Judaism, new levels of awareness, and they cannot be explained by reference to any antecedents.

Moreover, they were new not only in the days of Amos and Isaiah, but remained strange and unaccepted throughout the succeeding millennia. They were novel and distinctive not only against the background of the primitive ideas of the heathen and of the more refined conceptions of the Greco-Roman world— they remain distinctive against some of the prevalent religious ideas of the present day.

Once having come into possession of these ideas, the Jewish people never abandoned them, in spite of frequent "backsliding" on the part of some of the people. There were Jews in almost every age who were attracted to alien ways and patterns of thought, and who adopted them with too great avidity and too little discrimination. There were others who proved unworthy of their heritage. But the people as a whole remained steadfast. It is difficult to account for this remarkable steadfastness and for the vigor and inner force which propelled the people in its career of world-defiance. For long centuries they stood alone. In their precariously sheltered Judaean homeland they fought desperately to defend their faith, and when fortune favored them they looked beyond their borders and zealously sought to convert the world. They attacked the ancient world in the strongholds of its deepest attachments, its revered beliefs and its ancient codes and cults. Judaism by itself did not destroy paganism, but it unleashed forces which ultimately undermined it. Through Christianity and, later, Islam, vital elements of its message spread through the world and carved new highways for the spirit of man.

But in the process Israel remained a people apart. Friends and foes alike through the ages knew them as such. "Their laws are different from every other people" (Esther 3:8). "These men are Jews," was a cry which Paul heard in Macedonia, centuries later, "and they are disturbing our city. They advocate customs which it is not lawful for us Romans to accept or practice" (Acts 16: 20–21). And in Rome, the elder Pliny writes of the Jews as "a race famous for its insults to the Gods." They were slandered as misanthropes, as cannibals and atheists; and Tacitus rehearses all the libels against "this race detested by the Gods, whose customs are perverse and disgusting" and who "regard the rest of mankind with all the hatred of enemies." [87]

In order to carry out successfully the task assigned to it, Israel found it necessary to live in the world, but apart from it—on the other side, as it were. This, the Rabbis said, was implied in the very name "Hebrew" ('Ibri), from 'eber, the other side: "the whole world was on one side [idolaters] and he [Abraham, the Hebrew] was on the other side." Balaam, the pagan prophet of the Bible, who came to curse Israel but reluctantly remained to bless it, was deeply impressed by this fact: "Lo, it is a people dwelling alone, and not reckoning itself among the nations"

(Num. 23:9). To the leaders of Israel this was the keynote of their existence: "I am the Lord your God, who have separated you from the peoples. . . . I have separated you from the peoples that you should be Mine" (Lev. 20:24–26). The darkest heresy was the wish: "Let us be like all the other nations of the earth," a wish which would never come true (Ezek. 20:32). The Rabbis asked: "What made Jeremiah compare Israel to an olive tree?" (Jer. 11:16). "Because all liquids co-mingle one with another, but oil refuses to do so and keeps separate. So Israel does not mingle with the heathen." [88] It did not escape the Rabbinic homilists that the olive does not yield its oil until it is beaten and bruised, and they did not fail to draw the inference from this for the future of the people of Israel.

In three decisive moments in its history, Judaism was confronted with the attraction of fusion and syncretism which would have transformed it into something quite different from what it was, and in each instance it rejected this categorically: Baal-Yahwism in the days of the prophets; the Hellenistic-Judaic amalgam five centuries later in the days of the Ḥasidim and the Maccabees; and the Judaeo-Christological synthesis in the age of the Tannaim. It could not accept the orgiastic and licentious fertility rituals of the Canaanitish Baal worship. It detected in Hellenism a distinct threat to its own sober morality, its code of personal piety, and its prophetic tradition of social progress. It saw in Christianity, as we shall have occasion to point out, fatal eschatological overemphasis, an irrational antinomism, and an attenuation of monotheism in the concept of the God-Man.

Judaism consciously resolved to go its own way.

⮜V⮞

ON CLINGING TO EMINENCE

Professor Arnold J. Toynbee regards this "going its own way," this remarkable constancy, unparalleled in all history, of a people to an idea, as "the most notorious historical example" of what he calls the "idolization of an ephemeral self." He describes this "error of the Jews" as follows:

In a period of their history which began in the infancy of the Syriac Civilization and which culminated in the Age of the Prophets of Israel, the people of Israel and Judah raised themselves head and shoulders above the Syriac peoples round about in responding to the challenge of a 'Time of Troubles' by rising to a higher conception of Religion. Keenly conscious, and rightly proud, of their spiritual treasure which they had thus wrested from an ordeal that had broken the spirit of their Aramaean and Phœnician and Philistine neighbours, the Jews allowed themselves to be 'betrayed by what' was 'false within' into an idolization of this notable, yet transitory phase of their own spiritual growth. . . . They persuaded themselves that Israel's discovery of the One True God had revealed Israel itself to be God's Chosen People; and this half-truth inveigled them into the fatal error of looking upon a momentary spiritual eminence, which they had attained by labour and travail, as a privilege conferred upon them by God in a covenant which was everlasting. . . . Brooding over a talent which they had perversely sterilized by hiding it in the earth, they rejected the still greater treasure which God was now offering them. . . . And so it came to pass that

77

the Gospel of a Jewish messiah who was God Himself incarnate was preached by Galilaeans and taken to heart by Gentiles. . . .[1]

In thus deliberately refusing the opportunity that was offered to it of realizing its manifest destiny of flowering into Christianity by opening its heart to the gospel of its Galilaean step-child [*sic!*], Judaism not only stultified its spiritual past but forfeited its material future into the bargain. In declining to recognize its expected Messiah in Jesus, Judaism was renouncing its birthright in two great enterprises which eventually made the respective fortunes of two different daughters of Judaism by whom these enterprises were duly carried out in the fullness of time.[2]

Surveying the same scene—the first centuries of the Christian era—Professor George Foot Moore, who was not an impressionistic historian out on a global tour, gives no indication at all in his magnum opus *Judaism* that the Jews who lived at that time in Palestine had perversely sterilized their talent by hiding it in the earth. On the contrary, he finds the Jews of that epoch very dynamic—indeed, waging war with great energy upon polytheism and idolatry and carrying on an active propaganda for proselytes all over the pagan world. "There is no way of estimating statistically," he writes, "the results of Jewish propaganda in the centuries that fall within the limits of our inquiry [the first centuries of the Christian era] but they were indisputably very large, even if only proselytes in the proper sense be taken into account."[3] The Scribes and Pharisees who traversed "sea and land to make a single proselyte" (Matt. 23:15) were certainly not hiding their talent in the earth. "The Jewish community in Rome exhibited from its infancy such an aggressive spirit of proselytism as to determine the government to banish the chief propagandists from the city"[4] (139 B.C.). The composition of the noble postexilic psalms of exquisite spiritual sensitiveness, the tenderest minstrelsy of the human heart in communion with God; the Book of Job, the profoundest plumbing of human suffering and divine justice; the Wisdom literature of Bible and Apocrypha, so rich in moral insights and so sagacious; the creation of the synagogue, the most noble, original, and democratic religious institution in the ancient world; the establishment of a public school system for the training of children, rich and poor alike, and of a ritual of public worship devoid of sacrifices which was altogether unknown in the ancient world; the deepening of the universalistic motif in Judaism; the profound amplification of the concepts of charity, repentance, prayer, study, piety, and moral decorum, and, finally, the remarkable development of the Oral Law which provided new thoroughfares for the creative spiritual life of the people—these achievements of postexilic Judaism are certainly not evidence of any intellectual or spiritual sterility.

Certainly the Maccabean Revolt, the only successful revolt in defense of religion known to the ancient world, and the life-and-death struggle on the part of the faithful Jews to preserve their faith in the insidious amalgam of Seleucidian Hellenism gives no substance to the charge of spiritual stultification. Of this Professor Toynbee is fully aware. The Scribes and Pharisees had then "come to the front by taking the lead in heroic Jewish revolt against the triumphal progress of Hellenization." [5] But somehow the power and insight and courage deserted them in the time of Jesus! But how, where, and why? There is no evidence of any religious "blackout" following the Maccabean struggle. On the contrary, Judaism gained in power and in confidence with the resurgence of national pride following the Maccabean victories, and in subsequent years moved resolutely forward to win the hearts and minds of the heathen world. The period may well be said to have been the *risorgimento* of the Second Commonwealth. The victory of the Maccabees did for the spirit of the Jewish people in the second century what the victory of Marathon had done for the Greeks in the fifth. Even centuries later, when the Roman Empire was approaching what Gibbon characterized as "the happiest and most prosperous period in the history of the human race"—but which for the Jewish people was one of dark disasters and tragedies such as the insurrections of 115, the extermintaion of Jews in Egypt, Cyrene, Cyprus, and Mesopotamia and the final agony of rebellion in Palestine under Bar Kochba—

even in those desperate times the Jews carried on undismayed a brave and successful missionary activity in the pagan world in behalf of their faith.

Nor were the Jews thereby "idolizing an ephemeral self," or clinging to a "momentary spiritual eminence."

One detects here in Toynbee the same note of irritation which Nietzsche found to exist among certain people in relation to the Greeks:

Time after time hearty resentment breaks forth against the presumptuous little nation, which for all time dared to designate everything not native as barbaric. Who are they, one asks, who, though they have nothing to show but an ephemeral historical splendor . . . yet lay claim to the dignity and pre-eminence among peoples to which genius is entitled among the masses? [6]

The originality and uniqueness of the people of Israel are to be found not merely in the fact that they rose to a monotheistic conception of religion, head and shoulders above that of any other people, but in that they remained constant to it, defending it with their lives through long, bitter centuries, defying rulers and empires and enduring frightful persecutions because of it. Fortunately for mankind the spiritual eminence which Israel had attained proved not to be momentary, nor was their constancy to it ephemeral. Else the monotheistic vision of the founders of Judaism would have been one with the isolated proximate monotheism of Ikhnaton—a momentary flash followed by a returning darkness of superstition and idolatry. If it is true that Judaism reached the peak of its spiritual evolution in the prophetic era, in the eighth to sixth centuries B.C., the peak of Israel's effective contribution to the spiritual progress of mankind was still a thing of the future. For everything depended on whether Israel would remain faithful to that prophetic heritage, whether it would safeguard and propagate it in the face of constant opposition, whether it would overcome the many allurements of assimilation and compromise. The epic of Israel's struggle to preserve and transmit its revolutionary spiritual ideals, and its unparalleled power of resistance, are in their matchless valor as inspiring and unique in the world as the Torah itself. One should marvel at the rare quality of their constancy as much as at the peerless truths of their discovering.

To Professor Toynbee, Judaism has survived "only as a fossil" and Jews are among the relics of the Syriac civilization.[7] What a spry fossil and what a lively corpse! The challenging rôle which Judaism played in the life of Christendom throughout the centuries is surely known to every student of Christianity. No Christian theologian and no Church council ever made the mistake of regarding Judaism as petrified and Jews as negligible driftwood. From the time of Constantine onward, legislation was enacted by secular or ecclesiastical authorities to separate and isolate Jews from Christians and to restrict social intercourse between them out of fear of "Judaizing" influences. The Talmud and other Jewish books were ordered burned by papal bull and Church councils, lest they endanger the true faith. The prodigious literary polemics against Jew and Judaism through nearly all of the Christian centuries seem to suggest that the Church viewed them as serious antagonists, a force against which it must defend itself—but never as a relic. Professor Toynbee's violent onslaught on the amazing effrontery of the Zionists of the twentieth century in accomplishing successfully the reestablishment of the State of Israel is his own indirect acknowledgment that it is somewhat premature to speak of Jews as "fossils."

Nor was it a feeble relic of distant days which Hitler and the Nazis fought so furiously when they unleashed their wrath and thunder against the Jews and Judaism! Judging from the desperate violence of their campaign and the massive armaments which they employed, they must have been persuaded that they were facing some powerful enemy indeed, very much alive and very resourceful, whose continued existence was *the* supreme threat to all that they stood for and to the kind of world which they wanted to build. In the eyes of the Nazis, wrote Aurel Kolnai, "the Jews are odious inasmuch as they are bearers of the bacilli of liberty and progress. . . . What they [the Nazis] are engaged in persecuting is not so much the Jews as the Jewish spirit, and not so much the Jewish spirit as *the* Spirit." [8]

The Jewish people was encouraged by its spiritual leaders to think of itself as eternal and to keep alive within itself a sense of greatness. "All Israel are the sons of Kings." [9] While Israel proclaims, "Who is like unto Thee, O Lord, among the mighty" (Ex. 15:11), the Holy Spirit also proclaims, "Happy art thou, O Israel, who is like unto thee?" (Dt. 33:29).[10] There is no courage without pride, and no greatness without self-esteem. Israel was not unaware of the precious prerogatives of the unique spiritual leadership with which it had been invested. It was proudly cognizant of its rôle, and confident of the time when its ideas would fertilize the world. But this self-esteem was of a special brand. It was not provender upon which vulgar egoism, chauvinism, or imperialism could feed. Judaism provided Israel with no such pleasant rationalizations. Jews were there to serve God. They were not to glorify Israel, but to glorify God. They would either serve as instruments of the divine purpose, or they would suffer crushing retributive justice.

Whatever pride the Jews derived from the knowledge that they were the designated guardians of a precious and eternal truth was more than compensated for by the heavy price which they were prepared to pay and did pay for it in suffering and persecution. This is the reverse side of the medal. For it was more than a spiritual treasure which they had come to possess for their own private satisfaction. It was a hard challenge to live by their faith and to carry it to a hostile and intolerant world, and in the process to "be despised and rejected by men and to become acquainted with grief." Each succeeding age tells its own story of the price that was paid. Over and again the actual dread realities equaled or surpassed the earlier tragedies. In the middle of the seventeenth century, one-third of the Jews of Europe were massacred; in the middle of the twentieth, two-thirds. From the slave pens of the Pharaohs to the gas chambers of Hitler, the *via dolorosa* of this people of the immemorial crucifixion has stretched long and desolate through the weary centuries. Yet they remained faithful.

"Look down from heaven and see," rises the anguished cry from its litany of prayer, "how we have become a scorn and a derision among the nations; we are accounted as sheep, brought to the slaughter, to be slain and destroyed, to be smitten and reproached. Yet, despite all this, we have not forgotten Thy Name! We beseech Thee forget us not." What a rare diadem of proud sorrow is here, what strength and what humility!

And what shall be said of a people which through long, dark centuries of exile, outrage, and indignity could chant the refrain of a prayer so triumphant, so defiant, and so overflowing with gratitude as this: "Happy are we. How goodly is our portion, how pleasant our lot, how beautiful our heritage! How happy are we that we are privileged to proclaim at sunrise and at sunset, 'Hear, O Israel, the Lord our God, the Lord is One!' "

Let it be noted, too, that the religious guides of Israel throughout the centuries taught their people to attribute all their national misfortunes to themselves alone, to their own sins and backsliding, not to others or to a maleficent Providence. "Because of our sins were we exiled from our land and removed far from our country," is an ancient prayer embodied in the 'Amidah of all holy days. "Because of our sins and for the iniquities of our fathers, Jerusalem and Thy people are become a reproach to all that are round about us" is another self-recriminatory confession which is recited on certain weekdays by this proud and stiff-necked people. "Yet Thou hast been just in all that has come upon us, for Thou hast dealt faithfully and we have acted wickedly," is the keynote to the preamble of the covenant which was made by the exiles who returned to their shattered land in the days of Ezra and Nehemiah (Neh. 9:33).

The first Temple was destroyed, the Rabbis averred, because idolatry, immorality, and bloodshed prevailed. The second Temple was destroyed because hatred without cause prevailed among the people.[11] They wrought their national sorrows and misfortunes into humble confessions to a God Who does not willingly afflict His children. Later ages seized upon such expressions of noble self-reproach as self-indictments justifying the contumely which they heaped upon the Jews and the persecutions which they inflicted.

"The greatest offering that Israel made to God," writes Professor Hempel, "was the sacrifice of its pride in its own past in order to justify Him and His righteousness." [12] In their sacred books and in their historical writings the Jews never glossed over their national defeats, the faults of their national heroes, or their own shortcomings as a people.

The pagans were wont to reward their Gods for favors received and to blame and punish them when their petitions were denied. "They will pass through the land, greatly distressed and hungry; and when they are hungry, they will be enraged and will curse their king and their God" (Is. 8:21). Suetonius records that when reports of the greatly beloved Germanicus' recovery spread abroad in Rome, "a general rush was made from every side to the Capitol with torches and victims, and the temple gates were all but torn off, that nothing might hinder them in their eagerness to pay their vows." But when it was at last made known that Germanicus had really died, "the temples were stoned and the altars of the gods thrown down, while some flung their household gods into the street." [13]

It was for the sake of preserving and universalizing their faith, pure and intact, free from heathen admixture, that the Jews persisted in their separateness, and resolved to stand alone. It was not a case of "mere opposition" or "stage heroics" with which Marcus Aurelius charged the Christians of his day and with which Professor Toynbee is inclined to charge the Jews of the last two thousand years. The separateness of the Jews, to quote Professor Moore again, "accomplished its end in the survival of Judaism and therein history has vindicated it." [14]

◄ VI ►

ON REJECTING TREASURES

Nor did the Jews reject "the still greater treasure which God was offering them" in the coming of Jesus of Nazareth. What they rejected was the Messianism of Jesus, Paul's onslaught on the Law, his gospel of redemption through the atoning death and resurrection of Jesus, and the doctrine of God incarnate in man.

How could it have been otherwise? As a Messianic movement Christianity failed, as have all such movements in Jewish history and in the history of other peoples. The new order of things, the Kingdom of God, which was expected hourly, did not materialize. It has not materialized in the two thousand years which have elapsed since that time. The appearance of Jesus did not mark the end of history, and the mission and teachings of the Christian Church today are not greatly influenced by considerations of his Second Coming. The postponed Parousia has long since lost its theologic import for considerable sections of Christendom, even as the coming of the Messiah has for considerable sections of Jewry.

The Jews did not reject the God concept of Jesus, for that was Jewish in essence and Jesus derived it from the Torah. "The New Testament adds nothing to the content of the idea of God which is not already present in the literature and faith of Israel. It is often argued that Jesus held a unique conception of God, by which is usually meant the fatherhood of God. We have seen, however, . . . that the divine characteristics which the

85

term 'fatherhood' denotes are fully evident in the Old Testament." [1]

The ethics of Jesus, too, were standard Jewish ethics except as regards nonresistance, nonconcern with the material needs of life, and the love of one's enemies—extreme doctrines not part of normative Jewish thought. These ideas were undoubtedly entertained by some apocalyptic groups in Jewry, but were certainly not of a nature to take one out of Judaism. Jesus' moral code, with the exceptions noted, was the code of Pharisaic Judaism in his day. The morality which the Church taught the heathen world—again with the exceptions noted—and which appealed so strongly to it, was Jewish morality, the healthy-minded, clean, and regenerative morality of Israel.

"In what way did the teaching of Jesus differ from that of his contemporaries?" query the editors of *The Beginnings of Christianity*, and they reply:

Not by teaching anything about God essentially new to Jewish ears The God of Jesus is the God of the Jews, about whom he says nothing that cannot be paralleled in Jewish literature. Nor was it in his doctrine as to the Kingdom of Heaven that Jesus differed markedly from the Jewish teachers. . . . The differences which are important concern three subjects of vital and controversial interest, resistance to the oppressors of Israel, the fate of the People of the Land, and the right observance of the Law. On the first point he conflicted with the tendency to rebellion which ultimately crystallized into the patriotic parties of the Jewish war in C.E. 66; with the second and third he conflicted with the Scribes.[2]

As we shall have occasion to show, the pacifism of Jesus was not directed specifically to the Zealots, the Sicarii, those who sought to rebel against Rome. It was a thoroughgoing doctrine of nonresistance applicable to all of life's situations and directed to all men. On this score Jesus did differ from the prevalent prophetic-Pharisaic teachings of Judaism, although his views were surely not unknown in certain mystically-minded groups in Israel: "And if anyone seeketh to do evil unto you, do well unto him, and pray for him and ye shall be redeemed of the Lord from all evil." [3] It was not a doctrine which was calculated to arouse any widespread active hostility in his day. It was not until the war with Rome began a generation later that the advocacy of pacifism became contentious and dangerous.

As regards the fate of the "People of the Land"—the *'Ame Ha-arez*—the authors of *The Beginnings of Christianity* maintain that Jesus offered the opportunity of entering the Kingdom of God to publicans and sinners through a repentance which "could be obtained rather by attention to principles than by . . . an extreme and meticulous attention to the details of the Law, such as rendered repentance impossible to ordinary badly educated men."

There appears to be some confusion here between the repentance of publicans and sinners and the relation of the *'Ame Ha-arez* to matters of ritual purity and the tithes. The publicans and sinners were not necessarily the "People of the Land."

The publican was considered a moral outcast not because he did not observe meticulously all the details of the Law. He was, as a rule, an unscrupulous and pitiless taxgatherer, serving a hated and usurping government, who shamefully mulcted the people of their last extractable *prutah*. His repentance would be indicated only by a radical change in the conduct of his calling. This is the advice which John gave to the publicans who came to him to be baptized: "They said to him, Master, what shall we do? And he said to them: Extract no more than that which is appointed you" (Luke 3:12–13). This is the advice which any Rabbi of that day would have given them. It had nothing to do with scrupulosity in the matter of the observance of the laws of the Torah. If a man sinned he could readily repent and be forgiven. Restitution, wherever possible, and sincere contrition were all that was required. A man did not have to be a scholar, a saint, or a pietist to have his repentance accepted.

Jesus befriended publicans and sinners, and dined with them in the hope of leading them on to repentance. This is the act of a loving moral guide and teacher. He taught men, as he did in the parable of the Pharisee and the Publican (Luke 18:9–14), the superiority of sincere repentance over self-righteousness. This, too, is profoundly spiritual. It could hardly be maintained, however, that such attitudes and instructions were unknown and unshared by others, Rabbis and teachers, in his day. They could not have been subjects of controversy in the days of Hillel, a contemporary of Jesus and a leader of the Pharisees, who taught: "Be a disciple of Aaron, loving peace, and pursuing peace, loving all thy fellow-creatures, and drawing them nearer to the Torah." [4]

There is no mention in the New Testament of the technical term "People of the Land." The term "publicans and sinners" is not a synonym for it. There was no animosity between the "People of the Land" and the Pharisaic teachers in the days of Jesus.

The *'Am Ha-arez* is very often placed in the Mishna and the Tosefta in juxtaposition to the *Ḥaber* ("Associate" or "Fellow"). Both are technical terms. The *Ḥaberim* were the more exacting Jews, who formed themselves into associations or *Ḥaburot* for the sole purpose of being in a position to observe more strictly and with greater security the laws of ritual cleanness and of tithing. All those who did not join the *Ḥaburot*, whether priest or layman, were to that extent known as *'Ame Ha-arez*. In the eyes of the *Ḥaber* every Jew who did not obey the laws of Levitical purity and proper tithing in their highly developed form was an *'Am Ha-arez*. Such a man need not at all be a sinner or an ignorant man, or of a disposition inimical to the Sage or the Scribe. An *'Am Ha-arez* could be a teacher of the Law to the children of a *Ḥaber*.[5] The marriage of the son of a *Ḥaber* to the daughter of an *'Am Ha-arez*, or vice versa, is considered a matter of common occurrence.[6] The Tosefta relates that Rabban Gamaliel the Elder married his daughter to Simon b. Nathaniel—a priest and an *'Am Ha-arez*.[7] A *Ḥaber* and an *'Am Ha-arez* may belong to the same family. An *'Am Ha-arez* may at any time join a *Ḥaburah*, and the doors were always open to welcome him.[9]

The highly particularized laws of ritual cleanliness which entered so considerably into the daily life of the *Ḥaber* interfered perforce with close neighborly contacts with the 'Ame Ha-arez, but we have no reason to think that this led to animosity and bitterness—any more than we have reason to think, or any evidence to show, that the masses of the people resented the Pharisees, whose rigorous religious discipline they admired, even though they could not always follow their example. Josephus frequently emphasizes the fact that the Pharisees had great influence with the multitude,[10] that they were able greatly to persuade the body of the people,[11] and that the multitude sided with them against the Sadducees.[12]

The 'Ame Ha-arez included all the elements of the population who were not in Haburot. Just as the Haburot counted among their membership men from every walk of life, so did the 'Ame Ha-arez include men from all classes of society, the scholar and the priest, the merchant and the farmer, the rich and the poor. If Jesus defended the 'Ame Ha-arez, for which there is no evidence, he was certainly not defending the "common people" against any aristocracy either of wealth or of learning.

The bitter criticisms of the 'Ame Ha-arez which one finds occasionally in Rabbinic sources all date from the second century onward. The authorship of the statement, attributed to Hillel: "An 'Am Ha-arez cannot be a Hasid," is doubtful. In Abot De Rabbi Nathan [13] it is attributed to Akiba (2 c.), and we think with greater likelihood. A demoralization spread in the religious life of the people consequent upon the wars with Rome, the destruction of the Temple and the scattering of the priesthood, the Hadrianic persecutions and the closing of the schools and synagogues. Laxity in the observance of all laws set in. The Christian Church under Pauline inspiration was energetically pressing its attack on the Law generally. Pharisaic "legalism" became a controversial issue. The Rabbis therefore reached out for a stricter discipline and a greater stability in doctrine. Periods of great social decomposition create a desire among the faithful for a more vigorous discipline.

In the second century the center of the people's life was shifting from Judaea to Galilee. The religious laxity of the Galileans and their general ignorance of the Law were proverbial. Their religious standards and their educational facilities were inferior to those set by the Rabbis. The term *'Am Ha-arez* now came to include not only those who did not live up to the strict observance of Levitical purity and tithes as the *Ḥaber* understood it, but all those who disregarded moral and religious standards, who neither studied the Law nor taught it to their children, who would not cooperate in the heroic efforts of the Rabbis to save Judaism from total destruction.

All these conditions were non-existent in the days of Jesus. It is doubtful, therefore, whether the fate of the "People of the Land" could have been a subject of vital and controversial interest to him or to his contemporaries.[14]

On the matter of the right observance of the Law—the Sabbath law, for example, or the law of divorce—the attempts to draw a critical distinction between the teaching of Jesus on these subjects and that of the Rabbis have not proved convincing. On the subject of divorce, the Rabbis themselves differed as to the correct meaning of the Biblical law which grants a man the right to divorce his wife if "he found some unseemly thing in her" (Dt. 24:1). Jesus took the position also taken by Bet Shammai, that no man may divorce his wife, save on account of adultery. If Mark (10:1–12) represents the true position of Jesus, he seems to have been opposed to divorce altogether. This is doubtful. Matthew 19:9 appears to reflect his true position. Certainly the clear meaning of the law in the Torah was to make possible the annulment of an unsatisfactory marriage, not to prohibit divorce altogether.

As regards Sabbath observance—"that the Sabbath was made for man and not man for the Sabbath" (Mark 2:27)—this did not represent any break with the basic attitude of Pharisaic Judaism. In the second century of the Common Era, when Sabbath laws had been elaborated much further by the Rabbis and culminated in the thirty-nine chief categories of prohibited work, R. Jonathan b. Joseph (2 c.) employed the almost identical words of the Gospel: "The Sabbath is committed to your hands, not

you to its hands." [15] Both the Gospel and the Rabbis were probably quoting a popular folk saying long in vogue among the
people.

It was an established principle that in the case of danger to
human life, in war, in sickness or accident, all the laws of the Sabbath may be suspended. Even when the danger was not clear, the
Sabbath law was to be suspended. Quick action in its suspension
is praised, delay condemned.[16] Jesus' controversy with the
Pharisees over the charge that his disciples plucked ears of corn
unlawfully on the Sabbath day and ate them because they were
hungry (Mark 2:23–28) could have involved no real difference
of opinion as regards the law. Such action could quite properly
be justified under the law on the ground that it was necessary to
preserve life. This is true also of the other Gospel references to
the Sabbath. They are rather the reflections of the antinomist
controversy, developed in later times by other men, which sought
to establish that "the Son of man is Lord even of the Sabbath
day" (Matt. 12:8), that he could abolish the Biblical law of the
Sabbath altogether, as well as all other laws, and that "Christ
has redeemed us from the curse of the law" (Gal. 3:13).

Some Jewish rigorists sought to make the Sabbath a day of
total inactivity, even to the point of refusing to engage in self-
defense on it. But long before the days of Jesus, during the
Maccabean revolt, this strict view of Sabbath observance, which
was probably held by the Ḥasidim, had been relaxed.[17] It was
relaxed in other regards by the Sages and Rabbis of later generations in order to make it a joyous day as well as a holy day.
Numerous legal fictions and simple expediencies like the 'Erub
(enlarging the private domain within which certain activities on the Sabbath, otherwise prohibited, could be carried on)
were evolved to liberalize the inflexible Biblical injunctions not
to go out of one's place on the Sabbath (Ex. 16:29), not to kindle
any fire in one's dwelling place (Ex. 35:3), and not to do any
manner of work (Ex. 20:10). Here as in the case of Prosbul,
which Hillel instituted as an economic necessity to circumvent
the scriptural ordinance concerning the annulment of debts in

the year of release (*Shmiṭah*)—"for he saw that people were unwilling to lend money to one another" [18]—the motive was not "to bind heavy burdens, hard to bear, and lay them on men's shoulders" (Matt. 23:4), but to lift what in the course of time had turned out to be heavy burdens.

This, too, was the case with the dissolution of vows. Scripture makes no provision for it. Vows, often made thoughtlessly or under great stress, turned out at times to be chains too heavy for men to bear. The Rabbis accordingly declared that under certain conditions a Sage or three private persons could declare a vow invalid and absolve the taker of the vow from its consequences. The teachers of the Mishna knew that "the rules about release from vows hover in the air and have naught [in Scripture] to support them"; [19] nevertheless they prescribed these rules to make it easier for men. Similarly the Rabbis declared: "There never has been a 'stubborn and rebellious son,' and there never will be" and "there never was a condemned city and never will be." [20] They surrounded these inoperative Biblical laws which prescribed the death penalty for the rebellious son (Dt. 21:18–21) and for the city beguiled into idolatry (Dt. 13:13–18) with so many restrictions that to all intents and purposes they abrogated them. Other Biblical laws such as the ordeal by means of the Bitter Waters for the woman suspected of adultery (Num. 5:11) and the rite of the breaking of the heifer's neck in the case of the slain found in the field (Dt. 21:1f.) were likewise abrogated.[21]

To return to the Sabbath. The Jewish people throughout the ages loved the Sabbath and welcomed it as a queen and bride. It was not a day of gloom and austerity. "The Holy One, blessed be He, said to Moses: I have a precious gift in my treasure-house, called the Sabbath, and I desire to give it to Israel." [22] "They who keep the Sabbath and hail it with delight will rejoice in Thy Kingdom. The people who sanctify the seventh day will be filled and delighted with Thy goodness. For Thou didst find pleasure in the seventh day and didst sanctify it. Thou didst call it the most delectable of days, a remembrance of creation itself." [23]

It is of interest to note that the Sabbath had a strong attraction for many non-Jews in the pagan world, and it retained its hold for centuries upon Judeo-Christians. "The Church had to fight against the translation of the Jewish Sabbath into the Christian Sunday for nearly the whole of the first millenium of its existence." [24]

The above considerations lead one to the conclusion that there were no such decisive differences on the subject of law between Jesus and his contemporaries as to make inevitable a complete break. The break was due to other causes and was made inevitable by other hands.

Certainly the Jews did not reject Jesus because of his alleged total abandonment of the Torah, for Jesus never abandoned the Law in whole or in part. On the contrary, he made it abundantly clear that he came not to abolish the Law and the prophets but to fulfill them. "Whoever then relaxes one of the least of these commandments and teaches men so, shall be called least in the Kingdom of Heaven; but he who does them and teaches them shall be called great in the Kingdom of Heaven" (Matt. 5:17–19). Jesus did not oppose even those laws which the Scribes and Pharisees developed out of the Torah and which the Sadducees, for example, opposed. He denounced these teachers because he believed that they were not practicing what they preached—and what true prophet and teacher in Israel ever failed to denounce pretense and hypocrisy? "The Scribes and the Pharisees sit in Moses' seat; so practice and observe whatever they tell you, but not what they do; for they preach, but do not practice" (Matt. 23:2–3). He denounced them for giving tithes of mint and dill and cinnamon but ignoring "the weightier matters of the law, justice and mercy and faith; these you ought to have done, without neglecting the others" (Matt. 23:23). Centuries before, Amos and Isaiah had uttered the selfsame diatribe. Jesus' attack was certainly no new note to Jews who in their synagogues on Sabbaths and holidays listened to the readings from the prophets. They knew that Isaiah had said: "Bring no more vain offerings . . . I cannot endure iniquity along with the solemn assembly"

(Is. 1:13), and that Hosea had proclaimed, "I desire mercy and not sacrifice, the knowledge of God, rather than burnt offerings" (Hosea 6:6).

Jesus taught the Law "as one who had authority" (Mark 1:22), that is, not as the Rabbis taught it; not, for example, as Hillel taught it, in accordance with a generally accepted technique of Halachah employed in the Schools, but as a prophet would have taught it, *mi-pi Ha-Geburah*, on direct authority received from God. All the apocalyptists spoke in the name of revelation. Jesus saw his rôle as that of a prophet announcing the approach of the Millennium. He accordingly did not feel himself restricted to the Pharisaic technique of interpreting the Torah. It was generally accepted that with the coming of Messianic times prophecy would return to Israel. In fact, the return of prophecy would be one of the signs heralding the coming of the Messiah. A prophet was assured privileges under the Law which were not possessed by any other religious teacher. No prophet, of course, could advocate the abrogation of any fundamental Biblical law, such as the prohibition of idolatry, without branding himself a false prophet, deserving of death. But a prophet had considerable leeway in other matters. A prophet whose credibility was well established could, for example, order the temporary suspension of any law of the Torah (short of idolatry) in order to meet an emergency, and the people were obligated to obey him.[25]

Jesus evidently sought to exercise this prophetic privilege, but only in his exposition of the Law, for he announced no new laws nor did he attempt to abrogate any existing law, and he never questioned the authority of the Torah as such. When he told his disciples, "Do you not see that whatever goes into a man from outside cannot defile him?" (Mark 7:18), he was directing himself specifically to the criticism made by the Pharisees against some of his disciples who ate with hands unwashed, thus violating "a tradition of the elders" (Mark 7:2–3). The law of the washing of the hands was not a Biblical law and was not in common practice among the people. The inference drawn in Mark that "thus he declared all foods clean" (7:19) is clearly unwarranted and is not mentioned in Matthew 15 where the episode is also recorded. It is out of keeping with Jesus' consistent and positive attitude toward the Law. Mark here reflects the later Pauline influence. This seems to be the case also with the claim, attributed to Jesus, to forgive sins (Mark 2:5–12; Matt. 9:2–8). This has no basis in Jewish law. The core of Pauline Christianity was Jesus' rôle in the forgiveness of sin—by his death and during his life. This authority came with the possession of the Holy Spirit. According to John, Jesus bestowed the authority to forgive sins also upon the apostles, after he had breathed the Holy Spirit on them (John 20:23). Jesus' assumption of the rôle of prophet certainly did not please the Rabbis, but it was not on that score that the Jewish people rejected him.

The Jews would certainly not reject Jesus on the strength of his conception of the rôle of Israel in history. "Salvation is from the Jews" (John 4:22), he told the woman of Samaria. The charge which he gave to his disciples was specifically limited to Jews: "Go nowhere among the Gentiles, and enter no town of the Samaritans, but go rather to the lost sheep of the house of Israel. And preach as you go, saying: 'The Kingdom of Heaven is at hand' " (Matt. 10:5–7). His mission was exclusively to the Jews. This was a deviation from the prophetic tradition. The prophets of Israel never restricted their prophecies to the Jewish people. "I appoint you a prophet to the nations," was the word of the Lord to Jeremiah. "See, I have set you this day over nations and kingdoms" (Jer. 1:10). (The text of Matt. 28:19, "Go therefore and make disciples of all nations, baptizing them in the name of the Father and the Son and the Holy Spirit," is clearly of a later time.)

Jesus would not heal the daughter of the Canaanite woman who pleaded with him. He would not answer her. He was sent only to the lost sheep of the house of Israel. "It is not fair to take the children's bread and throw it to the dogs"—a sentiment which cannot be paralleled for severity in the whole literature of Judaism. It was only after the distraught mother pleaded,

"Yes, Lord, yet even the dogs eat the crumbs that fall from their master's table," that Jesus recanted: "O woman, great is your faith! Be it done for you as you desire" (Matt. 15:21–28).

It has been correctly observed "that Christianity in the first century achieved a synthesis between the Greco-Oriental and the Jewish religions in the Roman Empire." [26] Whether this synthesis was actually achieved in the first century or somewhat later is not of great moment. Three stages may be noted in its consummation—in the transition from Judaism to Christianity. The first stage is Jesus and the gospel of the Kingdom, the second is Paul and the piacular sacrifice on the cross, the third is the Gospel of John and the Word become flesh. Each was distinctive and all three were ultimately merged, though not without great controversy and confusion, in the final orthodox version.

Paul is the bridge between the Judaic gospel of Jesus concerning the coming of the Kingdom of God and the urgent need for repentance, and the thoroughly Hellenistic Logos gospel of John, wherein the Word which was God became flesh in Jesus, the Son of God, one with the Father, who was sent by God to overcome the dominion of Satan in the world and, having accomplished his mission, returned to God.

"When Jesus came into Galilee, spreading the gospel of the Kingdom of God and saying the time is fulfilled and the Kingdom of God is at hand" (Mark 1:14), he was voicing the opinion widely held that the year 5000 in the Creation calendar which was to usher in the sixth millennium—the age of the Kingdom of God—was "at hand." [27] Induced by the popular chronology of the day, the mass of the people came to believe that they were on the threshold of the Millennium. The advent of the Millennium carried along with it the appearance of the Messiah and his appointed activities. Jesus' essential mission was messianic, and he sought to save men from the "birth throes" of the messianic times by calling them to swift and thoroughgoing repentance so that they may be found worthy to enter the Kingdom.

There was nothing in Jesus' doctrine of repentance and the approaching Kingdom of God which the Jews of his day needed to reject in defense of their faith. There was nothing in it which endangered their faith. There were apocalyptically-minded Pharisaic Jews who believed that the order of the world was about to change and that they were on the threshold of the Millennium. There were those who did not believe it. It was not an issue involving a fundamental creed. To those who did believe in the approaching cosmic catastrophe, thoroughgoing repentance and austerities would logically recommend themselves.

Because there were many at that time who were expecting the coming of the Messiah, or his forerunner, to announce the beginning of a new age, the generation abounded in Messianic movements, each one fraught with grave political consequences for the peace of the nation. The Roman imperium was ruthless in the suppression of all such messianic claimants because they were suspected of seeking the overthrow of Roman authority and the reestablishment of Jewish independence. The Jewish Messiah, when he appeared, would be proclaimed King of the Jews.

When Jesus was put to death, his faithful followers were confronted with a dreadful dilemma and embarrassment. It was to them a crushing catastrophe. Their master had been arrested, tried, condemned, and crucified. Did that not prove that he was not the true Messiah, that he was no different from the many others who had recently appeared as pretenders to that rôle and who had been liquidated by the Romans? If Jesus were the true Messiah, why did he die? Was not his mission a failure?

Two answers were soon supplied by the faithful. He died, it was true, but he was soon resurrected. He was seen alive after his entombment. Where is he now? He ascended to heaven and will soon reappear on earth to complete his mission and usher in the Millennium.

But why did he die? In order to atone by his death for the Original Sin with which mankind was fatefully burdened since Adam. Jesus had called upon men to repent of their own personal sins in preparation for the Kingdom, but there was also a collective sin, it was argued, the primordial sin of Adam, in which all men shared and for which no individual could atone. It was necessary for the Messiah, who had been sent by God, to take upon himself the universal sin of mankind, and by his death to atone for it so that the tragic debt would be paid for all time. This was Paul's contribution to the theologic complex of Christianity—vicarious expiation, for which Biblical proof was soon sought and discovered in Isaiah 53. It was the second step in the development of Christian theology. With Judaism, Torah was central; with Jesus the Kingdom; with Paul it was the redemptive rôle of Jesus.

The third step was taken in the Diaspora in the course of the missionary preaching about the resurrected redeemer to the Roman world. Here the Hellenistic idea of the Logos was widely current both among Jews and among pagans—the Logos, the Word of God, the instrument by which God, the Transcendant, worked His will in the world. Logos took on many degrees of personification, from what might be called a pure abstraction among the Jews to a God subaltern and co-worker with the Supreme Deity. It was necessary to come to terms with this Logos idea, whether as attribute, instrument, or divine personality, if the Christian gospel was to be widely accepted. This fusing or reconciliation was achieved and is reflected in the Gospel of John. "In the beginning was the Word . . ."

This was the third stage. Jesus became the Logos, the incarnate Word of God, the God made flesh. Orthodox Christianity, after many bitter disputes, finally accepted and fused all three doctrines into one—the historic messianic rôle of Jesus, the resurrection and the atonement death of Jesus preached by Paul, and the Incarnation as reflected in the Fourth Gospel.

Paul marks the dividing line between Judaism and Christianity. He was a Jew of the Diaspora, a rigorous monotheist, and a bitter foe of all forms of idolatry. He had observed the ceremonial law of Judaism, but reluctantly, and at a later stage abandoned it and "died to the Law" (Gal. 2:19). His final disillusionment came when he saw that some of the very champions of the Law among Judeo-Christians, like Peter and Barnabas, were acting insincerely and inconsistently in the matter (Gal. 2:11–14).

Paul claims to have been extremely zealous, before his conversion, for the traditions of his fathers. But he must have been impatient with the Law even before he was converted or he could not have spoken of the Law as "a curse" from which men were finally redeemed by the atonement of Jesus. How could the vision of the resurrected Jesus on the road to Damascus have made him such a bitter and violent enemy of the Law? Certainly Jesus was not one. There must have been other Jews, even before the days of Paul, especially in the Hellenistic Diaspora, who fretted under the restraints of the Mosaic ceremonial code, who found the Law a serious hindrance to their free social and economic contacts with the non-Jewish world, and who in their hearts preferred a purely spiritual Judaism which was based solely on faith in the One God of Abraham, and not cumbered with the legislation which Moses ordained. But they had no authority upon which to base their views such as Paul found in Jesus the Messiah who by his appearance ushered in a new age and a new dispensation. In any event, it is clear that Paul wished to bypass Moses and the covenant of Sinai altogether and return to the original covenant of Abraham, to the universal monotheistic faith, which all the nations of the earth could share. Paul wanted to reject the Torah, but he could not reject it outright. The Torah was needed to substantiate and bear witness to Jesus and to his rôle in history. Paul therefore appealed from Moses to Abraham—from the Sinai covenant, which in his view was a restrictive, negative, and temporal covenant, to the covenant of Abraham which was universal and eternal.

Five hundred years later Mohammed adopted the same line of Paul in rejecting both Judaism and Christianity. He, too, went back to the universal monotheism of Abraham. To quote from a recent study:

He [Mohammed] stated that he did not come to abrogate the Old and New Testaments, but rather to fulfill the spirit and letter of the Book. He maintained that Abraham was neither a Jew nor a Christian, but the true expounder of ethical monotheism, and that the Koran, as revealed to him by Allah, through the angel Gabriel, embodied the true revelation which the Jews and the Christians had failed to follow. Tracing his genealogy to Abraham through his son Ismael, Mohammed claimed to be the rightful heir to Abraham's high rank.[28]

The Law which was given to Moses at Sinai was, according to Paul, a punishment for the sins of the people of Israel. The Ten Commandments were "a dispensation of condemnation." Any written code of laws kills; only the spirit gives life (II Cor. 3:6). The Torah is such a written code. It is not merely the law of the Rabbis which Paul condemns. Actually, the law of the Rabbis was not yet as extensively developed in his day as in the subsequent centuries. It is the laws of the Torah which he principally had in mind. "Where there is no law, there is no transgression" (Rom. 4:15).

At times Paul argues that while the Law itself is not sin, it suggests and arouses sin. "If it had not been for the Law, I should not have known sin" (Rom. 7:7). Paul here has in mind not merely the ceremonial law, but the ethical law as well. "I should not have known what it is to covet if the law had not said, 'You shall not covet'" (*ibid.*). At other times Paul argues that the Law is too weak to safeguard against the promptings of the flesh, the evil inclinations, within him (Rom. 8:3). At best the Law was a regrettable interlude, a custodian until the true faith was revealed. "Now that faith has come, we are no longer under a custodian" (Gal. 3:25).

Paul was not interested in the healing miracles and exorcisms which others reported about Jesus and which are found so plentifully in the Gospels. He shows little interest in the human career of Jesus altogether. The sole miracle which profoundly stirred and affected his life was the miracle of the resurrection. He knows nothing of Jesus as God incarnate, and nothing of the

Virgin Birth. He was especially eager to preach his gospel to the Gentiles and to convert them to the faith of "Christian" monotheism, thereby erasing all distinctions between Jew and non-Jew according to the promise made to Abraham: "in you all the families of the earth will be blessed" (Gen. 12:3).

The Law, as Paul saw it, was *the* stumbling block to the conversion of the Gentile world to the true faith. The demands of the Law—Sabbath observance, circumcision, the dietary regulations, the laws of purity—were sufficiently exacting to discourage many from accepting the faith. His passionate devotion to the resurrected Christ and the salvation which he was convinced flowed from him for all mankind, and his proselytizing zeal, made him bitterly intolerant of the Law. "Christ is the end of the Law" (Rom. 10:4). The covenant of Sinai is Hagar, bearing children for slavery. The covenant of Abraham is Sarah. "Cast out the slave and her son!" (Gal. 4:30)

Nevertheless, Paul was prepared to practice the Law himself, if by so doing he might win over those under the Law to the true faith (I. Cor. 9:2). For this reason he advised the faithful to avoid eating of food which might have been sacrificed to idols, a very grave matter in the eyes of law-abiding Jews, not because he regarded the act itself as unlawful, for "all things are lawful," but so as not to give offense and make the work of conversion more difficult (I Cor. 10:23–33). The faithful should not make an issue of food or Sabbath observance, of clean or unclean, or of circumcision, but "pursue what makes for peace" (Rom. 14:13f.).

Paul was thus ambivalent on the subject of the Law, even as he was on the election of Israel, his other troublesome theologic inconsistency. Paul assigned to the Jewish people a special rôle in the new dispensation. Like Jesus, he too evidently believed that "salvation is from the Jews." "God has not rejected this people whom he foreknew" (Rom. 11:2). "As regards the gospel they are enemies of God for your sake: but as regards election they are beloved for the sake of their forefathers. For the gifts and the call of God are irrevocable" (Rom. 11:28–29). It is an advantage to be born a Jew. "Then what advantage has the Jew? . . .

Much in every way. To begin with, the Jews are entrusted with the oracles of God. What if some were unfaithful? Does their faithlessness nullify the faithfulness of God?" (Rom. 3:1-3). "They are Israelites, and to them belong the sonship, the glory, the covenants, the giving of the Law, the worship and the promises; to them belong the patriarchs, and of their race, according to the flesh, is the Messiah" (Rom. 9:4-5).

The universalism of Paul was not free of local patriotism. Israel "after the flesh" was still the chosen people. At times there appears to be no contradiction in his mind between a national faith and its universal mission. At other times there decidedly is.

The total effect of Paul's disquisitions on the Law and his ambivalence was to denigrate its sanctity in the eyes of assimilation-minded Jews and to nullify it completely as far as Gentiles seeking conversion were concerned.

There was violent resistance among the early Judeo-Christian brotherhoods of Palestine and elsewhere to Paul's attitude toward the Law. They looked upon the Law—the Torah—as sacred and eternally binding upon themselves and their descendants, and not as a punishment but a privilege. The Jewish-Christian Ebionites, according to Irenaeus (2 c.), rejected Paul because he was an apostate from the Law.[29] The early Christians among the Jews saw no contradiction between their loyalty to traditional Judaism and their belief in the Messiahship of Jesus. They were aware of no new covenant or dispensation. Jewish Christians who observed the Sabbath and the festivals, circumcision, the dietary laws, and the laws of purity persisted well into the third century. Orthodox Christianity attacked them bitterly. "It is monstrous," wrote Ignatius (2 c.), "to talk of Jesus Christ and to practice Judaism."[30] Some Rabbis, on the other hand, like Simon the Pious (3 c.) and Simon ben Lakish (3 c.), defended these Judeo-Christians, and did not wish to exclude them from the Jewish community.[31]

The "burden of the Law" was regarded by loyal Jews not as a burden at all, but as a wholesome discipline. The purpose of the Law was to increase personal holiness [32] and to refine the spirit of man,[33]—not to make him aware of his inability to fulfil it and thus force him to rely exclusively upon grace and redemption. God wished to increase the merits of Israel, wherefore he multiplied for them laws and commandments.[34] The Jews found the Torah and its statutes and ordinances "perfect, reviving the soul; rejoicing the heart . . . enlightening the eyes . . . more to be desired than gold, even much fine gold; sweeter also than honey and the honeycomb" (Ps. 19:8–10).

With everlasting love hast Thou loved the House of Israel, Thy people. Torah and commandment, statute and judgment hast Thou taught us. Therefore, O Lord our God, when we lie down and when we rise up we will meditate on Thy statutes. We will rejoice in the words of Thy Torah and in Thy commandment forever; for they are our life and the length of our days. Blessed art Thou, who lovest Thy people, Israel.[35]

The Jewish people—Pharisees, Sadducees, and Essenes alike—could not have accepted Paul's conception of the Law under any circumstances. It was utterly alien to them, as it was to the Jewish-Christians of Palestine, as it would have been to Jesus himself, who did not oppose the Law at all and who did not seek to abrogate it for the sake of making proselytes among the Gentiles. Paul's position cut at the very roots of their faith. There has always been a debate among Jews as to the extent to which one is free to interpret the Written Law and by what technique, and whether the Oral Law is binding and to what extent. Orthodox, Conservative, and Reform Jews have continued the debate to this day. But no organized Jewish religious group ever maintained that the Law could be dispensed with altogether, that the Law was a curse or that faith alone was sufficient.

In fact, it was the Law around which the faithful in Israel rallied in the disastrous days which followed the destruction of the Temple and the collapse of the state, and again during the savage Hadrianic persecutions. The spiritual chaos of those times, the crushed and beaten morale of the people, the danger of complete prostration, are nowhere so movingly portrayed as in the Apocalypse of Baruch (2 c. C.E.), written contemporaneously with some parts of the New Testament; and its exalted faith, rising from amidst the ruins, reflects the indestructible strength and nobility of a Judaism based on Torah:

> "For the shepherds of Israel have perished,
> And the lamps which gave light are extinguished,
> And the fountains have withheld their stream whence
>   we used to drink,
> And we are left in darkness,
> And amid the trees of the forest,
> And the thirst of the wilderness."
> And I answered and said unto them:
> "Shepherds and lamps and fountains come from the Law:
> And though we depart, yet the Law abides.
> If therefore you have respect to the Law,
> And are intent upon wisdom,
> A lamp will not be wanting
> And a shepherd will not fail,
> And a fountain will not dry up." [36]

One is forced to the conclusion that not all the Jews who lived in the century in which Paul and other Christian antinomists preached regarded the Law as a curse! Many looked upon it lovingly, as a blessing and a refuge, even as centuries before it had been for the sorely afflicted "a lamp to my feet and a light to my path" (Ps. 119:105). One hundred and seventy-six verses are devoted in this psalm to an exuberant laudation of the Torah.

The Christian Church itself soon came to have laws—ceremonial laws—of its own, and in time they were codified into canons of religious and ecclesiastical practices—baptism, the eucharist, the sacraments, communion feasts, fasts and Sunday laws, penance and unction, priesthood and confession, ecclesiastical regulations and privileges, tithes, pilgrimages and shrines, rituals, incense and vestments—an Halachah quite as meticulous and burdensome as that of the Scribes and the Pharisees. The Church, too, came to acknowledge the importance of canons in the regulation of faith and discipline. The great experiment in building a Church on pure faith did not succeed!

Certainly, no one who is acquainted with the determined and persistent struggle for the pure monotheistic faith among the people of Israel since the days of Moses and the Prophets could have assumed for a moment then or since that Judaism would find lodgement for the concept of a God such as one finds in the Fourth Gospel, a God who came down to earth, assumed human form, and suffered death for the salvation of men—a doctrine which Jesus himself never taught. These ideas were known to the Jews long before the time of Jesus, and had been rejected by them. They were popular and current in the ancient world. As Professor Murray correctly states:

The idea of an "only begotten son" of God was regular in the Orphic systems, and that of a son of God by a mortal woman, conceived in some spiritual way, and born for the saving of mankind, was at least as old as the fifth century B.C. . . . That this Saviour "suffered and was buried" is common to the Vegetation or Year religions, with their dying and suffering gods; . . . That after the descent to Hades He should arise to judge both the quick and the dead is a slight modification of the ordinary Greek notion, according to which the Judges were already seated at their work, but it may have come from the Saviour religions. The belief in God as a Trinity, or as One substance with three "personae," . . . is directly inherited from Greek speculation. . . .[37]

Judaism had resisted these notions for centuries.

It is understandable that Fourth Gospel ideas should have found acceptance among those in the pagan world who had long been habituated to them through mystery religions, or among pagan proselytes to Judaism to whom such ideas would appear neither strange nor startling and among whom the Christian propaganda actually made its first converts. These concepts might not be strongly resisted by those who, in the Hellenistic world, entertained the current ideas of a Logos, the Word made flesh, the Incarnation of divine wisdom and the mediator between God and man. They certainly could not be accepted by Torah-trained Jews to whom the concept of the unity of God, simple and undifferentiated, was the very bedrock of their faith.

The Jewish people could not but reject such a doctrine unless it were prepared to abandon the most treasured and essential conviction for which it had struggled through the centuries and of which it believed itself to be the covenanted guardian and spokesman to the world. It could not accept a renewed mythologizing of God, which it had resisted for a thousand years, even though the concept of a born, dying, and resurrected God might now be presented as a metaphysical idea and not as a concrete event which took place on a specific date in history or as a trinitarian conception of monotheism. Judaism could find no room in its monotheism for the concept of Jesus as "Son of God, born of the Virgin Mary" (The Apostles' Creed), or as "Very God of Very God" (Nicene Creed), or as "Perfect God and Perfect Man" (Athanasian Creed).

It was not the rejection of the Rabbinic law which made of Christianity a Gentile faith; the Sadducees had also rejected it, and centuries later, the Karaites, who remained, however violently opposed, a minority within the borders of Judaism. Though some Rabbinic authorities would have nothing to do with the Karaites, others like Maimonides urged that they be treated as erring brothers and ministered to as members of the household of Israel. It was the rejection of *all* authority to the Law and the idea of a God incarnate which placed Christianity outside the bounds of Judaism. Here was the fork of the road!

Judaism rejected no treasure. Judaism rejected nothing in the teachings of Jesus which, if accepted, would have added one cubit to its stature or in any way reenforced its monotheism or its moral code. It was to the Gentile world that Christianity made its monumental contribution. It was upon the Gentile world that Christianity, profiting from the momentum of the frontal attack upon polytheism and idolatry which Judaism in its proselytizing activity had been carrying on, and equipped with much of Judaism's lofty and cleansing moral code, made its powerful impact. Where Judaism in its proselytizing efforts could attain only a limited success because it would not yield in its requirements for full acceptance of the Law on the part of those who sought conversion, Christianity, making no such requirements, scored heavily. Christianity was able to bring large sections of the Gentile world—then in the throes of a prolonged spiritual crisis resulting from the breakdown of its ancient beliefs and the failure of its ethical philosophies to satisfy the spiritual needs of men —to a vision of a noble faith and a clean way of life which it derived from Judaism. In so doing, Christianity contributed mightily to the spiritual progress of mankind. One cannot but salute in reverence and admiration its many teachers and leaders who through their devotion, courage, and often through their martyrdom, carried the message of their faith through the centuries to the far-flung corners of the earth.

Maimonides and other Jewish spokesmen regarded Jesus as well as Mohammed as divine instruments in preparing the way for mankind's universal conversion to faith in the one true God. Maimonides wrote: "All these teachings of Jesus the Nazarene and the Ishmaelite [Mohammed] who arose after him were intended to pave the way for the coming of the King Messiah and to prepare the whole world to worship God together as one." [38]

But it was not the pristine monotheism of Judaism which Christianity in its missionary zeal conveyed to the Gentile world, nor exclusively its sturdy, practical, this-worldly ethics. It was a syncretistic faith—strongly salvationist in character, with a major accent on the promise of immortality—far in advance of anything in the Greco-Roman world, but not the uncompromising monotheism of Judaism. Its moral idealism excelled anything the ancient world had to offer, but it was unlike Judaism in that it was oriented toward a Kingdom not of this world.

Thus a mighty stream of influence flowed out of Judaism at the beginning of the common era and, dividing from it, watered benignly many lands and cultures. Other streams were in time to flow out of it and, again dividing, were to pursue their independent courses through history. But the river which is Judaism, replenished by the ageless springs of its own inspiration, continued to follow its own course to its appointed destiny known only to God.

⊷ VII ⊶

ON AVOIDING ALTERNATIVES

The teachers of Judaism almost instinctively rejected a formula of Either/Or in assaying religious values. They avoided all sharp antinomies, all irreconcilables, which lead to a spiritual impasse. This may be seen, in the first instance, in their reflections on the nature and attributes of God. They approached the subject with the greatest diffidence. Here were doors to which no mortal man had the indubitable keys. But being deeply engrossed in their faith, they speculated in all reverence and reserve upon them. Is God a God of justice? Is He a God of love? Does He judge men according to their deserts or does He forgive men according to His great mercy?

Competitive theology has, almost from the beginning, assigned to Judaism a God of justice and to Christianity a God of love. Judaism never proclaimed that God is love. It never proclaimed that God is justice. Justice is no antonym for love; hate is. In the few places in the Bible where the attributes of God are enumerated, they are fairly well apportioned as between justice and love, with a marked bias toward the latter. The teachers of Judaism, knowing man's frailty, taught the love and forgiveness of God. Knowing also man's stubbornness and the frequency of his backsliding, they taught the justice of God and His sure and certain retribution. Social life cannot be constructed on the principle of love alone or on justice alone. Man must be accountable for his actions, but he must also be given the opportunity to repent. The two primary names for God in Judaism, YHVH and Elohim, the Rabbis took to designate Him as a God of mercy and as a God of justice.

Commenting on the verse (Gen. 2:4) "In the day that the Lord God—YHVH Elohim—made earth and heaven," a Rabbi said: "This may be compared to a king who had some empty glasses. The king said: 'If I pour hot water into them they will crack; if I pour ice-cold water into them they will also crack!' What did the king do? He mixed the hot and the cold water together and poured it into them and they did not crack. Even so did the Holy One, blessed be He, say: 'If I create the world on the basis of the attribute of mercy alone, the world's sins will greatly multiply. If I create it on the basis of the attribute of justice alone, how could the world endure? I will therefore create it with both the attributes of mercy and justice, and may it endure!' " [1]

The noted Hebrew essayist, Aḥad Ha-'Am, contends that the idea of absolute justice lies at the foundation of Judaism and that it represents a principal, if not *the* principal divergence from Christian ethics. His contention suffers, we believe, from the penchant of this brilliant writer for sharp antitheses and oversimplification. Aḥad Ha-'Am accepts the notion which has long been popularized by Christian apologetics that Jewish morality is based on justice while the morality of the Gospels is founded on love. He maintains, however, that justice is the higher principle, and goes to great lengths to demonstrate that Hillel's "negative" rule: "What is hateful to yourself do not do to your neighbor," is a sounder principle than that which Jesus phrased positively: "Whatever you wish that men would do to you, do so to them" (Matt. 7:12). He holds, moreover, that this represents a fundamental difference between Judaism and Christianity as to what constitutes the basis of moral conduct.[2]

This is far from certain. Jesus based his view on the authority of Lev. 18:18: "Love your neighbor as yourself," which he regarded as "the great commandment of the Law," like the com-

mandment to love God. On these two commandments "depend
all the law and the prophets" (Matt. 22:37). Akiba shared the
same view.[3] Hillel had worded it negatively. Other Jewish
teachers did not always employ Hillel's phrasing. Maimonides,
for example, interprets the verse "Love your neighbor as yourself," in the positive form, exactly as Jesus did.[4]

There is no authority either in Biblical or in Rabbinic theology
or ethics for the contention that the idea of absolute justice "lies
at the foundation of Judaism." In Judaism it was always justice
and love, with the accent, as a rule, on love. Jeremiah expressed
the classic Jewish concept of God: "I am the Lord Who practices kindness, justice and righteousness on the earth, and in these
things do I delight, says the Lord" (Jer. 9:24). So also the
Psalmist: "Righteousness and justice are the foundations of Thy
throne, loving kindness and faithfulness go before Thee" (Ps.
89:15). The prophet Jonah complained bitterly that God's love
was so boundless as actually to interfere with the operation of the
laws of justice (Jonah 4:2). In Rabbinic literature the term
Raḥaman, the Compassionate One, is often used as the name of
God. He is the *Ab Ha-Raḥamin*—the Father of Compassion.

Certainly "no man should ruin his own life for the sake of
another," and "to preserve your own life is a nearer duty than
to preserve your neighbor." [5] But what is "one's own life?" What
and whom does it include? When a man makes supreme sacrifices
for wife or child or friend or country or an ideal, is he really
ruining his life for the sake of "others," or is he fulfilling the
deepest potentialities of his own being? Where are the boundaries
of mine and thine? Some Rabbis characterized men who based
their conduct on the principle: What is mine is mine, what is
thine is thine, as belonging to "the common type," and others
characterized them as belonging to "the type of Sodom." [6] "The
Torah begins with an act of loving kindness and ends with an act
of loving kindness." [7] It is the virtue of *gemilut ḥesed*—"the practice of kindness," altruism—which many Rabbis extolled above
all other virtues. R. Judah, compiler of the Mishnah, declared:
"He who repudiates the doctrine of *gemilut ḥesed*, it is as

though he repudiates the cardinal doctrine of Judaism (the unity of God)." [8] It is higher than justice; it is higher than charity, declared R. Eleazar.[9] Men should not insist on the strict letter of justice but go beyond it. "Jerusalem was destroyed only because they based their judgments strictly upon Biblical law, and did not go beyond the requirements of the law." [10]

The Either/Or approach was avoided not only as regards the attributes of justice and love in God, and as regards the operation of these ethical principles in man; but also with respect to the problem of the one and the many. Judaism maintained a balance between the individual and society. It aimed to give man a sense of spiritual security and dignity in his personal life, and society an ordered way of justice, peace, and progress. It granted no complete autonomy to the individual, even in his quest for holiness; but neither did it consent to his total submergence, even to achieve the most efficient society.

More than any other religion of ancient times, Judaism stressed the idea of community. Most religions concerned themselves with the individual's private fate, both here and hereafter. Judaism's accent was on the organized social body, the people, which it regarded as the matrix of the individual's personal life and destiny. The personal relationship of man to his Maker and his private duties and responsibilities are, of course, never overlooked. But preponderately it is the people—its history, its relation to God and to the world, its collective mission and responsibility—which figures so prominently in the Bible. "Hear, O Israel!"

This is one of the reasons why the social message has remained so strong in Judaism. It derives from the advantage which is enjoyed by a religion which is bound up with a particular and a covenanted community, obligated to mutual aid and aware of a collective responsibility toward its own members as part of its mission toward the rest of mankind. Such a religion has the potential of developing high concepts of interpersonal relationships and social ideals.

But the rights of the individual were never overlooked in the emphasis which was placed on group solidarity. Faith in the worth of the individual and of human personality is an essential element of Judaism. Man has immense significance in the scheme of things. Man is very important to God in the unfoldment of His purpose—each man, every man, rich or poor, wise or simple, saint or sinner. Sin is abandonment of status, degradation, voluntary descent into unworthiness and paltriness. Sin is not—as some theologic Existentialist writers of the school of Kierkegaard and Barth would have it—the refusal of man to admit his "nothingness"; and history is not "the revelation of the wrath of God upon the sinful pride of man." [11] Sin is failure to live up, in each given situation, to the highest moral potentialities in one's self. Man must live and act always as if his life were tremendously significant, as if his soul and mind were boundless in their capacities and in their influence, reaching distant shores and extending far into the future.

God is not displeased by man's "competitiveness," or by his failure to acknowledge his "creatureliness" or by his desire to construct a better future for himself and his children. God does not humble the mighty simply because they are mighty. The gods of the ancients were jealous of man. Their struggles and rivalries with the children of the earth and the cruel punishments which they inflicted upon mortals who, in one way or another, ruffled their dignity occupy a prominent place in mythology. Prometheus, out of compassion, stole fire from heaven and bestowed it upon man, wherefore the fury of Zeus was vented upon him and he was riveted to Mount Caucasus and, daily, a griffon vulture tore at his liver.

The second and third chapters of Genesis retain traces of these early cosmic myths and their theme of rivalry, although the emphasis is less on divine jealousy than on man's disobedience. But in the first chapter these traces are entirely obliterated. Here, God created man in His image, and blessed him and said: "Be fruitful and multiply and fill the earth, and subdue it; and have dominion over the fish of the sea and over the birds of the air and over every living thing that moves upon the earth" (Gen. 1:27-28). Man was challenged to exercise dominion! Man's reaching out for mastery over nature, his enterprise, his prosperity, and his belief in his high destiny were never regarded by Judaism as *hybris*, as *gabbut*—as haughtiness or pride. On the contrary! Judaism wanted man to think of himself as a partner of God in creation, finite and limited to be sure, but within his limited domain a creator. "I say, 'you are God's sons of the Most High, all of you'" (Ps. 82:6). Only godlessness is regarded as sinful pride, the arrogant belief that man can get along without God and can accomplish his purposes without Him.

Judaism, of course, admonished man to be humble, not because God is jealous of man's pride but because "man's pride would bring him low" (Pr. 29:23). It leads to contention, cruelty, and self-destruction (Pr. 13:10). In wanting man to be modest in spirit, Judaism did not thrust upon him a degrading sense of guilt, a perennial reminder of a sinfulness which is forever at the very core of his personality, and a conviction that he is not capable of helping himself through effort, education, and social activity to a better and nobler life.

The universal moral law which Judaism proclaimed demands much of man in terms of duty and sacrifice, but it also gives much to him in terms of high and independent status and dignity. "Every man has the right to say," declared an ancient teacher in Israel—basing himself on Genesis 5:1, "this is the generation of man" ['man' in the singular]—"for my sake was the whole world created!" [12]

Judaism thus endeavored to give man a sense of greatness in a universe in which he is very small. The world to the ancients was, of course, far smaller in scale than our universe of expanding immensities, wherein man's racial history is less than a moment of geologic time. Yet, even in relation to their vastly smaller universe, man appeared to them pitifully puny, lost, and unimportant. This feeling at first dominates the Psalmist when he declares: "When I look at Thy heavens, the work of Thy fingers, the moon and the stars which Thou hast established—What is man that Thou art mindful of him, and the son of man that Thou dost care for him?" (Ps. 8:4-5). But no moral aspiration can be looked for in man as long as he regards himself as insignificant and of little account. No ethical strivings ever spring from the soil of self-belittlement and disesteem. Hence, the Psalmist climaxes his hymn with an apostrophe to man's unique distinction and dignity, and with the assurance of his worth in the world which God created for him: "Yet hast Thou made him little less than God, and hast crowned him with glory and honor. Thou hast given him dominion over the works of Thy hands; Thou hast put all things under his feet" (Ps. 8:5-6).

It is man's high and noble estate, deriving from kinship with God, which imposes upon him the obligation of imitating His ways. "Be ye holy, for I, the Lord your God, am holy" (Lev. 19:2). Judaism therefore never proclaimed that God is all and man is naught, that "If God is Lord then man is His slave . . . in the core of his being a disloyal slave." [13] "Ye are children unto the Lord your God" (Dt. 14:1), declared Judaism. Children, not slaves! The covenant between God and Israel on which Judaism based its faith is a voluntary covenant, a compact built on consent! In a covenant, status is recognized as well as mutuality and corresponding obligations. Covenants are not made with men utterly devoid of worth or trust or competence, men who are forever conscious only of their own nothingness!

But, however important the individual is in the eyes of Judaism, he is not all-important. Man is never superman, never *Übermensch*, any more than he is merely *Auchmensch*. There is no cult of the Ego in Judaism, any more than there is a cult of the State. The importance of the great personality, the seer and pathfinder in human history, is not underestimated. But while he is praised and extolled, he is never adored. Adoration belongs to God alone. Judaism is not a religion about any man in whom the fullness of God made itself manifest. Moses and the prophets were great and inspired teachers, messengers and instruments of God, some greater than others; but none is faultless, and all share the common fate of man. The adoration which the followers of

Buddhism, for example, came to bestow on Gautama, or the Christian world on Jesus, was never given by Jews to Moses or to any other man. The major interest of Judaism always centered in the way and the goal rather than on the guide.

Along with the individual's inalienable rights, assured to him by virtue of his categorical relationship to God, there are his obligations which spring from his inextricable relationship to society, in the fulfillment of which lies the key to his self-fulfillment. Self-realization comes through social cooperation. Judaism has very little sympathy for the hermit in quest of personal salvation. When a man effaces himself for the sake of a greater cause, he becomes transfigured into something greater than himself. But the religious recluse never effaces himself; even in the midst of his extreme mortifications he remains self-centered. Judaism rejoices in a service of God which is "in the midst of the congregation" (Ps. 22:23). Nearly all the prayers of Israel are in the plural: "Bless *us*, O our God, *all of us together*, with the light of Thy countenance."

The individual was called upon to seek the good life through active participation in the responsibilities of community life. The community, as such, was required to set up such political and social institutions of justice and equity as would assist the individual in his quest for freedom and the good life. Thus Judaism maintained a reasonable balance between individual and society. Any monolithic corporate society which demands *Gleichschaltung*, *Vermassung*, totalitarianism, would be viewed by Judaism as disastrous to the spiritual growth of the individual.

It was never Either/Or in Judaism with reference to faith and knowledge. Judaism faced the inevitable limitations under which man's faith must function, but it never permitted these shortcomings to force it away from its balanced position and to acknowledge defeat in agnosticism or atheism. It did not stand helpless before the impassable boundaries of reason and speculation, immobile in the presence of confounding paradoxes. It went beyond doubt with open eyes, and chose the way of complete

faith in the face of incomplete knowledge. What is paradoxical
to the mind need not prove a block to moral action. A paradox is
not necessarily an immobilizing self-contradiction. It is the confession of bafflement in the presence of a meaning not yet grasped,
perhaps never to be fully grasped, by man's limited mind. Judaism frankly confronted the paradoxes which exist in theologic
and philosophic thought. But while its Sages wrestled with them
on the plane of inquiry, they did not for a moment slow down
the pursuit of their moral objectives. Thus, for example, R. Jannai
(3 c.), confronted with the paradox which tore at the heart of
Jeremiah and Job, accepted with resignation the impenetrable
enigma and admitted: "It is not in our power to explain either the
well-being of the wicked or the sorrows of the righteous." [14]
However, such bafflement did not prevent this famous Rabbi
from founding a school for the expounding of the Torah and for
the raising of many disciples. Akiba could not solve the paradox
of God's omniscience and man's free will, nor that of grace and
works.[15] This did not prevent him from dying a martyr for his
faith. The teachers of Judaism were constantly engaged in working out a program for the life of man and society within the given
terms of reference. Their moral earnestness far exceeded their
speculative curiosity, and their practical minds were not permanently halted at the threshold of defective definitions. They
did not start with rationalism and move on to skepticism and
despair, as did many religious philosophers of both the ancient
and the modern world. They began with a revealed Law and a
binding covenant—spiritual and ethical truths which did not
emerge from skillful dialogues at pleasant symposia but as a
revelation, as a "burden" and a summons.

Talmudic literature makes it abundantly clear that the Rabbis
did not avoid the challenge of man's intellect. As we have seen,
neither they nor other educated Jews of their day lived in a
cultural vacuum. The Greco-Roman world, of which Palestine
was an integral part, abounded in philosophic schools and scholars
in the early centuries of the common era. It was alive with sects,

wherein these very problems were vigorously debated. The keen minds of the Rabbis, so subtly trained in dialectics, and confronted daily with matters of religious doctrine and with the tasks of instruction, could not remain impervious to them. Undoubtedly they speculated much and brooded long over the dilemmas of human thought. They experienced the anguish of intellectual bafflement, but they moved beyond such perplexity to compensatory duties. They knew that true faith is never without uncertainties. They were left wondering but not skeptical.

The inevitable limitations of religion are, in a sense, analogous to the limitations of science, and no more constricting. There was a time when scientists were confident that they would soon achieve the total solution for the riddle of the universe. In our generation, scientists are far less confident. The most profound among them freely acknowledge that objective reality may forever elude the intellectual grasp of men.

But although man has been denied the knowledge of ultimate reality—the how and why of things—he is nevertheless permitted to learn much, very much, about the relations which exist between things and forces in the universe. While man may never be able to explain—because he may never be able to understand—the nature and origin of electricity or gravitation or magnetism, he may come to understand a great deal more about their operation and thus be enabled to use them to his advantage —to increase his power and his well-being in the world. It is in this field of research and investigation into the relationships of things and forces, in learning how they operate and how we can use them, that man finds great reward and satisfaction. Thus, even though scientific knowledge may never be absolute for man and the principle of indeterminacy may increasingly invade its domain, it nevertheless offers him a world of enterprise, challenge, and meaning which can satisfy a purposeful and victorious scientific life.

This is true also of man's spiritual life. It is not within the range

of man's capacity to learn the true nature of God or fully understand His ways. "Canst thou by searching find out God? Canst
thou find out the limit of the Almighty?" So Job is admonished;
and the foremost of the prophets was told: "No man can see me
and live" (Ex. 33:20). Nevertheless, though man may never
come to know God—"Truly Thou art a God who hidest Thyself," declared Isaiah—he may learn much about the operations
of God's laws of justice, love, and truth in the world and, living
by these laws, he may prosper.

Thus, within a hard, unyielding framework of the unknown
and the unknowable, there is yet a vast world of ascertainable
moral truth and of opportunities for moral and spiritual action
wherein man can find a challenge to his noblest ambitions, as well
as deep satisfactions. It is on these values that Judaism concentrated.

Because of this concentration on ascertainable truth and moral
tasks, Judaism, except in those periods of narrow self-enclosure
which resulted from fear and persecution, did not punish unorthodox opinions. The wrong kind of *conduct* was punished—
when the community possessed the authority to punish—not the
wrong kind of opinion. For example, an Elder who rebelled
against a decision of the High Court in Jerusalem, not found ex-
plicitly in the Torah but based on their interpretation, was to be
put to death; but he was liable to the death penalty only if upon
hearing the decision of the High Court, sitting in the Chamber of
Hewn Stone in the Temple grounds, he returned to his own city
and gave practical decisions concerning what should or should
not be done which were in clear defiance of the Court ruling. He
was not culpable if he merely continued to hold to his former
views without acting upon them.[16]

A Jew could question the existence of God, be a *kofer be'ikar*,
and go unpunished by any court or any legally constituted
authority. It was only the man who cursed God, or who turned
to idolatry or led people astray into idolatry, or the false prophet
who prophesied what he had not heard and what had not been

told him, who was subject to the penalty of death. No one could be punished by any earthly tribunal for not believing in Providence, or the Hereafter, or Resurrection, or the Messiah, or the divine origin of the Torah. The authorities were content to leave the punishment of such heretics to Heaven. Jewish courts of justice in Talmudic times never tried cases of heresy,[17] though we find occasionally bitter utterances in Rabbinic literature against the heretic, as we do against the informer and the apostate.[18]

Among the twenty-four categories of those who will have no portion in the world to come, the Rabbis included heretics (*minim, apikorosim, koferim* and *mumerim*).[19] For heretics who actually did not believe in a world to come this was hardly a punishment. . . . There were no Inquisitions in Israel and no autos-da-fé. There are references in the Talmud to excommunications (*Niddui, Ḥerem*) and to certain individuals who were excluded for longer or shorter periods by the Rabbis as a disciplinary measure. Some noted Rabbis like 'Akabia ben Mahalalel, Eliezer ben Enoch and Eliezer ben Hyrcanus were punished in this manner by their colleagues; however, in no instance was the punishment due to any heretical view which these Rabbis entertained, but to disagreements over practical rules, especially rules of ritual purity.[20] Subsequently, forms of excommunication were employed by Jewish courts of law to compel unwilling defendants in lawsuits to appear before them and to abide by their decisions. In the Middle Ages excommunication was invoked to compel individuals to comply with urgent regulations which the community adopted for its social or economic security. Especially in the period of the Geonim did the practice of employing excommunication as a disciplinary measure increase.

In later times and in certain countries of the dispersion where the position of the Jewish community had become precarious, or where the theologic heresies of any of its members might not only endanger its own solidarity in the face of the enemy but might provoke hostile action on the part of the dominant faith, the ban of excommunication was on occasion imposed upon those holding heterodox opinions, and at times grossly abused, as was the case with Uriel Acosta and Baruch Spinoza.

Where the range and scope of ideas were concerned, Judaism again rejected Either/Or. It did not set out to pursue an idea, even a good idea, *à outrance*, relentlessly to its logical conclusion; it did not aspire to any ideological consistency regardless of consequences. This often leads to a *reductio ad absurdum*. A spiritual concept or an ethical ideal is desirable only to the extent that it is serviceable to man and society.

Thus, for example, Judaism held high the ideal of peace. It was the first religion to think of an international order, to proclaim peace as an ideal for mankind, and to summon nations to "beat their swords into ploughshares" and "learn war no more." Yet it never passed over into pacifism. Judaism was convinced that the theory could not sustain the practice.

It was so also with the Messianic idea. Judaism entertained the hope of a national Messiah who would bring to Israel freedom and independence, and to mankind universal justice and peace. This hope of national redemption has been treated by some theologians as something narrow and unworthy, especially when they contrast it with the "spiritual" Kingdom which Jesus, according to their interpretation, preached. Nationalism, patriotism, and the love of freedom are deplored in the case of Jews by writers who extole such ideas as supreme virtues among their own people. The very men who pray for their country's victory in time of war and the success of its arms, who bless its flag and who teach men that "it is sweet and glorious to die for one's fatherland," somehow deem it reprehensible for Jews to have entertained similar sentiments. It was not "spiritual" for Jews to have longed to free themselves from the oppressive Roman tyranny and to have looked forward to the coming of a leader who would liberate them from its galling yoke. The heroic struggles of the Jews against the Romans in behalf of their political independence are characterized by Toynbee as "the Satanic Jewish *émeutes*," and he seems to be holding high carnival at the discomfiture of those intractable Jews who were responsible for them.[21] But the same historian treats the resistance of his own country and of other free nations to Prussian militarism and Nazi imperialism in an altogether different manner:

By rising to the Warrior's level in the world wars of 1914–18 and 1939–45, unaggressive peoples did exercise the cardinal virtues in War to such good effect that they twice defeated a militarist empire's long prepared attempt to conquer the World; and, in winning these successive victories at a fearful cost in blood and tears, they twice bought for our society an opportunity to get rid of War by a better way than submission to a world-conqueror's forcibly imposed Pax Oecumenica.[22]

Why do theologians and theologic historians become so sanctimoniously international and "spiritual" when it comes to the national interests of the Jewish people, while remaining so patriotically national and "worldly" when it comes to the interests of their own people?

But while entertaining the hope of the coming of a Messiah, the Jewish people never accepted any specific Messiah. They sensed that the idea, inspiring as a hope, was hopeless as a reality. An actual Messiah is always an unfulfillment, an anticlimax, and his appearance in history has had, time and again, disastrous consequences for the people.

Judaism does not stand or fall with the belief in a Messiah, declared Albo (15 c.): "The belief in the coming of the Messiah is not a fundamental principle, denial of which nullifies the entire Torah. . . . He who denies it should not be called an infidel." [23] It is certainly not the keystone in the arch of Judaism. There were even some independent spirits among the Rabbis, like the Amora Hillel (4 c.), who denied the coming of the Messiah altogether! "The Jews have no Messiah to expect, for they have already had him in the days of Hezekiah." [24] There were others, like R. Samuel, who stripped the Messianic idea of all its apocalyptic accretions. Said he: "There is nothing that will be different in the Messianic times from the present except freedom from foreign domination." [25] The social order will be the same.

Nor did Judaism wish people to occupy themselves too much with the subject of the Messiah, or be impatient about his coming, or calculate the time of his appearance. "Blasted be the bones of those who calculate the End." [26] The time of the End is with God. Men, by their repentance and good works, may hasten it.

Similarly, while Judaism made social justice and the economic rights of men central in its teachings, it never preached communism or the abolition of private property or the wrong of possessing property—all leading ideas in some other religions. It never proclaimed: "Woe to you that are rich, for you have received your consolation" (Luke 6:24). Lycurgus, who legislated for Sparta, and Plato, who wrote a constitution for an ideal Greek republic, took communism as their model. Communism seems to have been a widespread Aryan practice in earliest times. Not a trace of it is to be found in any of the Biblical legal codes. None of the Hebrew prophets—the foremost champions of social justice—advocated communism in any form. They did not make social justice synonymous with equalizing the distribution of the goods of a community and the establishment of a communistic society. In Jewish law and in Jewish tradition, the rights of property were safeguarded within the framework of social responsibility and the well-being of the community. Judaism is not committed to any dogmatic economic system. It was concerned with the safeguarding of humane principles which each age must be challenged to translate into such economic arrangements as would best meet its changing needs. There are essential human rights at stake in every economic system, and religion must remain free to defend these rights for which no system provides adequate guarantees.

Judaism warned against both the temptations and the misuse of wealth, but it never commanded man, in order to inherit eternal life: "Go, sell what you have and give it to the poor, and you will have treasure in heaven; and come follow me" (Mark 10:21). Joḥanan b. Zakkai, founder of the Jabne Academy, thought otherwise. The business of life should not be neglected even when the Messiah appears: "If you hold a sapling in your hand and someone cries, 'Lo, the Messiah comes,' plant the sapling first and then go to meet him." [27]

It was not long before many of the leaders even of the Christian Church abandoned their original communism and their attitude toward property and riches. Once the belief gained ground that the end of history was not in sight and the establishment of the Kingdom of God was not imminent, that this world, as it was constituted, would endure for an indefinite time, the Church compromised with the world and proceeded to rediscover and restate many of the traditional ethical values of normative Judaism—values unrelated to eschatology—at the expense of the "crisis" ethics based on the Parousia. Thus Clement (2–3 c.), employing the favorite Alexandrian technique of allegorizing sacred texts, devotes his entire work *The Rich Man's Salvation* to give "spiritual" meaning to the advice which Jesus gave to the man who wished to inherit eternal life:

It is not what some hastily take it to be, a command to fling away the substance that belongs to him and to part with his riches, but to banish from the soul its opinions, its attachments to them, its excessive desire. . . . For it is no great or enviable thing to be simply without riches. . . . How could we feed the hungry and give drink to the thirsty . . . if each of us were himself already in want. . . . We must not then fling away the riches that are of benefit to our neighbors as well as ourselves. . . . Wealth is an instrument. You can use it rightly; it ministers to righteousness. But if you use it wrongly, it is found to be a minister of wrong.[28]

This is old Jewish wisdom, which the Church came to appreciate, although not wholeheartedly. Throughout subsequent centuries the ideal of poverty continued to be preached and extolled in the Christian world, and communism was the established way of life in all of its monasteries and nunneries.

Judaism's natural tendency to avoid irreconcilable attitudes is evident even where the laws of the Torah are concerned. The Bible had ordained that there must be nothing added to it or subtracted from it (Dt. 4:2). Nevertheless, the teachers of Judaism —true to the spirit of the Bible, but desirous at the same time to keep it viable and contemporaneous, to save its laws from obsolescence—found ways of interpreting it in such fashion that without doing violence to its essential integrity, much indeed was added and much subtracted from it. The *apikoros* might gibe at the Rabbis: "Of what use are the Rabbis to us? They have never permitted us the raven [prohibited by Scriptures], nor forbidden us the dove [permitted by Scriptures]." [29] In actual practice, however, as we have seen (see page 91 f.), the Rabbis did permit much that was prohibited and in some instances prohibited things that were permitted. In times of emergency a law of the Torah was amended, or set aside altogether, to serve the higher interests of the faith. Basing himself on the Biblical verse, "It is time to work for the Lord; they have made void Thy law," R. Nathan (2 c.) declared: "They have made void Thy law because it was a time to work for the Lord." [30] Certain sects in Israel resisted this practice, some of them very powerful sects, like the Sadducees, men of hard conservatism and opposed to all reform, and in later times the Karaites. The Sages and Rabbis however, in spite of opposition, proceeded to develop an elaborate exegesis, which made abundant room for legal growth and for ethical deepening and enrichment. By means of it, and without abandoning the dogma of plenary verbal inspiration, they were able to deal with the anthropomorphisms, the improbable narratives and the contradictions of the Bible, as well as to satisfy the demands of an advancing life upon a closed canon. All was implied in the Torah, they argued, so that all could be deduced from it.[31] "Just as a rock may be split into many pieces, so may one Biblical verse convey many teachings." [32] Every word and phrase of the Bible had, of course, a clear surface meaning, but there were also inherent meanings which called for decipherment at the hands of skilled initiates and trained scholars.

The Rabbis not only derived new laws from the Written Law by a system of interpretation, but they claimed to be in possession of ancient laws not found in or derived from the Written Law, but which were nevertheless also to be accepted as "the Halachah of Moses from Sinai." But in their exegesis they were careful not to ignore the simple *p'shaṭ* or *emet* (truth)—the clear, literal meaning of the text. The principle laid down was: "No text can be torn away from its clear simple meaning." [33]

To maintain a proper balance between text and interpretation was no easy matter, and the road of the Pharisaic teachers was full of pitfalls. Hence their repeated insistence upon a thorough discipleship, upon the study of the Torah under the expert tutelage of some master of the Law and on personally ministering to him through many years in order to learn "his way in holiness." They declared: "Greater is the service of the Torah than the study thereof," [34] and they pointed out: "When the disciples of Shammai and Hillel multiplied who had not served their teachers sufficiently, dissension occurred in Israel and the Torah became like two Torahs." [35] The Rabbis recognized the limitations of the self-educated scholar. He was in danger of missing that discrimination which comes only as a result of a long cultural tradition and a close apprenticeship with the expert bearers of it.

This danger may be seen in the case of Philo. He applied the mode of allegorizing, which was very popular in Alexandria among pagan expositors of Hesiod and Homer, to the laws of the Torah. He sought to present the Torah as a system of exalted religious philosophy and to justify by means of allegory those laws and narratives of the Torah which the intellectuals of his day might find objectionable. Philo himself accepted the binding authority of the laws of the Torah and he observed them. Others, however, especially among Judeo-Christians, who adopted the same technique, translated all the ritual and ceremonial laws of the Torah into pure allegory and symbolism, and drew the conclusion that they need not be observed at all. Thus the *Epistle of Barnabas* (1–2 c.), originating probably in Alexandria, em-

ploys this subjective allegoric, *midrash* technique, and concludes
that the dietary laws, circumcision, Sabbath, and all other laws
of the Torah are to be understood *only* in their spiritual sense
and are not to be observed at all. The prohibited foods are
prohibited vices, circumcision is not of the flesh and the Sabbath
refers to the seven thousandth year of creation when the Messiah
Jesus would appear. This elastic technique is used in the New
Testament and is abundantly followed in Patristic literature.
Justin's *Dialogue with Trypho* is an outstanding example of it.
Allegory served the purpose of the Church Fathers admirably,
and they took to it avidly. Allegory, in fact, turned out to be the
battleground of Christian and Jewish apologetics.

Philo used the methods of allegory to an extent which the
Rabbis would have deprecated. His doctrines were orthodox
enough, but his exposition lacked the distinctive Hebraic grain;
it had the earmarks of a theologic colonialism. It was Judaism in
a foreign idiom. That is why Philo's influence on Judaism remained negligible, while his influence on the development of
early Christian thought was enormous. No reference to Philo is
found in Jewish literature until the time of Azariah di Rossi in
the sixteenth century.

The Rabbis of Palestine and subsequently those of Babylonia
were not primarily concerned with apologetics, with justifying
Judaism to the non-Jew, or with establishing the fact that Plato
borrowed his ideas from Moses. They were concerned with
teaching Judaism to the Jew. They employed allegory, to be sure,
but they forbade the use of this method in interpreting Scriptural
passages which contained laws and commandments.[36]

Characteristic, too, was Judaism's attitude toward the Temple
and the institution of sacrifices. The sacrificial cult remained in
Israel until the destruction of the Second Temple, eight hundred
years after Amos and his fellow prophets had thundered forth
that God had not spoken to the people nor commanded them
when He brought them out of the land of Egypt concerning
burnt offerings and sacrifices (Jer. 7:22; Is. 1:10–17; Micah

6:6–8). The Deuteronomic Code, though compiled under prophetic influence, had nevertheless kept the institution of sacrifices. The Temple in Jerusalem retained its sanctity in the eyes of all Jews, regardless of their attitudes toward the institution itself. It was the holy national shrine, the symbol of their universal faith, "the sanctuary, O Lord, which Thy hands have established" (Ex. 15:17). It was in the Temple that Isaiah received the vision which consecrated him a prophet of God. Jeremiah, who was tried for blasphemy because he had prophesied the destruction of the Temple and had warned the people not to put their trust in its physical buildings, nevertheless prophesied that it would be rebuilt (Jer. 33:18). Upon their return from Babylonian captivity the people rebuilt the Temple and resumed the sacrifices, although they had been taught by the prophets of the exile that prayer could well take the place of sacrifice and that God could be worshiped elsewhere than in His sanctuary in Jerusalem, for God is everywhere and everywhere are His unwalled Temples. "Thus says the Lord God: Though I removed them far off among the nations, and although I scattered them among the countries, yet I have been to them as a little sanctuary in the countries where they have come" (Ezek. 11:16).

But the Temple was precious in the sight of the people. Except for a few decades, during the Babylonian exile, it had stood on Mount Zion for a thousand years, "beautiful in elevation, the joy of all the earth" (Ps. 48:2). Pilgrimages were made to it by Jews from all over the Diaspora, who brought their offerings and sacrifices. There is no criticism of the cult of sacrifice in the New Testament. Jesus, his parents, and Paul brought offerings to the Temple (Luke 2:24; Acts 21:26).

And yet the Temple was not enough! Revered, sacred, the duly prescribed place of divine worship, and the incontestable symbol of the faith, leaders and people alike knew that it did not completely satisfy them nor fully express the inner spirit of their religion. Much else was needed. Hence alongside the Temple, the people came to have another place of worship, no longer a *Bet Mikdash*—a Sanctuary, but a *Bet Ha-Keneset*—a

Meeting House, a Synagogue. Here was the throbbing heart of the faith. Here was focused the variegated life of the community; here the youth of each generation was molded into the Jewish way of life, trained into loyalty and discipline. No priests and no sacrifices, no features of cult and no ecclesiastical authority were here. This was the domain of the Sage and the scholar.

The synagogue had been growing in strength and influence throughout the centuries of the Second Commonwealth. By the beginning of the common era it could be found in every Jewish community inside and outside Palestine, even in the courts of the Temple itself. It had become the dynamic center of Jewish life and faith—its impregnable spiritual fortress. When the Second Temple was destroyed, regretted and lamented though the event was, it made no appreciable difference to Judaism, except insofar as it established the synagogue as the exclusive center. The destruction of the Temple was not quite as crushing a blow as might be imagined. There was full confidence that Judaism could survive without a central national shrine.

In their attitude toward Temple and synagogue, as in other matters, the leaders of Judaism sought to reconcile the Law and the prophets, the letter and the spirit. They tolerated no sharp breaks with the past. They built bridges leading from past tradition to present needs.

Similarly, it was never a case of Either/Or as between Halachah and Haggadah, between Law and Lore. The vast literature of Judaism, from the Bible to the latest *midrash*, contains many homilies and rich deposits of ethical lore and folk tales. The homiletical interpretations of the Rabbis and their ethical expositions contain at times bizarre and imaginative tales, the proliferation of a rich, creative fancy. It should be borne in mind that the Rabbis were not only teachers of law, but preachers as well. Apart from students bent on acquiring a knowledge of the Law and all the intricacies of legal dialectics, the masses of the people who sought guidance and edification also turned to them. On the very face of it, many of these Rabbinic tales and discourses cannot be taken literally. They were intended to challenge attention, to attract the listener, or to convey a moral lesson by way of an arresting story. It may well be that some of the Rabbis and many of their listeners, children of their time, actually gave credence to these miraculous tales, just as some of them undoubtedly believed in demons, spells, dreams, and the influence of the stars.[37] The superstitious beliefs and practices which are attributed to some Rabbis of the Talmud were the source of considerable consternation to the Rabbis of later times who, like the author of the *Sefer Ha-Ḥinuch* (13–14 c.), found themselves under the necessity of explaining the apparent contradiction which existed between them and the clear intent of the Biblical injunctions against charms, sorcery, and all forms of wizardry and divination.[38]

The masses of the people hungered for the simple homily, the captivating parable, the honeyed wine of some legendary tale. They longed for a world wherein they could abide, if only for a brief respite, with all cares banished and all desires satisfied. Their tired hearts welcomed the Haggadah. They were too spent by daily toil to follow the knotty problems of legal discussions. They would at times turn away from the Rabbi who discussed Halachah to one who entertained and instructed them with Haggadah.[39] The famous Haggadist R. Levi (3 c.) declared: "In former times when a *pruṭah* was still to be had, men would sometimes want to listen to a word from the Mishnah, the Halachah or the Talmud; but now that the *pruṭah* is gone, and men are heartsick because of oppression and subjection, they long to listen only to words of blessings and comfort." [40]

Part of the Haggadah of the Rabbis was also aimed at answering the attacks which were made on the Bible, on Jewish doctrines, or on the people of Israel by Gnostics like Marcion, and other critics, both Christian and pagan—attacks which in many instances appear to us today as incredible as the refutations they provoked.

Some Rabbis, like R. Joḥanan and R. Simon b. Lakish (3 c.), regarded Haggadah highly and read books of Haggadah on the

Sabbath when only holy books should be read.[41] There were others like R. Zera who did not relish Haggadah at all and who compared its books to the writings of sorcerers.[42]

But whatever the individual attitudes of the Rabbis might have been, it is clear that Haggadah was never used by them as a basis for Rabbinic law, any more than the Prophetic Writings or the Hagiographa were ever used for that purpose.[43] No Halachah was ever derived from an Haggadah. Haggadah had no authority whatsoever. It was never part of a creed or a code. The informal conversations of the Rabbis (*siḥat ḥulin*) with which the Talmud abounds and which, it was held by some, merited study [44] were never regarded as sources of Halachah.

Time and again Rabbis and expositors of Judaism in the Middle Ages, under Christian and Karaite attacks, found themselves under the necessity of drawing attention to the sharp distinction which exists between Halachah and Haggadah. The noted statesman and Talmudist, Samuel Hanagid (10–11 c.), who stands at the headwaters of the glorious Renaissance of Hebrew learning among Spanish Jews, wrote in his *Introduction to the Talmud* that where the Haggadah is concerned one is free to accept whatever appeals to his reason. Judah Halevi (11–12 c.), pre-eminent poet of Spanish Jewry and author of the famous apology for Judaism, *The Kuzari*, explains to the King of the Khazars the nature and purpose of Haggadah, but makes it very clear that it is in no way related to law.[45] In the thirteenth century Moses Nachmanides made the same point in his public disputation with Fra Pablo Christiani in Barcelona (1263). Midrash and Haggadah, he maintained, are allegorical and legendary. If one cares to believe in them, well and good; if not, no harm is done.

It is the Halachah which, in the main, preserved the structural distinctiveness of Judaism. The Haggadah frequently wandered far afield, though in its ethical ranges it sometimes reached towering heights. Folklore in Judaism is one thing; doctrine and code are quite another. Thus, for example, no reference to angels is found anywhere in the Mishnah, though they are abundantly mentioned in Biblical and Rabbinic folklore. Belief in angels is no dogma in Judaism, as it is, for example, in the *Imān* of Islam, where it is included among the six major principles of religious belief. None of the medieval Jewish philosophers, with the possible exception of ibn-Daud, includes this belief among the essential articles of faith.

Quite a number of folk concepts are found in the Haggadah—angels, Satan, Original Sin, and evil spirits, but they were ideas which belonged to the faith only tangentially. They were never part of doctrine. In Christianity some of these folk concepts became central dogmas, and Haggadah ascended the throne.

The same controlled position is reflected in the attitude of the Rabbis toward prophecy and miracles. They did not and they could not deny their place in Judaism, or the possibility of their manifestation at any time. The Bible clearly accredited both. But they were not willing to stake the future of their faith on the chance appearance of men who might pretend to superior divine authority and who might utter prophetic oracles not in keeping with the long-established principles of Judaism, perhaps even in defiance of them. They were unwilling to base law or doctrine upon reputed miracles which might be exploited to confirm heresies. They therefore maintained that prophecy actually ceased in Israel with the last three Biblical prophets, Haggai, Zechariah, and Malachi. The Holy Spirit departed then,[46] and thereafter only the *Bat Ḳol*, a divine Voice—an inferior form of divination—remained. The *Bat Ḳol* was made manifest, in some instances, by interpreting words casually uttered by children in the synagogue, or in some chance reading of a passage in a sacred book which might then be viewed as an omen.[47]

Oracles and seats of oracular worship which were so popular in the pagan world throughout the Hellenistic age disappeared from Israel in postexilic times along with many other forms of divination. The official Urim and Tummim, the oracle by lot which was used on occasion by the High Priest, was no longer in the Second Temple.[48] R. Abdimi of Haifa (3–4 c.) declared: "At the time of the destruction of the First Temple, prophecy was taken away from the Prophets and given to the Sages." [49] R. Johanan went much further: "At the time of the destruction of the First Temple, prophecy was taken away from the Prophets and given to fools and children." [50] He had in mind perhaps the widespread "prophetic" practices among the early Judeo-Christians, practices which were encouraged by Paul and others: "Now I want you all to speak in tongues, but even more to prophesy" (I Cor. 14:5). This was in keeping with the conviction that with the approaching End the spirit of prophecy would return in overflowing measure (Joel 3:1-2). But the Christian Church itself, which came to be plagued by "false prophets," impostors, and pretenders who endangered its orthodox doctrines, soon put prophecy under restraint.

The position came to be held in normative Judaism that the Sage, the skilled interpreter of the Torah, was superior to the prophet. [51] The purpose of the Rabbis was not to deny the prophetic spirit, but to insist that whatever further truth or new insights were required by subsequent ages could very well be drawn by trained and devout minds out of the deep well of the Torah whose waters were inexhaustible.

This attitude also determined the course of Jewish mysticism throughout its history and distinguished it from Christian and Moslem mysticism. In Jewish mysticism the stress was not laid on private mystical experience, on an inner illumination, or on experiencing God through ecstasy and revelation, but on discovering recondite truth by probing deep into the inner meaning of Scriptures, into the text, the letters of the text, their numerical value, combination, and permutation (*gymaṭria, noṭriḳon*). Through a lavish system of Biblical allegory conjoined with borrowed ideas, mostly Neoplatonic, of spheres and emanations, Jewish mystics developed their theoretic and practical cabala. Even the appearances and revelations of Elijah with which some Jewish mystics were favored or the Voice of a *Maggid* (mentor) had as their objective largely the elucidation of some particularly difficult text of the Bible or some baffling legal intricacy. There were exceptions, of course, and in high-tensioned times of Messianic expectations there were men and women who were emotionally roused to outright prophecy. But as a rule the Jewish mystic was not trained to wait in quiescence of mind for an inner voice or an inner light.

Miracles, too, though not theoretically disputed, could not be employed to establish an Halachah. R. Eliezer b. Hyrkanus (1–2 c.) had a dispute with the Sages over an oven, the famous oven of Aknai, which was built of separate layers instead of one piece, and involved some question of ritual cleanliness. R. Eliezer brought forward all the arguments which he could muster to prove his point, but the Sages did not agree with him. Whereupon he said: "If the Halachah is as I state it, let this carob-tree prove it." The carob-tree was torn a hundred cubits out of its place! "No proof can be brought from a carob-tree," the Sages retorted. Again he said: "If the Halachah agrees with me, let this stream prove it." Whereupon the stream flowed backwards. . . . Again he urged: "If the Halachah agrees with me, let the walls of the schoolhouse prove it." Whereupon the walls inclined to fall. . . . Again he said: "If the Halachah agrees with me, let it be proved from Heaven!" Whereupon a Heavenly Voice (*Bat Ḳol*) cried out: "Why do ye dispute with R. Eliezer, seeing that in all matters the Halachah agrees with him?" But R. Joshua arose and exclaimed: "It is not in heaven" (Dt. 30:12). What did he mean by this? Said R. Jeremiah (3–4 c.): "The Torah has already been given at Mount Sinai; we pay no attention to a Heavenly Voice; Thou hast long since written in the Torah at Mount Sinai, 'after the majority must one incline' " (Ex. 23:2).[52]

Judaism, in its historic evolution, did not move from prophecy to apocalypse, but from prophecy directly to the men of the Great Synagogue, from the Torah to its interpretation at the hands of the Scribes and the Sages. Folkist beliefs and superstitions, native or alien, in postexilic as in preexilic times, did infiltrate and at times even threatened the authoritative faith. There always existed the danger of a relapse into the mythological in all areas short of outright polytheism. Mysticism and the apocalypse could always pave the way for such a relapse, and normative Judaism was on guard against a return of the "turmoil of imaginings" of the primitive world from which it had escaped. Judaism sought to guard itself against such dangers by curbing and, to all intents and purposes, outlawing all prophecy subsequent to the postexilic restoration.

Even before it finally banned all apocalypses, Judaism must have been suspicious of them because of their wildness of fantasy, their waywardness and randomness, as well as their overemphasis on eschatology. The Book of Ezekiel was almost excluded from the canon or withdrawn from public use in schools and synagogues because of its mystical and apocalyptic elements.[53] Prophetic and Rabbinic Judaism was predominantly interested in the progress of man and society, while the apocalypses were interested in the timetable of the approaching End. The one sought a moral reformation of society; the other hoped for its miraculous transformation through divine intervention. The prophets tried to make their message and their visions crystal-clear to men: "Write the vision; make it plain upon the tablets, so he may run who reads it" (Hab. 2:2). The apocalypses, much like the equivocal pagan oracles, wrapped their visions in mystery and ambiguity—"Shut up the words, and seal the book" (Dan. 12:4)— and purposely made their utterances cryptic, allusive, and in need of decipherment.[54]

There is a remarkable balance and pragmatic quality in Judaism which, while not proscribing deviation either into the mystical or into the pietistic, nevertheless kept these, as it were, within bounds. The periphery was never confused with the center; and the surface eddies were never mistaken for the deep-carrying channels of the faith.

◄(VIII)►

ON BEING REASONABLE

Many scholars have commented on the temperate quality of Judaism, its wholesomeness and whole-mindedness, eschewing, as it does, all extremes. Some have disparaged this sobriety; others have extolled it. There are those who have a liking for religion with a hairy shirt, a penchant for hallowing with harrowing. The normal human craving to be well fed and warmly clad and sheltered is to certain lofty souls evidence of some grave moral shortcoming. For them social, political, or economic progress, if not a delusion, is of slight importance. If there is any possibility of happiness in this world at all, they insist that it is in no way related to the enjoyment of God's material blessings.

Judaism in its seasoned wisdom was never superior to man's material needs and to their satisfaction, to what has been condescendingly referred to as "humanistic meliorism," or more contemptuously by Aldous Huxley as "the advertising man's apocalyptic faith in Progress towards a mechanized New Jerusalem." One detects a measure of affectation in this disparagement of modern society which, according to the belittling summary of T. S. Eliot, is engaged in "devising the perfect refrigerator and working out a rational morality." This finical attitude is not convincing. One cannot be a true lotus-eater and at the same time, for health's sake, carefully watch one's calories. . . . To disdain in principle all scientific knowledge and social progress and in practice welcome all that flows from them in terms of the conquest of disease, the reduction of illiteracy, the elimination of poverty, the protection of the young and the aged, and the vast extension in the benefits of the applied sciences, is "to break the cask and keep the wine from spilling" [1]—a prodigious feat indeed, if one is able to accomplish it.

Judaism is not too high-pitched for ordinary human needs. To be sure, "man does not live by bread alone" (Dt. 8:3), but without bread man does not live at all. "If there is no flour there is no Torah." [2] Judaism viewed man in all his dimensions and sought to establish harmony in all his legitimate needs.

Jewish ethics is nowhere motivated by the conviction that "this is the last hour" (I John 2:18), that the present order of the word is about to end cataclysmically, that a new order is about to be ushered in by the miraculous intervention of God, and that men should therefore concentrate intensively on extreme acts of self-purification. Judaism does not reflect the anxious mood of an age of crisis, even as it does not build its ethical doctrines on a concept of the radical malevolence of human nature, or on man's impotence to "save" himself.

The teachers of Judaism constantly stressed the fact that Judaism is a livable faith, not too difficult for man or beyond his reach. It did not demand the impossible of man. The good life, acceptable to God, is within the reach of all. The standard of conduct demanded of man was not inordinately difficult of attainment:

For the commandment which I command you this day is not too hard for you, neither is it far off. It is not in heaven, that you should say, "Who will go over the sea for us, and bring it to us, that we may hear and do it?" But the word is very near you. It is in your mouth and in your heart, so that you can do it [Dt. 30:11–14].

The task of building the good society is difficult, but no one man is called upon to bear the entire burden alone. Each man is required to do what he can to the best of his abilities. R. Ṭarfon (c. 100) said, "It is not your responsibility to complete the work, but neither are you free to desist from it." [3]

Judaism had faith in human perfectibility, but it took a reasoned and long-range view of it. Human perfection is a goal, not a present reality. Judaism therefore outlined a considered regimen of moral tasks and duties and a deliberate course of training for the conduct of the good life. "Love your neighbor as yourself," is not the beginning of such a course but its consummation. We do not climb a ladder by starting at the top. A premature demand for maximum moral performance on the part of the individual is as fatal to his development as a similar demand made upon the physical exertions of an athlete. Hence Judaism offered an ordered manual of training—the educative laws of the Torah.

In contrast may be cited the severe requirements which Jesus exacted from those who would enter eternal life. "For the gate is narrow and the way is hard, that leads to life, and those who find it are few" (Matt. 7:14; Luke 13:24). The same thought is expressed in *II Esdras*, an eschatological work of the second century c.e.: "There be many more of them which perish, than of them which shall be saved."[4]

In Hindu thought the single span of a human life was not regarded as long enough to attain perfection, which task required many incarnations. The ideal figure of the Stoics, the Wise Man, was also an impossible ideal. "The Stoics admitted that he was as rare in the real world as the phoenix."[5]

Judaism does not attempt to alter human nature or to suppress human instincts. Its aim is to guide them. It is deeply perceptive of man's capacities, but also of his limitations. Judaism teaches man to love his neighbor as himself (Lev. 19:18), to love the stranger as himself (Lev. 19:33), not to hate his brother in his heart (Lev. 19:17), not to take vengeance or bear any grudge (Lev. 19:18). It teaches man to *help* his enemy (Ex. 23:4). "If your enemy is hungry, give him bread to eat; and if he is thirsty, give him water to drink" (Pr. 25:21). Judaism could endorse every magnificent word on love which Paul wrote to the Corinthians (I. Cor. Chap. 13). They are a superb and unique epitome of Biblical and Pharisaic teachings. But nowhere is the command given in the Bible to *love* one's enemy! This is contrary to human nature, and as such it is impossible of fulfillment. To require men to fulfill the impossible is to bring confusion and frustration into their spiritual lives and possibly to cause them to recoil in despair even from those duties which are capable of accomplishment. "As far as reason is concerned," declared Saadia, "it demands that the All-Wise does not charge anyone with aught that does not lie within his competence or which he is unable to do." [6] The Torah was not given to ministering angels,[7] but to men—mortal, fallible men.

The Christian Gospels themselves demonstrate how impossible of fulfillment was Jesus' mandate to love one's enemy when, time and again, he, who was otherwise so tender and forgiving, is portrayed as denouncing the Scribes and Pharisees as "a brood of vipers" (Matt. 12:34), "blind fools" (Matt. 23:17), "hypocrites and serpents" (Matt. 23:13, 15, 23, 33), and consigning them to damnation, woe, and hell (Matt. 23:33; Luke 10 *passim*). He used a whip of cords to drive the money-changers out of the Temple, pouring out their coins on the ground and overturning their tables (Matt. 21:12–13; Mark 11:15–17; John 2:15).

If controversy can arouse such bitterness in the most idealistic of men, how can one expect ordinary mortals who are entangled and tossed about in the fierce conflicts and rivalries of daily existence to love their enemies?

Judaism does not regard extremes in piety with favor. "Be not righteous over-much" (Eccles. 7:16). The man who is excessively pious is characterized as a *ḥasid shoṭeh*—a pious fool. R. Joshua (2 c.) was wont to say: "A pious fool brings destruction upon the world." [8] The Talmud frowns upon seven types of Pharisees—"the plague of Pharisees"—men who are in one way or another addicted to exaggerated piety, real or affected.[9] Judaism was suspicious of all that was florid and baroque, overstrained and exaggerated in the realms of spiritual thought and exercise. It mistrusted mystic inebriation, agitated hysterical religiosity, a debauch of piety. It held its ethical demands in the firm grasp of human competence and experience.

No one was called upon to be altruistic to the extent of devoting *all* of his possessions to the Lord.[10] A man should give *of* all that he has (Lev. 27:28), not *all* that he has. Judaism urged a due and liberal measure, but not to the point of self-impoverishment. "In Usha they ordained that one who wishes to distribute his possessions must not go beyond one-fifth of them. It happened that one wanted to distribute more than one-fifth, and his colleagues would not permit him to do so." [11] By giving more than he can afford, a man might himself come to be dependent upon the charity of others.[12] But exceptions are approved in cases of extreme urgency. Monobaz, King of Adiabene (1 c.), who embraced Judaism, was praised because in a year of great drought and scarcity he distributed all the accumulated treasures of himself and his fathers among the people. When confronted by the members of his household with the charge that he had squandered the wealth which his ancestors had accumulated, he replied: "My fathers stored up treasure below and I am storing up above . . . my fathers gathered treasures of money, but I have gathered treasures of souls. . . ." [13]

Inner disposition in the carrying out of a commandment or in the performance of a meritorious act was held to be very important, for "God requires the heart." [14] It was the opinion of R. Ashi (4 c.), the editor of the Babylonian Talmud, that "if a man thought to fulfill a commandment and did not do it because he was prevented by force or accident, Scripture credits it to him as if he had performed it." [15] But extreme inwardness, which regards the act itself as of little or no account, is alien to Judaism. A meritorious act is important even without *kavanah*, without the correct inner intent, without its having been done *li'shmah* —for its own sake. By performing it the agent may ultimately come to acquire the correct inner attitude [16]—for men learn by doing and are affected by whatever activity they are engaged in, and a moral act per se has a social utility, quite apart from the agent's intent. God rewards those who do good even when the motive is not of the highest. Their status, of course, is inferior, and the reward is less. Of such, the Torah states, "God's mercy is great *unto* the heavens" (Ps. 57:11); but of those who perform

God's behest for its own sake, "His mercy is great *above* the heavens" (Ps. 108:5).[17]

Prayer without inner intent is, of course, of little worth. Men were admonished not to make their prayers routine. Religious observances and the fulfillment of the commandments however are not invalidated by lack of a proper disposition. "Commandments do not require *kavanah*." [18] Some later authorities applied this principle to Rabbinic ordinances alone, and not to the Scriptural.

Melanchthon, a leader of the Reformation, was thoroughly disgusted with all moral acts which did not spring from the purest and noblest of motivations. "How stinking are the moral virtues, how bloody are the rags of righteousness of the saints!" The Rabbis were never so severe or contemptuous of good actions, even when these were not performed out of the loftiest motives, out of complete rightness of purpose.

R. Safra (3 c.) on concluding his prayer added the following: "May it be Thy will O Lord our God, to establish peace . . . among the disciples who occupy themselves with Thy Torah, whether for its own sake or from other motives; and may it please Thee that all who do so from other motives may come to study it for its own sake." [19]

The *Zaddik*—the righteous man—was not the perfect man. No man is or can be perfect. Commenting on the statement of the Mishnah, "If a man performs but a single commandment, it shall be well with him," Rab Judah declared: "This is its meaning: He who performs a single commandment in *addition* to his equally balanced merits, it shall be well with him and he is as though he had fulfilled the entire Torah." [20] This was not a mechanical method of determining ethical status or of arriving at an evaluation of virtue by a process of simple measurements. It was a profound way of indicating that perfection is not within the reach of man. "There is no man who sinneth not"—and very few indeed in their lifetime fulfill the Torah from *Alef* to *Tav* —but when the balance is struck, if a man's good deeds preponderate, even by so much as a single deed, he is accounted as *altogether* righteous.

It is possible also for one extraordinary good deed to raise a man to great heights. "There are such as acquire eternal life in a single hour, while others acquire it only after many years." This was a favorite saying of Judah Hanasi (2 c.), the redactor of the Mishnah.[21] A single commandment, properly performed in purity of heart, may cause one to inherit eternal life. A single deed may be of such great merit as to atone for a lifetime of sin and raise a man to the level of a saint. R. Abahu (4 c.) heard a voice in a dream declare: "Let Pentakaka [a by-word for one who commits as many as five sins daily] pray and the rains will fall and the drought will be ended." Pentakaka prayed and the rains came. R. Abahu summoned the man. "What is your occupation?" he asked. "I commit five sins daily," he replied. "I hire harlots, I am an attendant at the theatre, I take the clothes of the harlots to the bath-house, I dance and caper before them and beat the drum." "And what good deed have you performed?" "Once, when I was cleaning the theatre a woman came and stood behind the post and wept bitterly. 'What's wrong with you?' I asked her. She said: 'My husband is in prison. I came here to hire myself out as a harlot to find money to set him free.' Whereupon I sold everything I had, including my bed and bedding. I gave her the money and told her to go ransom her husband and keep herself free from sin." R. Abahu said: "You have merited that your prayers for rain should be answered." [22]

It is to Hebrew ethical thought rather than to Greek that one must go for a fruitful concept of the golden mean. Judaism did not recommend as the ethical goal a mathematically calculated counterpoise between undesirable extremes, one of excess and the other of defect, but a driving forward toward holiness and self-perfection along the temperate ways of moral progress. The golden mean is not a measure of computation but a wise technique toward a life of continuous and mounting aspiration.

Maimonides stresses the fact that the golden mean, the middle of the road, is the true "way of God" and that we are commanded to follow that road in all matters except as regards humility and anger.[23] For those who are sick of soul and who require drastic treatment it is sometimes necessary to prescribe an extreme regimen, in order to enable them to return after a time to the normal way of life which avoids all extremes. The middle of the road is the way of the *Hacham*, the wise man. A slight deviation in the direction of a more rigorous practice of virtue is permitted to the man who wishes to be a *Hasid*—a very pious man. "But we are commanded to follow the middle ways for they are the good and correct ways concerning which it is said: 'and you shall walk in His ways.' " [24]

Maimonides also calls attention to the goal toward which this middle road must lead. The ultimate aim and purpose of human life is to seek the practice of loving-kindness, judgment, and righteousness, in imitation of the moral attributes of God.[25] Thus man is given a criterion by which he is enabled to determine what is the real mean. Herein lies the sharp distinction, as Ahad Ha-'Am correctly points out, between Aristotle's formulation of the doctrine of the mean and Judaism's:

Aristotle did not set up a higher moral criterion by reference to which the mean point could be determined in every case. For him all virtue was really but a code of good manners to which the polite Greek should conform, being enabled by his own good taste to fasten instinctively on the point equidistant from the ugliness of the two extremes. But Maimonides, as a Jew, made this principle the basis of morality in the true sense, because he couples with it a formulation of the supreme moral end. This moral end, for which the virtues are a preparation, compels us and enables us to distinguish between the extremes and the mean.[26]

Virtue is not the middle course between opposing vices, but the determined ascent along moderately graded levels of self-improvement toward a fully sufficient moral life none too steep and accessible to all.

But while Judaism is preeminently a practical and livable religion, a constructive idealism, it is not an "easy" religion. Nor is its code of conduct reduced to calculated prudence or a self-complacent morality. It is an ethics of quest and fervor. Its reasonable, practical idealism is of a revolutionary quality, an explosive moral common sense. It is a religious humanism which is actively and passionately intolerant of all moral deception and self-deception and of all forms of injustice and human exploitation. It is especially intolerant of them because its demands and expectations are *not* excessive. The oppressors of mankind can get along much more easily with mystics and visionaries, with dreamers and perfectionists, than with determined people possessed of an obdurate morality of common sense, who know what they want and who are convinced that it can be had.

For Judaism the moral life involves struggle against forces within and without. It is an earnest and arduous quest. One must *"press* on to know God" (Hos. 6:3). One must *seek* Him "with all your heart and with all your soul" (Dt. 4:29). It is not enough to know what justice is; one must *seek* justice (Is. 1:17). "Justice, justice, you shall *pursue!"* (Dt. 16:20). One must be "swift to do righteousness" (Is. 16:5) and one must *pursue* righteousness (Is. 51:1). It is not enough to know truth; one must *"seek* truth" (Jer. 5:1). One must *"seek* peace and *pursue* it" (Ps. 34:15). Judaism is a summons not so much to ethical knowledge as to ethical action and mission.

The Bible nowhere calls upon men to go out in search of peace of mind. It does call upon men to go out in search of God and the things of God. It challenges men to hunger and thirst after righteousness, to relieve the oppressed, to proclaim liberty to the captives, and to establish peace in the world. These objectives must be elaborately sought. As often as not, such enterprises are attended by persecution and suffering. Judaism as a prophetic religion could not offer its faithful the compensation of peace of mind, except insofar as the confidence of faith lessens the tensions of doubt and despair; but it did offer them other and more precious compensations—the nearness of God, an uplifting interest in life, a nourishing pride and dignity and, on occasion, the ineffable ecstasy that derives from moments of spiritual daring and adventure. There is a lyrical vibrancy to such moments when man drinks of the wine of life and partakes of the very manna of heaven.

Personal sacrifices are often involved in the pursuit of the good life. Sometimes even martyrdom is called for. The moral commitments of the faithful are never of a limited liability. The Jewish people gave the first religious martyrs known to mankind, and through many dark and weary centuries of exile and persecution its noblest sons and daughters never denied God the supreme tribute of martyrdom. True love of God is to serve Him "with all your heart, with all your soul and with all your might" (Dt. 6:5). Akiba defined the term "with all your soul" to mean "even if He takes away your life." He attested it with his own martyrdom:

When R. Akiba was taken out for execution, it was the hour for the recitation of the *Shem'a*. When they combed his flesh with iron combs, he accepted the Kingdom of Heaven [he recited the *Shem'a*]. His disciples said to him: "Our teacher, even to this point?" He said to them: "All my days I have been troubled by this verse 'with all your soul' (which I interpreted to mean) 'even if He takes your life.' I asked myself: When shall I have the opportunity of fulfilling this commandment? Now that I have the opportunity shall I not fulfill it?" [27]

Strange "legal formalists," these Rabbis who underwrote their dry exegesis with their tortured bodies and their martyrdom!

To the threatened and persecuted Jews of Yemen who in 1172 sought guidance from the "Light of the Exile" when they were confronted with the choice of apostasy, martyrdom, or exile, the "rationalist" Maimonides replied:

My Brethren! Hold fast to the covenant, be immovable in your convictions, fulfill the statutes of your religion. . . . Rejoice ye that suffer trials, confiscations, contumely, all for the love of God, all to magnify His glorious name. It is the sweetest offering you can make. . . . Should ever the necessity of fleeing for your lives to a wilderness and inhospitable regions arise—painful as it may be to sever oneself from dear associations, or to relinquish one's property—you should still endure all.[28]

Martyrdom was mandatory in cases where a man was ordered to transgress the laws against idolatry, incest, and murder. But only in such cases. This was the decision reached by the Rabbis at the time of the Hadrianic persecutions.[29] R. Ishmael believed that under certain circumstances a man may even worship an idol in order to save his life, for the Torah was given to man that he might *live* by it, and not die because of it (Lev. 18:5).[30] It was the same R. Ishmael who declared that no regulation should be enacted by which the majority of the people cannot abide.[31] But the law followed the opinion of R. Eliezer who declared that a man must accept martyrdom rather than practice idolatry. He believed as Akiba did that a man should serve God with all his soul, that is, with his very life.[32] Some Rabbis held that in time of religious persecutions, when the faith is threatened or when the transgression must be performed in public and demonstratively, a man must incur martyrdom even for a minor precept—"even to change one's shoe strap" [33] (from the white worn by Jews to the black worn by heathens). But in all other instances, a man may, nay *must*, transgress the law to save his life. Otherwise his blood is upon his own head.

The Rabbis warned against an eagerness for self-immolation. The two disciples of R. Joshua are commended for having disguised themselves during the Hadrianic persecutions in order to save their lives. No purpose would have been served by allowing themselves to be detected and killed.[34] Ignatius' (2 c.) longing for martyrdom—"I no longer wish to live after the manner of men," "Permit me to be an imitator of the passion of Christ" [35] —would have been frowned upon by his Rabbinic contemporaries, and the mad yearning of the Donatist sect of Circumcellions for self-destruction would have been abhorrent to any sect in Jewry.

At the same time, the common-sense morality of Judaism stemmed from a very uncommon passionate religious dedication. Jews "gave their backs to the smiters" and died as martyrs not so much for their sound, practical moral code, which they treasured, but "to sanctify the name of God." Judaism was never

merely a moral philosophy. It was always a passionate faith. The
Torah was a "fiery law" (Dt. 33:2). The fires of God flamed
within it. "The Ten Words were written with black fire upon
white and were wrapped up in flame." [36] The Torah was given to
the people of Israel, declared the Rabbis, because they were indomitable and tenacious, because they were prepared to die for
it. On this and on this alone it was a case of Either/Or—"Either
Jew or be crucified!" Such a people was fit to receive a faith
which was likened to a burning fire.[37]

One wonders whether this burning fire is not the unconscious
heritage of those sons and daughters of Israel, so tempestuous
of soul and of such fierce devotions, so passionately eager to
redress the world's wrongs, who are so often found in the van-
guard of the revolutionary movements of the world, storming
the citadels of political and social tyranny and evil. How else can
one explain these early, eager swallows who are so frequently
frozen and destroyed in the many premature springtides of the
world's quest for justice and freedom? Theirs is perhaps the very
fire which the prophet Jeremiah experienced—"a burning fire
shut up in my bones; I am weary with holding it in, but I cannot"
(Jer. 20:9). These idealists are not prophets, but assuredly they
are the descendants of prophets; and their love of justice, their
righteous anger and impatience are part of a heritage of which
they themselves may not be fully aware.

In pointing out the preponderant emphasis in Judaism on rea-
sonableness, it is not suggested that less "reasonable" moods are
not to be found in the far-flung domains of Jewish literature,
wherein through the ages ritualists and pietists, rationalists and
mystics, traditionalists and reformers, priests and prophets all
recorded their views. Some overemphasized one and others another tenet, and in so doing upset the balance, the unique ethical
and spiritual equipoise which distinguishes their historic faith.
But insofar as they were extravagant, their views never constituted essential ideas in Judaism. For the technique of Judaism's
unique religious humanism was to sift and screen these copious
beliefs and finally to reject all that was extreme and excessive, all

that was overgorged either with sensuality or spirituality, all that denied reality or was blinded by it, all that deified man or degraded him. Judaism has been a movement of purification and equilibrium, achieving for the religious life of man what Greece achieved for his artistic and intellectual life—a sobriety of measure and order which we are wont to call classicism.

~◀ IX ▶~

ON SOCIAL PROGRESS

Among the religions of mankind Judaism was quite unique in relation to the idea of human progress. With the exception of Zoroastrianism, this idea is not present commandingly, if at all, in other faiths—in Hinduism, Buddhism, Confucianism, Taoism, Christianity, or Islam. Indeed, it belongs only to a small portion of the human race. The predominant mood of most historic religions is either despair or distrust of progress.

This is true of the early myths of mankind, whose mood is one of fatality. The myths of chapters two to eleven of Genesis, filtered and reworked ethically and monotheistically though they were, do not escape the inevitable tragic dénouement characteristic of all ancient mythology. Adam and Eve are cursed with death and expelled from Eden. Abel is slain, and Cain is fated to go through life a branded fugitive. The Flood destroys mankind and all living things except Noah and those who find sanctuary in the Ark. The men who set out to build the Tower and the City in the plain of Shinar are halted in the midst of their proud and confident enterprise and are scattered in a confusion of tongues over the face of the earth.

It is only when myth ends in the Bible and history begins, when the ethical motif enters with the story of Abraham and the other Patriarchs, that the overhanging pall of fatality is lifted. Thereafter life and hope, will and freedom, struggle and progress, come to dominate the scene.

History could not begin for the Biblical annalist, nor the ethical drama of Israel and mankind unfold, until man's place was made secure in an enduring universe of moral rationality and consistency. Man had to be convinced that the will which governed his world was a moral will which faithfully executed in the governance of mankind the same moral mandates which it prescribed for man. The unpredictable caprice of the mythological powers took no account of man and gave him no security (see page 44). In the face of a possible total destruction of his world at the hands of an arbitrary and impulsive power, all ethical strivings on his part were meaningless. It is only in a continuing and orderly universe that the aspirations of mankind can have any validity. Accordingly, as if to indicate the approaching transition from myth to history, the Bible records that God made an everlasting covenant with the earth and with every living creature upon it, proclaiming "that never again shall all flesh be cut off by waters of a flood," and though man may sin again—"for the imagination of man's heart is evil from his youth"—God will never again "curse the ground because of man" and "never again destroy every creature as I have done." There will from now on be an orderly process in creation: "while the earth remains, seedtime and harvest, cold and heat, summer and winter, day and night shall not cease" (Gen. 8–9).

Man is also reassured not only as to his important place in this world, but as to his moral security in it since it is governed by a just lawgiver and not by a whimful power whose unpredictable actions are not always commensurate with human guilt or merit. This is the full import of the amazing colloquy which takes place between Abraham and God (Gen. 18). "Wilt thou destroy the righteous with the wicked?" Abraham persistently inquires of God. "Shall not the Judge of all the earth do right?" It was only after Abraham was assured and reassured that the righteous will not fare as the wicked do even in the midst of the wicked heathen city of Sodom that Abraham was prepared to "charge his children and his household after him to keep the way of the Lord by doing righteousness and justice" (Gen. 18:19).

In such an enduring universe, mankind could build confidently and be justified in making provision for the future. It could be urged on to high and rewarding ethical adventure. God's covenant with the earth is soon followed by the covenant with Abraham: "Walk before Me and be blameless. And I will make my covenant between Me and you . . . and your descendants after you." This covenant did not preclude appropriate retribution for wrongdoing, but there would be no disproportionate punishment—certainly no utter destruction. "For this is like the days of Noah to me: as I swore that the waters of Noah should no more go over the earth, so I have sworn that I will not be angry with you, nor condemn you utterly" (Is. 54:9). This is the note on which the heroic drama of Israel's and man's spiritual pilgrimage begins.

Because the classical world had no belief in human progress, it was little concerned with the amelioration of man's lot. Most classical writers regarded human history as an endless series of cycles, a continual repetition of the familiar phenomena of recovery and decline. Since the fabled Golden Age in the dawn of mankind's existence on earth, the goodness and nobility of life had been running down through successive stages of degeneration. Perfection belonged to the past. Decay features the present. There is no hope for the future.

In his essay on "The Melancholy of the Greeks," Professor Butcher draws attention to "the peculiar vein of constitutional sadness which seems to belong to the Greek temperament, to the pervading note of melancholy in Homer, Mimnermus, Theognis, Pindar, and the Greek tragedians and philosophers." [1] The author correctly attributes this sadness to the fact that Greek thought turned mainly to the past, and that its political ideals "reflected the prevalent distrust of the future" and were devoid of hope and of any ideal of progress. In this respect Professor Butcher discovers one great difference between the classical Greeks and the Hebrews:

In the darkest hour of adversity the Prophets did not despair of Israel. . . . Through the Prophets an ideal and glorified national sentiment was created, transcending local limits, and intertwined with the highest hopes that could be conceived for humanity. They looked to a spiritual restoration and triumph which should be for the world at large, the beginning of a glorious future.[2]

Aristotle was convinced that "there was nothing new under the sun"—a view of which Judaism was prepared to take careful note, but which it did not adopt. "It is indeed true that these and many other things have been invented several times over in the course of ages, or rather times without number," Aristotle declared.[3] Plato, too, believed that many destructions of mankind had taken place, with few survivors, and that man's arts perished with them to be subsequently recovered.[4]

Marcus Aurelius, too, dwells on the theme "there is nothing new under the sun."

It [the rational soul] extends itself into the infinity of time, and embraces and comprehends the periodical renovation of all things, and it comprehends that those who come after us will see nothing new, nor have those before us seen anything more, but in a manner he who is forty years old, if he has any understanding at all, has seen by virtue of the uniformity that prevails all things which have been and all that will be.[5]

His fellow Stoics thought of progress in terms of the individual's advance toward serenity and calm, which in their eyes constituted the supreme moral achievement. Man's moral activity was centered not in social purposes and building the good society, but in the self, in rigorous self-discipline to achieve a life of correct inclinations, choices, and intellectual judgments. The Stoic system undoubtedly included altruism among the actions appropriate to a human being, but not to the extent of a man involving himself emotionally in the lot of his fellow men. There must be neither sympathy nor pity, for these destroy one's detachment and inner tranquillity. A man should care for nothing that is not under his direct authority and control. He should accept all else with quiet resignation. "Endure and Renounce!"

The Stoics did not conceive of progress, as the Jewish Sages did, in terms of "perfecting the world according to the pattern of the Almighty." They did not believe in the possibility or, for that matter, in the desirability of such progress; for this involved struggle and conflict, things not conducive to calm and serenity. This was the case also with the Neoplatonists:

Neither with Plotinus nor with any of his successors is there the least doubt that the contemplative life is in itself superior to the life of action. Here they are Aristotelian. The chance that the philosopher as such may be called on to reform practical life seems to them much more remote than it did to Plato.[6]

In Judaism the life of contemplation or of study was of significance only insofar as it led to action. "The goal of all wisdom is repentance and good deeds." [7] R. Ṭarfon and the Elders were once reclining in the upper story of Nitza's house in Lydda, when a question was propounded: Is study greater than action? R. Ṭarfon answered, "Action is greater." R. Akiba answered, "Study is greater, for it leads to action." Then they all answered: "Study is greater, for it leads to action." [8] The famous poet Judah Halevi warns men not to be beguiled by a species of Greek wisdom "which produces flowers but no fruit."

Where there is no belief in the reality of progress, there is no summons to social action. One finds a mature, philosophical concept of ethics among the best classical writers, but there is no *passion* for righteousness among them, no missionary urge to improve the conditions of life of whose inhumanity and injustice they were fully aware. What scant thought did the various systems of the pagan world and their gifted exponents devote to the slave and the poor, and to all the pitiful and degraded victims of the social injustices of their day! Struggle and sacrifice to help build the good society were beyond their ken. "Do not disturb thyself. Make thyself all simplicity. Does anyone do wrong? It is to himself he does the wrong." [9] The Cynic—"the Stoic of the slum and the street-corner"—was contemptuous of social life altogether. And the Epicurean was engrossed in personal happiness.

In Hindu religious speculation social progress was of no moment at all, and efforts at social improvement, which implied concern with mundane existence and with the development of human personality, were not to be attempted. The idea of progress in any temporal, social sense is alien to Hindu thought. Its religious tradition knew of four ages of the world, each inferior to its predecessor—the golden age, followed by one in which righteousness (*dharma*) decreased by one-fourth, this in turn followed by one in which righteousness decreased by one-half, and the present age in which righteousness has decreased by three-fourths—the most evil of all ages.[10]

Buddhism's great thesis was Enlightenment, and its supreme objective was deliverance and rest. To meditate on the formless in profound tranquillity—this is the supreme achievement of life. This, essentially, was also Taoism. The ideal conduct for man is quiescence and non-action.

Christianity, drawing inspiration from Jewish sources, had a Messianic conviction of progress, but away from earthly existence toward the Heavenly City and eternal life. The Kingdom of Heaven was not of this world. Some of the exalted teachings of the Sermon on the Mount were not viewed as a program of practical living for a society continuing indefinitely on earth, but were intended to prepare men quickly and intensively for the Kingdom of God which was near at hand and which only the purified could enter. "For here we have no lasting city, but we seek the city which is to come," is the message of the Epistle to the Hebrews. Those who died in the faith acknowledged "that they were strangers and exiles on the earth . . . seeking a homeland" (Heb. 11:13-14). In *The Shepherd of Hermas*, a second century Apostolic writing, the Shepherd, who was the angel of repentance, conveyed to Hermas the thought

that you, as the servant of God, are living in a strange country, for your city is far from this city. If then you know your city, in which you are going to dwell, why do you here prepare lands and costly establishments and buildings and vain dwellings?[11]

This was probably a common metaphor among the mystics of all faiths and also among the apocalyptically minded Jews inside and outside Palestine. Philo uses this same metaphor:

For in reality a wise man's soul ever finds heaven to be his father-land and earth a foreign country, and regards as his own the dwelling place of wisdom, and that of the body as outlandish, and looks on himself as the stranger and sojourner in it.[12]

Occasionally one comes upon a recorded contemplation of a Rabbi which also suggests that this world is like a vestibule to the world to come: "Prepare yourself in the vestibule that you may enter into the banqueting hall." [13] But the emphasis here is on preparation, and this preparation is to be achieved not through renunciation of this world but through moral effort and self-improvement on earth by obeying the laws of the Torah.

Among the early Christians there was no attempt to reform or to reconstruct society in any mundane sense. The Christian re-nounced the world at baptism. Thereafter he was in the world but not of it. He was a foreigner in it, and took no interest in government and public affairs. The social order, for so long as it lasted, was to be accepted with resignation. "Slaves, obey in everything those who are your earthly masters," advised Paul (Col. 3:22; see also I Pet. 2:18). "Slaves, be obedient to those who are your earthly masters, with fear and trembling, in single-ness of heart, as to Christ" (Eph. 6:5). The Kingdom of God was at hand, and all wrongs would then be righted. Until then— "Render therefore to Caesar the things that are Caesar's, and to God the things that are God's" (Matt. 22:21).

Christians remained people apart. The Jews, too, remained apart, in order to preserve their monotheistic faith and to guard themselves against the moral contamination of paganism. Chris-tians, however, remained apart not only because they wished to safeguard their faith and their way of life, but also because they wished to remain isolated from the world generally and from all worldly affairs, the better to prepare themselves for the Messianic Kingdom. The mood of Christian thought and its way of life in relation to organized society and government were dominated by otherworldly considerations. "Let grace come and this world pass away" is the prayer of the *Didache* (2 c.), recited probably at the *Agape*.[14] "Christians live in the world, but they are not of the world" is the central idea of the *Epistle to Diognetus* (3 c.). For three centuries and more, until the Church under Constantine and his successors integrated itself finally within the State, retreat from the world and renunciation of all worldly interests and pursuits were the primary requirements of the Christian discipline. When as a result of the new political accommodation this austere discipline began to fall into disuse and Christians became reconciled citizens of this world, the more devout among them, mindful of the original Christian summons to a life of poverty, penance, and prayer, resolved to seek retreat and seclusion even from the new Christian secular society in monasteries and nunneries. Hence the sharp rise of cenobitic monachism in the fourth and the following centuries.

The idea of progress is rejected today by some Existentialist theologians on the theory that in Christ history came to an end. "Time still goes forward, of course, but history only seemingly continues. Any genuine development has ceased. In the presence of God it has terminated." [15] The future will not bring anything that is essentially new, they insist.

In Islam, too, the motif of social progress is wanting. Gustave von Grunebaum wrote:

Islam is eminently human, in that it takes man for what he is, but it is not humanist in that it is not interested in the richest possible unfolding and evolving of man's potentialities, in that it never conceived of the forming of men as civilization's principal and most noble task. Man is to be directed and guided toward salvation rather than educated to develop himself in developing this world as the deed most deserving of everlasting reward.[16]

Judaism alone preached social progress as a reality, as desirable, and as the supreme challenge and opportunity. This is the very essence and meaning of Hebraic prophecy. Judaism did not approve of a spiritual egocentrism which sought fulfillment not in humanity and social enterprise but in a detached salvationism, non-action, or otherworldliness. It demanded inner change, of course, but it did not lightly dismiss the social imperatives. It did not accept a worship of God which does not involve the service of humanity. In matchless eloquence the prophets of Israel called upon men and women to think less of their rituals and their solemnities, the new moons and sabbaths, and more of the weak and the wronged in their midst, the orphan, the widow, and the oppressed. They urged them to believe that society *can* be improved, if men will but walk in the light of the Lord. Zion *can* be redeemed by justice and righteousness. The good society *can* be built here on earth, free from war, from exploitation, from fear (Is. 2:1-4; Mic. 4:1-4).

Judaism tolerated no moral neutralism. The fact of evil led other religions to reject the world. It led Judaism to efforts to remake the world. Man sins when he cultivates a habit of unconcern in the face of the remediable evils of life. Judaism never admonished men to be subservient to their master, to king or state until the coming of the Kingdom. Jerusalem was destroyed, a Rabbi asserted, only because the men of that generation did not rebuke one another. They shut their eyes to the evil which existed among them and moved like a herd, "the head of one at the side of the other's tail." [17]

Whoever can remonstrate against the sins of his household and does not, is seized [held responsible and punished] for the sins of his household; whoever can remonstrate against the sins of his fellow townsmen and does not, is seized for the sins of his fellow townsmen; and of the whole world, he is seized for the sins of the whole world. [18]

In only one book of the Bible—Ecclesiastes—is the reality of human progress questioned. "What has been is what will be, and what has been done is what will be done, and there is nothing new under the sun . . . that which is crooked cannot be made straight" (Ecc. 1:9, 15)—a view which Judaism rejected, as it rejected other ideas of the author of Kohelet. The repetitious cycle observed in the physical world, and its revolving seasons, moved Kohelet to conclude that a similar cycle of nonprogressive repetitiousness exists also in the moral and spiritual life of mankind, and that the transient character of a man's life in a world which endures forever is proof of the vanity of all human effort and aspiration. The Rabbis entertained serious doubts as to the inclusion of Ecclesiastes in the Canon. "The Sages wanted to store away the Book of Ecclesiastes [exclude it from the Canon] because they found in it ideas that inclined towards heresy." [19] The book of Kohelet does not defile the hands, maintained R. Meir (a sacred book of the Bible called for the washing of the hands after being handled). According to R. Simeon b. Menasia (2 c.), Kohelet contained only the *wisdom* of King Solomon, and was not composed under the inspiration of the Holy Spirit.[20]

It is a tribute not only to the range of mood of the Bible, but also and especially to the wide tolerance of the Rabbis that the book was finally included in the Canon. In no way, however, did the Rabbis associate themselves with all its views. They tolerated rather than approved Kohelet. They justified its inclusion thus: "Its beginning is religious teaching, and its end is religious teaching." [21]

Judaism's objectives in the quest of the good society are clearly defined: the end of war, universal peace, international cooperation under the reign of law, the eradication of poverty, the security of the individual against all forms of social oppression, the achievement of unity and freedom among men, the practice of compassion, of cleanness and of sobriety in living—all difficult but not impossible ideals.

◄(X)►

THAT MEN NEED TO BE SAVED

Judaism is not constructed around any drama of redemption. There is no term in the Hebrew language for "salvation" in a sacramental, redemptive sense. In Judaism the soul of man requires no "liberation," because the soul of man is not enchained. The idea that man needs to be "saved" either from the toils of life or from some Original Sin or from the prison house of matter or from baleful astrological influences is not part of Judaism. The Bible knows of no such concept as "redemption from sin." The term *ga-ol*, when used in Biblical sources refers to redemption from slavery, from an enemy, from imminent danger or death or exile. It also has legal implications. But in no instance does it refer to redemption from sin. This is true also of the terms *pa-doh* and *hoshe-a*, which mean help and deliverance from trouble, affliction or danger. "And He will redeem (Yifdeh) Israel from all his iniquities" (Ps. 130:8) simply means that if Israel is truly repentant he may count on God's forgiveness to save him from the punishments incurred "for with the Lord there is steadfast love" (cf. Ps. 25:22).

Saviour and Redeemer in the Christological sense are not to be found in the Bible.

Jewish theology accepts no doctrine affirming an inexorable round of rebirths in which the human soul is trapped and from which, in one way or another, it must be saved. Nor does it accept the doctrine of man's corrupt origin, "that all man descended from Adam contract original sin from him, and that this sin is transmitted by way of origin." [1] We have had occasion to note in other connections that such ideas, so widespread in the non-Jewish world, were not unknown to Judaism, and that references to them are to be found in its extensive literature. But they were never incorporated into the essential tenets of the faith.

The cornerstone of Hindu speculation as developed in the Upanishads and the Vedānta is the irremediable evil and misery of human existence, and the manner of man's deliverance (*moksha*) from the bondage and suffering of this world (*dukkha*) and from the chain of all future existences into a "final going out as a flame in water" (*parinibbāna*). It is a quest of salvation (deliverance) from existence itself. The way of salvation is through renunciation and "knowledge"—in the technical "gnostic" sense. To be saved is to forego all desire, all ambitions, even good ambitions, and to seek the dissolution of selfhood and individuality, as a drop of water loses itself in the ocean.

That the soul of man must pass through a succession of rebirths in atonement or in order to achieve deliverance was never a tenet of Judaism. Metempsychosis is not found in the Bible. Although very widely taught in Egypt and in the mystery religions of the Greco-Roman world, and accepted by Plato, no traces of it are found in the Talmud. This belief, under the influence of Moslem mysticism, found adherents among the Karaites, and later among the cabalists. It gained currency among the masses in the seventeenth and eighteenth centuries in Ḥasidic circles. Related ideas also made their way among the masses: the "impregnation" of souls (*'ibur*)—one soul returning to earth and uniting with the soul of a living man in order to perfect itself or to help the living man to perfection; *dibbuk*—a disembodied and restless soul taking refuge in the body of a living person and "possessing" him, to be dislodged only through mystic exorcism.

Metempsychosis is first mentioned in Jewish literature by Saadia (9 c.) who devotes quite a section of his Treatise on the Soul to its refutation and calls it "nonsense and stupidity." [2] There were some Jewish mystics who accepted this idea. But in

no instance did it become orthodox and supplant the basic doctrine that man is a free moral agent and that the law of retribution is not inexorable. "Repentance, Prayer and Charity avert
the evil decree." [3] "Repentance and good deeds are a shield
against punishment." [4]

In nearly all the mystery religions of mankind one finds myths
touching some perpetrated act of dread and monstrous propor-
tions, some primal misfortune which took place at the beginning
of creation and which had a disastrous effect upon all subsequent
human life. It ushered guilt, suffering, and death into the world.
Some gross crime of sacrilege or impiety or disobedience in
which the first of men was involved brought down a curse upon
all his descendants; all men must atone for it and must be
redeemed before they can find happiness here or hereafter.

In the Gilgamesh Epic the hero insultingly rejects the amorous
advances of the goddess Ishtar. The enraged goddess calls upon
her father Anu to avenge her. The Bull of Heaven is sent to
attack Gilgamesh. He and his friend Enkidu kill the bull, whereupon Ishtar curses Gilgamesh. Death is decreed for Enkidu, who
had tossed the right thigh of the Bull of Heaven in Ishtar's face.
Enkidu dies, and Gilgamesh, mourning his friend but wishing to
escape his fate, sets out to find Utnapishtim in order to learn the
secret of eternal life. At the end of his quest he is informed that
he must not entertain any hope of immortality.[5]

In Egyptian religion the god Osiris is murdered and dismembered by Set, his brother. His wife-sister, the goddess Isis, mourns
for him and gathers together his dismembered and scattered
limbs, whereupon he is restored to life, to become ruler of
the dead.

In the Eleusinian mysteries, it is Kore who is abducted and
ravaged by Pluto, and it is her mother Demeter who descends
from Olympus to find her and succeeds in bringing her back
from Hades.

In the Orphic mysteries it is Dionysus Zagreus, son of Zeus by
Persephone, who is plotted against and attacked by the Titans at
the instigation of Zeus' jealous wife Hera. The Titans slay him,

tear his body to pieces, and eat of his flesh. Zeus, in anger, hurls his thunderbolt and destroys the Titans. From their burned remnants springs the race of mortal men. Men therefore share in the impious act of the Titans, and from this guilt they must be redeemed by a prescribed secret ritual.

Similarly in the Phrygian mysteries centering in the Great Mother Goddess Cybele, Attis, her consort, is slain by a boar, or, according to another account, destroyed by self-mutilation, and is later resurrected.

In all these dramas of dying and resurrected deities, man is closely involved. The cultic rites were intended not alone to ensure fertility for the soil, but to purify the worshiper so as to bring him as an initiate into close communion with the deity in order that he might partake of the god and thus ensure himself safe passage and everlasting bliss in the realms of the afterlife.

In the Genesis story of the Bible (chapters 2-3), Adam and Eve disobey the command of the Lord not to eat of the tree of knowledge. They are punished for their disobedience. Eve is cursed with the pangs of childbearing, and the ground is cursed for Adam. Henceforth he will have to till the earth in hard toil, and with the sweat of his brow eat his bread. They are expelled from the Garden of Eden. Thus, man fell from his original state of innocence and happiness into a state of toil and suffering. It is not indicated in the Paradise story whether Adam and Eve were to have enjoyed immortality in Eden, and whether death became their lot as punishment for their transgression.

Adam's disobedience has come to be known as the Original Sin. That his guilt was transmitted to all his descendants became a pivotal doctrine in Christianity. Paul was responsible for placing this Genesis myth at the core of Christian doctrine. He explained the death of Jesus as the sacrificial atonement for the Original Sin of Adam which had led to the condemnation of all men (Rom. 5:12, 18-19). Those who believe in Jesus share in the atonement of his death, as previously they had shared in the guilt of Adam. They are forgiven and "saved" for eternal life (Rom. 6:3-4, 6).

Paul's gospel differed in this essential regard from the gospel of Jesus. Jesus nowhere speaks of an Original Sin. With Paul it is central in the soteriological drama which he envisaged.

Paul was keenly aware of the distinction between his gospel and that of John. He baptized not according to "John's baptism" which was "the baptism of repentance" (Acts 19:4) but "in the name of the Lord Jesus" (Acts 19:3–5). To Paul it was insufficient to know "only the baptism of John" (Acts 18:25–26). The resurrection of Jesus was the heart of his message: "If Christ has not been raised, then our preaching is in vain and your faith is in vain" (I. Cor. 15:14).

The early Church Fathers accepted and developed the idea of Original Sin, although not uniformly and not without some dissenting voices. In Augustine the doctrine of Original Sin and of man's total dependence upon God for salvation received its most complete and dogmatic enunciation. The soul was not initially imprisoned in the body but became so as a result of the sin of Adam; man cannot by his own free will escape the prison of that fatal sin.

The creeds of the Christian churches, from the First Council of Nicaea (325 C.E.) on, all incorporate the idea of salvation through Jesus. The official teaching of the Church of Rome on the subject was restated fully in the decrees of the Council of Trent (1545–1563):

The decrees of that Council affirm that the Fall caused loss of original righteousness, infection of body and soul, thralldom to the devil, and liability to the wrath of God; that such original sin is transmitted by generation, not by imitation; that all which has the proper nature of sin, and all guilt of original sin, is removed in baptism.[6]

The Protestant Reformation of the sixteenth century made no substantial change in this doctrine. Indeed, in Luther and Calvin it takes on an even more severe character, while in the modern school of Christian Existentialism, which reverts to them and to Paul, it assumes a startlingly didactic truculence. In defense of the theologic doctrine of Original Sin, modern apologists have seized upon the complexes and the hidden feelings of guilt in men which psychoanalysis has brought to light. Few people, indeed, are entirely free of some neurosis, and many suffer from serious psychotic ailments. Therapeutic techniques are being developed to help such people in their afflictions; but these illnesses are not *sins* in any sense and their treatment does not belong to the religious or theologic field, although religion's message of hope and trust is very often a great help in the cure of the sufferer. Such attempts to reinstate the concept of Original Sin—to give it a scientific stamp by identifying it with the terminology of psychoanalysis, with father-son mother-daughter rivalries, suppressions and death-wishes—are wide of the mark. Feelings of guilt unfortunately persist even among people who have accepted the Christian dogma of mankind's redemption from Original Sin. They are not dissipated by a theologic formula.

Dean Inge's statement that "the biblical doctrine of the Fall of Man, which the Hebrews would never have evolved for themselves, remained an otiose dogma in Jewish religion" [7] is quite correct, subject only to one amendment—that it was never a dogma at all. The idea of an Original Sin derivative from Adam, in which mankind shared, makes its first appearance in Jewish literature very late, in the apocalyptic *II Esdras* (1 c. C.E.) which shows definite Gnostic and Christian influences: "O thou Adam, what hast thou done! For though it was thou that sinned, the fall was not thine alone, but ours also who are thy descendants!" [8] However, in II Baruch, an apocalyptic contemporary of *II Esdras*, we find a flat contradiction to this theory:

For though Adam sinned and brought untimely death upon all, yet those who were born from him, each one of them has prepared for his own soul torment to come, and again each one of them has chosen for himself glories to come. Adam is therefore not the cause save only of his own soul, but each of us has been the Adam of his own soul. [9]

Paul certainly did not derive his doctrine of Original Sin, of humanity's involvement in it, and the manner of its atonement, from any authoritative Pharisaic source:

In asserting a direct causal relation, which he does not describe, between the Fall of Adam and the sin of all men in Romans 5.19 he [Paul] goes beyond the teaching of the Rabbis who were careful to insist on the full responsibility of every individual for his sin despite the effects of Adam's fall.[10]

The creation story in chapters two and three of Genesis is, as we have indicated earlier, a borrowed creation myth which was rewritten and reinterpreted by the Biblical author and which is not entirely screened and expurgated of its pre-Judaic elements. It represents an effort to explain etiologically the phenomena of death, pain, and struggle in human existence. But the creation account which is given in the first chapters of Genesis (1-2:3) represents the final Biblical recension and is entirely purged of all mythological elements. It knows nothing of any Garden of Eden, of any tree of life and tree of knowledge, of the creation of Eve out of the rib of Adam, of any beguiling serpent, of any disobedience on the part of Adam and Eve, of any divine curse or of any expulsion from Eden. It is in sharp contradiction to chapters two and three, both as to the manner by which the ancestors of the human race were created as well as to the tasks which were assigned to them by their Creator.

In the final version, man and woman were created as a pair, simultaneously. God did not intend them to remain in a state of ignorance concerning good or evil, or in a state of "innocence." They did not have to acquire the faculty of moral knowledge by wrenching it forcibly from an unwilling and jealous deity. It was a gift bestowed upon them from the very beginning by their Creator. This thought is quite pointedly repeated again in Genesis 5:1-2, which is the logical continuation after Chapter 2:3: "When God created man He made him in the likeness of God. Male and female He created them and He blessed them." This is the very antithesis of Genesis 3:22, where the Lord expresses anger at the thought that "man has become like one of us, knowing good and evil." God is pleased to make man in His image!

Nor is sexual knowledge regarded as sinful, acquired by man in disobedience of God's expressed command. On the contrary, all living things were created to be fruitful, all plants to yield seed and every tree with seed in its fruit (Gen. 1:29). Immediately upon their creation, God blessed Adam and Eve and said to them, "Be fruitful and multiply" (Gen. 1:28). No immortality was bestowed upon them which they later forfeited. The privilege of reproduction for the race of men excludes immortality; otherwise, the earth would not be able either to contain or to support them. The purpose of man's creation was not to provide God with a keeper to tend His Garden in Eden, but to rule the earth!

This account knows nothing of the story of Cain and Abel. It carries man's genealogy from Adam through Seth and Enoch, as does the author of I Chronicles (I Chr. 1:1). As was the case with other duplicate or triplicate narratives found in Genesis, the two creation narratives, the two different *Toledot* (Gen. 2:4; Gen. 5:1), were retained quite unreconciled (an attempted link between the two seems to be Gen. 4:25–26), giving rise to considerable controversy among generations of theologians and schoolmen. There is no mention of the Eden story of Genesis 2–3 anywhere in the Hebrew Bible and no further reference to Adam and Eve or Cain and Abel, though a description of the garden of God as a place of stately trees and precious stones guarded by a cherub is found in Ezekiel (Ezek. 28:13; 31:8–9) and in poetic similes elsewhere. The drama of the Garden of Eden and its actors do not make their reappearance in Jewish literature until the late apocalypses of the first century B.C. In the Haggadah of the Rabbis the scenes and characters of the Genesis paradise saga appear not infrequently. They provided the preachers of the day with rich homiletical material. They also provided the critics of the Bible and the enemies of Judaism, who insisted on reading the story quite literally, with abundant polemical material for their attacks, to which the teachers of Judaism had to reply—sometimes with arguments as fanciful as those of their opponents.

However, no doctrinal consequences were ever drawn from the Garden of Eden legend for Judaism as was the case for Christianity. Original Sin is mentioned neither in the Mishnah nor in any Rabbinic code. Primal myths have nothing to do with the history of the Jewish people which begins with Abraham, or with the religion which Abraham founded and which Moses and the prophets developed after him. The Genesis myths were in no way decisive for the theology of Judaism.

Nowhere is the Jew summoned to atone for an inherited burden of guilt. No sacrifices were ever offered in the Temple to expiate such a sin; no rite of propitiation or penance was ever prescribed for it. Nor is the hope expressed that God would in some manner intervene in the life of a doomed humanity to lift the curse of this guilt from off the shoulders of the descendants of Adam and to cleanse men of their original taint and corruption. The human race did not lose its moral freedom and initiative because of Adam's sin.

Judaism is much concerned with the moral issues involved in man's sins, but not with Original Sin, which is a nonmoral concept of mythological origin. Explanations are offered here and there in post-Biblical literature to account for the origin of sin as well as of evil in the world—problems which trouble a monotheistic faith much more than a dualistic or polytheistic one. Judaism accepted neither a Parsee nor a Gnostic dualism to account for the existence of evil, nor a Neoplatonic denial of any reality to evil. The reality of evil is acknowledged, and explanations are ventured by one or another teacher as to why God created it. No one is obligated by his orthodoxy to accept any one of these theories. In popular folklore the principle of evil was at times personified in Satan or the Devil, but Satan plays no rôle in the theology or creed of normative Judaism such as he assumes in orthodox Christian dogma. He is no divine or demonic power with whom God is in eternal combat. He is not the author of evil and has not the power of death (Heb. 2:14). In the prologue to the Book of Job, Satan appears among the Sons of God as the adversary of man but not as God's antagonist, and he does not possess the power of independent action. He figures more frequently in the Apocrypha, the Apocalypses and in Rabbinic literature, but belief in his existence is never an article of faith.

Judaism's primary concern was to teach man not how sin came into the world, but how to avoid sin and how to repent of sin once having succumbed to it. All men are capable of sinning because all men are endowed with free will.

Judaism did not caricature life into something banal and absurd, fallen and tragic, to make room for some miraculous redemption. It placed no such burdens and handicaps and introduced no such apprehensions and despair into man's moral life. If man has committed a sin, he may repent and be forgiven. The initiative, however, must come from man, not from God. God's love will meet man more than halfway, or, to use the superb imagery of Judah Halevi, "When I go forth to seek Thee, I find Thee seeking me." The Psalmist too finds that "God is near unto all who call upon Him, who call upon Him in truth" (Ps. 145:18). But the call must come from man. "Return to me, and I will return to you, says the Lord of Hosts" (Mal. 3:7; Zech. 1:3). The slightest effort on the part of man is met by God's ready and gracious cooperation. "God says to Israel, open the door of repentance even if only the width of the eye of a needle, and I will open it for you wide enough for carriages and wagons to pass through." [11] Redemption begins with self-redemption, but man's anxiety for a sin committed may properly end there. "Wash yourselves, make yourselves clean . . . though your sins are like scarlet, they shall be white as snow" (Is. 1:16–18).

Dr. Niebuhr may be correct in stating that the central message of the Gospel deals with sin, grace, forgiveness, and justification.[12] The central message of Judaism, however, deals with "doing justly, loving mercy and walking humbly with your God" (Micah 6:8). "And now, Israel, what does the Lord require of you, but to revere the Lord your God, to walk in His ways, to love Him, to serve the Lord your God with all your heart and with all your soul, and to keep the commandments and statutes

of the Lord which I command you this day for your good"
(Dt. 10:12–13).

Judaism applied itself to the task of helping men to face and
overcome their specific and individual sins, as well as the specific
social evils which result from their collective misdeeds. On the
Day of Atonement men are summoned to confess and to enu-
merate these sins, one by one, before God and to seek forgiveness for "having turned away from Thy good commandments and
ordinances to our hurt." Man is never confronted with the fact of
a total and irrevocable depravity demanding total regeneration—
rebirth into a new man. Men do fall into sin, but Man, the race,
has not fallen. Judaism thinks of Man as rising from imperfection
to higher levels. Occasionally a poetic hyperbole in the Bible, as
in Psalm 51, seems to suggest some inborn sin. "Behold I was
brought forth in iniquity and in sin did my mother conceive me"
(Ps. 51:7). But, as Dr. Cohen has correctly pointed out, the
thought of this verse is not that the marital act is sinful or that
the child inherits sin. Rather the Psalmist confesses here that he
has not resisted the sins to which all men are liable by virtue of
their humanity, and prays for forgiveness.[18]

The Decalogue's concept of punishment for the sins of parents
and forebears, retroactive to the third and fourth generations
(Ex. 20:5), has, of course, nothing to do with Original Sin; but
even so it is vigorously opposed by the prophets Jeremiah and
Ezekiel. They hold otherwise even though the same commandment declares that God's mercy extends unto the thousandth
generation of those that love and keep His commandments. "In
those days they shall no longer say: 'The fathers have eaten sour
grapes, and the children's teeth are set on edge.' But everyone
shall die for his own sin," Jeremiah prophesied (Jer. 31:29–30).
And Ezekiel declared: "The soul that sins shall die. The son shall
not suffer for the iniquity of the father, nor the father for the
iniquity of the son" (Ezek. 18:20). The Rabbis limited the application of the principle of inherited guilt in the Second Commandment to such instances where there is no repentance, where

—to quote the Targum—"the children carry on the evil deeds of their fathers." Where, however, repentance takes place, all sins are forgiven. "Inherited sin" is, therefore, neither impenitent nor inescapable.

Even the concept of inherited merit—"the Merit of the Fathers"—was brushed aside by some of the Rabbis even as Ezekiel had done (Ezek. 14:12-20). "Let not a man say, my father was a pious man; I shall be saved for his sake. Abraham could not save Ishmael, nor Jacob save Esau." [14] Whatever reservoirs of merit had been laid up by the Patriarchs had already been exhausted, according to the views of other Rabbis, in the days of Hosea, Hazael, Elijah, or Hezekiah.

Of course, neither Jeremiah nor Ezekiel, nor the Rabbis of subsequent centuries questioned for a moment the shared responsibility of men for the wickedness of their society or of their people. There is a collective responsibility for national apostasy and wrongdoing over and above individual responsibility for one's own conduct. There is an interlocking destiny in the shared life of a community whose moral consequences no individual member can escape, least of all members of a covenanted community who are pledged singly and collectively to abide in eternal loyalty to their God and to His commandments. But this is not Original Sin.

This attitude toward sin is bound up with the prominent place which *Teshubah*—repentance—holds in Jewish religious thought. The prophet Ezekiel, who gave the most vigorous expression to the doctrine of individual moral responsibility, is foremost among Biblical teachers in stressing the concept of repentance:

Say to them, as I live, says the Lord God, I have no pleasure in the death of the wicked but that the wicked turn from his way and live; turn back from your evil ways; for why will you die, O house of Israel [Ezek. 33:11]. Again though I say to the wicked, "You shall surely die," yet if he turns from his sin and does what is lawful and right, if the wicked restores the pledge, gives back what he had taken by robbery, and walks in the statutes of life, committing no iniquity, he shall surely live, he shall not die. None of the sins that he has committed shall be remembered against him; he has done what is lawful and right, he shall surely live" [Ezek. 33:14-16].

Repentance was one of the seven things which, according to the Rabbis, preceded the creation of the world.[16] The first-born man became a murderer—the assassin of his own brother! His dread punishment—to be a fugitive and a wanderer on the face of the earth. But when Cain cried out in anguish of soul, in contrition and in fear: "My sin is greater than I can bear! . . . I shall be hidden from the face of God and whoever finds me will slay me!"—God sheltered Cain, the repentant fratricide. He put a mark on him, lest any man who came upon him should kill him.

On the verse "Thou turnest man to the dust" (Ps. 90:3), R. Meir commented: "Up to the time that a man is crushed to the dust [his time of death] is the repentant sinner received." [17] On hearing these words, the dying heretic Elisha b. Abuyah, burst into tears. Whereupon R. Meir, his former pupil and his faithful friend, rejoiced and said, "It appears that my master passed away in the midst of repentance." [18]

In Greek philosophy repentance is not held up as a virtue.[19] In Judaism it is among the highest of virtues. No other religious literature is so eloquent on the subject of repentance—its nobility, its efficacy: "In the place where the repentant sinner stands, even the righteous who have never sinned cannot stand." [20] It was not something mysterious. It did not imply any mystic transformation in the individual, as if through some sacramental act he were "born anew," putting off his old nature and putting on a new nature (Eph. 4:22-24). This conception is traceable to the rites of initiation in the mystery religions where the novice underwent a mock death and was then reborn to a new life, and to the Christian doctrine that Jesus died as a sacrifice for the remission of the sins of men and that all who accepted him died with him and were reborn to a new life. Thereafter, if they sinned again, "there no longer remains a sacrifice for sins but a fearful prospect of judgment" (Heb. 10:26)—"As one baptism, so one penance." [21] The act of penance may not be repeated. "The gate of forgiveness has been shut and fastened up with the bar of baptism." [22] However, since the Devil is "never deficient in stumbling-blocks or in temptation," a second repentance is allowed "but now once for all, because now for a second time, but never more because the last time it had been in vain." [23] The rigor of this position was later mitigated by the Church. In Jewish teaching the gates of repentance are never shut.[24]

Public penance for sinners and open acknowledgment in assembly of grave sins committed by the individual—a nigh universal requirement in the early Church—were unknown in Judaism until the late Middle Ages. The sinner did not have to beat his breast in public or confess to anyone but God. Judaism has no confessors and no confessionals. No procedure was prescribed for a man's repentance such as bowing before the feet of the presbyter or kneeling in self-condemnation before the congregation of the faithful. No acts of self-abasement were imposed by Rabbinic authority, nor ascetic acts of penance.

The way of repentance is fully defined in Judaism. There must be acts of restitution and reparation wherever possible. There must be sincere confession, not to man but to oneself and to God. There must be the firm resolve not to sin again. One of the Sages declared:

If a man is guilty of sin and confesses it and does not change his way, what is he like? He is like a man who holds a defiling object in his hand even while he is immersing himself in purifying waters. All the waters in the world will not avail him. He remains unclean because he clings to his defilement.[25]

The authoritative teaching of Judaism was and remains: "My God, the soul which Thou hast placed within me is pure. Thou hast fashioned it in me. Thou didst breathe it into me." [26] A Haggadah of R. Simlai (3 c.) puts it this way:

Before a man is released for birth he is admonished, "Always bear in mind that the Holy One, blessed be He, is pure, that His ministers are pure and that the soul which He gave you is pure; if you preserve it in purity, well and good, but if not, I will take it away from you." [27]

It is for *man* to keep his soul pure. The body of itself does not defile it. Man's *misuse* of his body defiles it. The Scriptural blessing, "Blessed shall you be when you come in, and blessed shall you be when you go out" (Dt. 28:6), was interpreted by R. Johanan to mean: "May your exit from the world be as your entry into it; just as you entered it without sin, so may you leave it without sin." [28]

Judaism affirms that while there is evil in the life of man and of society, it can be overcome by moral effort and exertion to a degree where man's life on earth may yield him a large measure of happiness and satisfaction. Man is born with a capacity for both good and evil, for he is born a free agent. Man may sin or refrain from sin. He is born not perfect but perfectible, and his destiny is to perfect himself within the framework of his humanity. His task is not to eradicate his evil inclinations by mortifications, but to control them by following the prescriptions of the Law. He is capable of fulfilling his destiny or of rejecting it. He may make the effort or he may refuse to make it. There are forces within him which urge him to rise through moral effort to higher levels, and there are also forces which tempt him to sink to lower levels of greed and lust and indolence.

The commandments were given to man to help him and he is capable of fulfilling them. In his efforts to do so he need have no uneasy conscience about some primordial sin whose taint is forever within him. He need not mourn for some lost paradise or break his heart in reaching for the unattainable. He should not try to get out of his skin. By sincere efforts toward self-improvement, man will be fully justified. "And it will be righteousness for us if we are careful to do all this commandment before the Lord our God, as He commanded us" (Dt. 6:25).

Because there is no Original Sin, there is no need for a Redeemer. The doctrine of atonement through the suffering of another is nowhere found in the Hebrew Bible. "There is not to be found a single instance in the entire Hebrew Bible where the suffering of a prophet atoned for the sins of a group. Nothing could have been further from the spirit of the prophets' teachings." [29] The "servant of the Lord" in Second Isaiah was the covenanted people of Israel who in the fulfillment of its divine mission would endure much suffering for the healing of the nations. This is superb poetry, not dogma, and has no bearing upon the sins of the individual and the means of their atonement. No man can absolve another of his sins.

Man does not need saviours. Nor does man need mediators between himself and God. "No one comes to the Father, but by me" (John 14:6) is a concept alien to Judaism. Man needs help in his moral struggles—encouragement, hope, confidence. Such help comes from turning to God, and it is at all times available. Through repentance and amendment man's moral effort becomes the channel for the in-flow of the grace of God.

"Blessed are ye Israel," declares A. Akiba, "before whom do you purify yourself from your sins and who purifies you? Your Father Who is in Heaven." [30] "If trouble befalls a man let him not pray to Michael or Gabriel, let him pray to Me, and I will answer him at once." [31]

Man, according to Judaism, needs teachers and guides. He needs to activate his own will. A man rises and is brought nearer to God by sincere actions and good works. It is "deeds which make atonement for man." [32] His deeds also, not mere faith, are the final measure of a man's spiritual merit—deeds which spring from the depths of a willing heart and a full, free inclination. It is not so much what a man's belief is, but how that belief expresses itself in conduct. "Thou dost requite a man according to his works" (Ps. 62:12) is an oft repeated teaching of the Bible. "One cannot obtain rewards except for deeds." [33] Reward is given for setting out to perform the deed as well as for actually accomplishing it. Even the sincere commitment to *undertake* a good deed is not without its reward. But the accent is always on action.[34] Faith is important—"Great indeed is faith before Him who spoke and the world came into being" [35]—but it is not a substitute for action, nor is it in invidious contrast to it.

The prolonged theologic debate—faith versus works—which agitated the Christian world for centuries and which has not subsided even in our day finds little room in Jewish thought. A similar controversy raged in Moslem theologic circles. The puritanic Kharijites rejected the doctrine of faith without works. The Murji'-ites, on the other hand, maintained that all that mattered was faith in the unity of God and the apostleship of Mohammed. "To them faith was an entity in itself: grievous sin could not impair it nor could good works increase it." [36]

Faith (*Emunah*) in Judaism has little of ideological or confessional content. It is not creed or belief in the accepted usage of these terms. It is rather steadfastness to a course prescribed, firm and zealous adherence to a code of moral practice revealed to man, and confidence in the right outcome of all things willed by God and of all action acceptable to Him. *Emunah* derives from the same root as *aman*, master workman—it is inseparable from action. "I have chosen the *way* of *Emunah*, I have set Thy ordinances before me. I cleave to Thy testimonies, O Lord. . . . I will run in the way of Thy commandments" (Ps. 119:30–32). The term is applied in the Bible to God as well as to man. He is a God of *Emunah* (Dt. 32:4), steadfast and sure to execute justice and loving-kindness. "All His work is done in *Emunah*" (Ps. 33:4). *Emunah* is a way, the technique for fulfilling the laws of God (Ps. 119:30). To be forever wholehearted in the service of God and never to doubt His full power and promise—that is faith. If the promise seems slow, "wait for it; it will surely come, it will not delay." This is the faith by which the righteous man shall live (Hab. 2:3–4), and such was the faith of Abraham, which was accounted to him as righteousness (Gen. 15:1–6).

Among the Rabbinic compilers of the precepts of the Bible, there were those, like the author of the code *Halachot Gedolot* (8 c.)—the first to attempt such a compilation—as well as Saadia, Nachmanides, and others, who did not include a belief in God among the 613 commandments. Logically, of course, such a belief is at the very root of Judaism, but no one was commanded to believe, and no one was punished by an earthly tribunal for not believing.

A man is not "justified" by his faith. The term "justified" when used in a theologic sense as acquittal from inherent sin has no equivalent in Hebrew. The key Protestant doctrine of Justification by Faith alone, and not through good works, finds no place in Judaism, nor does the Catholic doctrine that man is justified by faith and works, where faith is restricted technically to the redemption which Jesus by his sacrifice wrought for mankind. Equally alien to Judaism is the doctrine so sharply enunciated, though not originated, by the leaders of the Reformation— that faith itself is not self-willed, that it comes only through the grace of God, and that even those who believe and do good are not necessarily saved unless God wills it so. Utterly incomprehensible to Jewish thought are these ideas which were included among the ninety-five theses that Luther nailed on the church door at Wittenberg: "The just man sins in every good work"; and "our best good work is a venial sin."

Judaism did not impale man on the horns of the dilemma—the "unaffected" grace of God and the "ineffective" works of man. Indeed, the only form of atheism known to the Bible is not the denial of the existence of God but the assertion that God is unconcerned with the actions of men and does not requite them accordingly (Ps. 14 and 53). In Judaism a man is made upright both by his faith in God and by his good works, the former being demonstrated by the latter. His spiritual life is not consummated by faith in God—it begins there, and it is ethical conduct which brings him near to God.

Not even a belief in Judaism is a requirement for such "salvation." It is open to all men, even to those who do not accept Judaism. Gentiles who avoid the grave moral offenses of murder, incest, adultery, robbery, the eating of the flesh of living animals, idolatry, and blasphemy—the so-called seven laws of Noah—are in the same category as the most pious among the Jews who observe the 613 commandments. Maimonides wrote in his Code:

Not only is the tribe of Levi [God's portion] sanctified in the highest degree, but any man among all the dwellers on earth whose heart prompts him and whose mind instructs him to dedicate himself to the services of God and to walk uprightly as God intended him to, and who disencumbers himself of the load of the many pursuits which men invent for themselves.[87]

Those Jews who accepted the Messiahship of Jesus, but in all other regards remained loyal to Judaism in doctrine and in practice, waged a bitter war against other members of their fellowship who substituted faith for works and who offered "salvation" to men solely through faith in Jesus. James, the brother of Jesus, evidently took sharp issue with the Pauline position. "What does it profit, my brethren, if a man says he has faith but has not works? . . . Faith by itself, if it has no works, is dead" (James 2.14f.). As if answering the great apostrophe to faith in Hebrews 11, "By faith Abraham, when he was tested, offered up Isaac," which reflects Paul's insistence on Abraham's justification through faith alone (Rom. 4:1–5), James declared: "Was not Abraham our father justified by works, when he offered his son Isaac upon the altar?" (James 2:21). It is James, too, who reaffirms the vital Jewish doctrine that the moral initiative must come from man: "Draw near to God and He will draw near to you" (James 4:8). No wonder Luther, for whom faith was everything and grace exclusively the free gift of God, called the Epistle of James "an epistle of straw!" Christian social reformers, on the other hand, in all ages—like William Langland in fourteenth century England, in whom the prophetic zeal was greater than the theologic—found sanction and inspiration in the teachings of James. "James the gentle said in his writings, 'Faith without fact is nothing worth, as dead as a door-tree unless deeds follow. Faith without works is dead.' "[88]

Pagan philosophers debated extensively the question not of faith versus works, but of thought versus action. They were inclined to give priority to philosophic contemplation. According to Aristotle, the object of life, the supreme End is happiness (*eudaimonia*), and happiness is an activity of the soul in accordance with reason. The perfection of the intellect is man's supreme task and purpose in life. Metaphysical speculation is the noblest occupation, just as mystic contemplation was held to be the noblest endeavor in the eyes of the Brahman. As we have seen, both viewpoints lead to detachment from the world and indifference to the needs of society. Even the philosophy of the Epicurean, which made pleasure the supreme good to be sought in the satisfaction of the senses as well as in the interests of the mind, led men away from active participation in citizenship and social obligations.

Not so Judaism. In Judaism thought could never be an end in itself. Learning and teaching were from the earliest times highly prized and revered among the Jews, and this explains, in part, their very active intellectual and cultural interests throughout the ages, their reverence for erudition and the achievements of the mind, and their passion for education. They were perhaps the first people in the world to establish a universal system of education. By the first century before the common era there was hardly a town or village in Palestine which did not possess its public school where children, rich and poor alike, were taught the Torah. "The study of Torah was supreme among all the meritorious acts, the fruits of which man enjoys in this world, while the stock remains for him in the world to come." [39] R. Meir declared: "Even a non-Jew who is engaged in the study of the Torah is like unto the High Priest." [40]

But however exalted the study of the Torah was regarded, it was not enough. Ḥanina in the name of R. Huna declared: "He who occupies himself with the study of the Torah only is as if he had no God." [41] R. Ḥiyya said: "If a man studies the Torah without the intention of fulfilling it, it were better he had never been born." [42] Simeon, the Son of Rabban Gamaliel, declared: "Not the expounding of the Torah is the chief thing, but the doing of it." [43]

It is not study which is paramount, but right conduct. Whether a man is righteous or wicked is far more important than whether or not he is a scholar. Even the foremost exponent among Jewish philosophers of the supremacy of intellectual perfection regards such perfection only as a means: "Having acquired this knowledge he will then be determined always to seek loving-kindness, judgment and righteousness and thus imitate the ways of God." [44] Men are to be rewarded not for being good thinkers, or good mystics, or good students of the Torah, but for doing good in the world.

Even God subordinates Himself to the fulfillment of His commandments. There is a remarkable statement by one of the Rabbis which sums up this characteristic attitude of Judaism. God said: "Would that they would forsake Me but keep My Torah!" [45]

Sometimes the people of Israel, facing grave danger, would pray for deliverance in utter dependence on God: "We do not lay our supplications before Thee because of our righteous acts, but because of Thine abundant mercies." [46] This is a poetic way of humbly expressing complete trust in God's goodness and compassion. It cannot be taken literally as a formula for obtaining God's help. The nearness of God is an achievement, not a grant.

The classic position of Judaism is defined by Akiba: "The world is judged by grace, yet everything is according to the amount of good works." [47] Faith is within man's originative spiritual competence, and is available to all men. Man can by his manner of life and conduct prepare himself to receive the grace and favor of God. True piety, Zwingli held, is born only when man sees that he has absolutely no means of pleasing God. According to Jewish doctrine, however, man definitely has means of pleasing God—by obeying His commandments! "The Lord will again take delight in prospering you, as He took delight in your fathers, if you obey the voice of the Lord your God, His commandments and His statutes which are written in this book of the Law" (Dt. 30:9–10).

In recent decades the doctrine that man is helpless to save himself, as reformulated by Existentialism, has won many adherents in Christian circles, and more recently, even among some Jewish theologians of the school of Martin Buber and Franz Rosenzweig, who would not themselves consent to be classified as Existentialists but whose basic assumptions, in strange Judaic livery, clearly belong to it. Among disciples in the English-speaking world, these ideas of Existentialism appear even more exotic, lacking, as they do, the transcendental German philosophic idiom which accommodates itself so neatly to its elusive and inconsecutive disquisitions. Existentialism is a philosophy grounded in deep pessimism and disillusionment. Its mood is crisis; its idiom, death. Man cannot escape the predicaments in which his existence is involved; his mind is snared by irresolvable paradoxes. His efforts at social and ethical improvement will not bring the Kingdom of God any nearer. It is even suggested that the very thought of man cooperating in its establishment is presumptuous and is but another evidence of his besetting sin of pride. Man needs a redeemer. For the Christians it is the redemptive Christ; for the Jew, it is the grace of God or the grace of the Torah. This pessimism has been deepened by the disillusionment with the scientific, social, and political movements of our day, which promised so much but which yielded such a large measure of anguish and human suffering. This mood underlies also the secular branch of this philosophy of the school of Jean-Paul Sartre, which frequently verges on intellectual and moral nihilism.

Such an exaggerated pessimism is diametrically opposed to Judaism's conception of man's nature, endowments, and achievements. Judaism does not build God's absoluteness on man's nothingness. Man can, to a large degree, make his own world; and man has, to a large degree, made it. In spite of frequent and tragic setbacks, it has been a progressing world. Man has moved forward to more knowledge, to higher standards of living, to greater social justice, to better health conditions, to more intensive efforts toward the eradication of poverty. In its wide perspective of human history, Judaism is able to see definite progress; and though the pace is slow, and the direction occasionally reversed, it sees man rising by the power of will and effort from the jungles of barbarism, slavery, poverty, and disease, to higher degrees of enlightenment, mastery over environment, justice and freedom. There is an ascending curve in the long evolutionary record of mankind.

Judaism maintains that man is finite and yet not helpless. Man cannot think as God but he can think about God. He does not know the ultimate answers, but in faith he can work with relative truth and find satisfaction and happiness in his work, provided it is well intentioned and directed toward God and the good of his fellow men.

Man cannot wait and should not wait to do the things which need to be done until he sees the road clearly ahead. Sometimes he must move forward through mist and fog. He must act with the material and the opportunities which are at hand, trusting that what he is sincerely striving to do will prove to be within the pattern of the abiding design of human progress and God's purpose.

"Yours is not the duty to complete the task, neither are you free to desist from it." [48] "Share your burden with God and He will sustain you. He will never suffer the righteous to be moved" (Ps. 55:23).

Pessimism is a form of atheism, for it omits God from man's calculations, and ignores the spirit of God that is in man. Man should continue to strive and aspire and build—again and yet again—upon the ruins of his many broken hopes and dreams. This is the wisdom of a people that has known many sorrows and disillusionments, and many stark tragedies, and has become too schooled for impatience and too old for despair. Men cannot see beyond the horizon of their own times. What lies ahead no one knows. But Judaism constantly reminds man that beyond all horizons there is God.

The stars and planets were there, and all the moving constellations, before man ever recognized them. In the dark imprisoned mind of the human cave dweller, there already lay impounded, as it were, all the marvelous achievements of man that were to come, all that he could not see or grasp or understand—all that he would have refused to believe—the inventions and discoveries, the power and mastery, the worlds of music and poetry, philosophy and science. In the brain of the primitive cave dweller there were already contained, as in a seed, all the blossoming and flowering civilizations that were to be, but he could not see the shape of things to come. He could not penetrate the curtains which enshrouded his visible and empirical world. He would have been justified in a total pessimism about the future of mankind—far more than men of later generations. For these already had a long recorded past to contemplate, a past which, in spite of all its turns and windings, did lead mankind forward to amazing progress and prospects.

Judaism admonished men not to despair of the future, nor of their own strength, nor of mankind's inexhaustible spiritual resources nor of God's cooperation. Long and hard is the way, but there is a way, and there is a goal.

The moral life and human aspirations are the "sacraments" of Judaism. It recognizes no others. There are no beliefs which "save" men. There are no ceremonial or ritual acts the very performance of which bestows supernatural grace and saving power. There are visible symbols in Judaism, signs of the covenant, memorials of fidelity, but no sacraments. From earnest and faithful quest of the good life, in all ways, great or small, flow all divine grace and power.

∽⟨ XI ⟩∾

THAT MEN SHOULD NOT
ENJOY LIFE

It seems strange that the question whether a man should enjoy his life should at all be raised. Yet, this is the very question which many religious and ethical philosophies do raise; and, oddly enough, the prevailing answer is in the negative—negative in two ways: that man does not, and that man should not, enjoy life.

Man has always been afraid of life, and there is much in life to make him afraid—much that is mysterious and evil, much of pain and sorrow; and overshadowing all towers the dread and ineluctable fact of death! Man was never quite equal to the tribulations of his existence and never able to master the forces which determined its course. He could not understand himself or his world, his origin or his destiny. The vast impersonal occurrences in nature—floods, storms, droughts, earthquakes, plagues—frequently crushed and overwhelmed him; and the destructive social forces which he could not control—wars and invasions, tyranny and oppression—undermined his confidence in himself and filled his life with anxiety. Apprehension was not limited to primitive societies or cultures. Enlightened, even sophisticated, civilizations experienced it. It is certainly not alien to our modern atomic age, which is so often called The Age of Anxiety.

We have already noted that many of the great systems of human thought and belief stressed the sadness and the futility of

life. Some religions regarded the very fact of life itself as evil
and the cause of all human suffering. Man was therefore advised
to renounce the love of life and seek the extinction of his selfhood. Preparatory steps to such self-disintegration are reclusion
and asceticism.

The ascetic motif finds its highest and most elaborate expression in Hinduism. It is perhaps the main source of most of the
systems of asceticism both of the Orient and of the Occident.
Hinduism defined an elaborate system of tapas, self-mortifica-
tions, to serve as the means of deliverance and escape from sam-
sāra—the wheel of life. It enjoined physical mortification upon
all men as a religious duty. This is an obligation incumbent not
only upon the Brahmans, but upon the Kshatriyas and the
Vaisyas as well. Even the despised Sudras came in time to be
included in the privileged discipline of tapas.

A man should pass the first stage of his life as the student and
disciple of some Brahman teacher, and the second as a house-
holder performing the duties of founding a family. Thereafter he
should abandon home, family, and possessions, and repair to some
forest to lead the solitary life of a hermit and practice austerities
of such rigorous and increasing intensity that by the time he
reaches the fourth and last stage he will have abandoned everything. He will go quite alone, without any companion, without
fire, without an abode. He will live among roots of trees, possessing only a dish, a stick, and a water jug and begging his food;
utterly indifferent, utterly detached, desiring neither life nor
death, letting the machinery of life run down. He then becomes
a sannyasi—one who has abandoned everything. This is the highest goal and supreme achievement of human life.[1]

The reform movement of Buddhism in no way moderated the
severe asceticism of the Hindu religion. Its pessimism is even more
thoroughgoing, and its renunciation of the world even more
complete. It is, in fact, a movement of monastic asceticism. The
four noble truths of the Buddha are: that all existence is suffering, that the cause of all suffering is craving, that the way to end
suffering is to end all craving, and that the way to end craving

is to follow the eightfold path of moral cultivation. To free oneself from the world of the senses, to tear desire out by the roots, to deaden the will to live, and to seek self-extinction in nirvana—this is the formula of blessed release for mankind.

Other systems of religion and philosophy did not find the root of all evil and unhappiness in the fact of life itself, but in the duality which exists in life and in the conflict between body and soul. According to them matter is irremediably evil. The human soul is imprisoned in the body, chained by its instincts, passions, and desires. It must seek escape from its physical thralldom. Holding the body in contempt, subduing the flesh, repudiating all its urgings and promptings, practicing austerities, fasts, and self-castigation, removing oneself from society itself—this is the way to the emancipation of the soul. The saint is the man who has achieved it.

Already in Babylonian mythology one finds a cosmic dualism, a struggle between the realms of light and darkness, but these are not yet distinguished as contending ethical principles. In Zoroastrian dualism the ethical contrast is emphasized. There are two co-equal divine forces: Ahura-Mazda, the god of light, who is also the god of good, and Ahriman, the god of darkness and evil. Ultimately the god of light will triumph and will destroy the god of darkness and evil. These beliefs gave Zoroastrianism the character of a quasi-monotheistic faith, definitely optimistic in outlook. Zoroastrianism never proclaimed matter as such to be evil. Asceticism therefore never found any foothold in its system.

Not so with the religions of Greece and Rome. We are not accustomed to associate asceticism with the Greeks and Romans. With respect to the Greeks especially, many are wont to think of a highly idealized Periclean Age suffused with "sweetness and light," and characterized by balance in all things and a great love for life. But the fact is that the popular religions of Greece and of the ancient Mediterranean world, as well as their most widely accepted religious philosophies, from the sixth century B.C. to the end of the pagan era in the fourth century C.E.

taught contempt for the human body, and included many ascetic practices in their rites. They were concerned largely with the nether world and the hereafter, with ancient guilt and expiation, and with dark magic and spells designed to save men from countless unknown terrors.

In the first three centuries of the common era, asceticism belonged to the thought and practices of nearly every philosophic school.[2] For six hundred years prior to that time all the mystery religions of Greece and Rome, beginning with Orphism, were eschatological in the main, surcharged with dualistic doctrine and self-mortifying practices. Whether these ideas were native with the Hellenes or imported from the East in post-Homeric times it is difficult and, for our purpose, not essential to determine. The Near East had completed a cycle of religious and social development before the Greeks emerged from their age of barbarism in the eighth century. The Greeks were certainly very susceptible to the ideas emanating from the peoples of Asia, as were the Romans centuries later. The orgiastic worship of the chthonic deities, the frenzied Bacchic rituals, the ecstasy of intoxicated worshipers, consummating in the rending alive of the sacrificial animal—the god incarnate—and the devouring of its flesh—these were not gay, lighthearted effusions of overflowing joy on the part of a life-loving people. They were rather the ways of a dark and dread religious mystery, the ways of lustration from dread, sin, and guilt. Men here sought redemption from a primal and inherited curse, release through manipulated ecstasy from the misery and pain of earthly existence, which in itself was looked upon as punishment. All the mystery religions were of a "salvationist" character. They offered man the correct ritual and the rules which would "save" him, which would deliver him from the world's sorrows, and ensure for him a safe journey to the next world and release from its punishments and torments. In some of these mystery religions one finds also the promise of release from reincarnation, from the endless cycle of birth and death, from what they, as well as Buddhism, called the "wheel of life."

In nearly every instance, the rites of initiation (*teletai*) into the mystery religions and the way of life prescribed for the initiates were ascetic in character.

> O happy he by fortune blest
> Who knows the mystic rites divine
> Who makes his life one long austerity

chants the Chorus in Euripides' *The Bacchae*.[3]

"Orphism was a way of life, and an ascetic one," writes Professor Guthrie.[4] The Orphic believed that

> The source of evil lay in the body with its appetites and passions, which must therefore be subdued if we are to rise to the heights which it is in us to attain. . . . The belief behind it is that this present life is for the soul a punishment for previous sin, and the punishment consists precisely in this, that it is fettered to a body. This is for it a calamity, and is compared sometimes to being shut up in a prison, more times to being buried in a tomb.[5]

In the official Eleusinian mysteries the initiates were instructed in the rules for reaching the next world safely and enjoying the bliss of the afterlife. These rules were of an ascetic nature. Pythagoreanism, which arose in Italy in the sixth century B.C., was closely related to Orphism in doctrine. It was dualistic in thought, and in practice, ascetic. Among the pre-Socratic philosophers, Empedocles preached asceticism.

Plato borrowed many of his ideas about the soul from Orphism. His philosophy, too, is sharply dualistic. Matter is evil in that it resists the Idea, the perfect Form. The soul is "entombed," "encaged." It is ever desirous to escape to its true home with God.[6] Only death can give the soul a chance to discover pure knowledge and real happiness.

> For the body is a source of endless trouble to us by reason of the mere requirement of food; and is liable also to diseases which overtake and impede us in the search after true being: it fills us full of loves, and lusts, and fears, and fancies of all kinds, and endless foolery, and in fact, as men say, takes away from us the power of thinking at all . . . and, last and worst of all, even if we are at leisure and

betake ourselves to some speculation, the body is always breaking in upon us, causing turmoil and confusion in our enquiries, and so amazing us that we are prevented from seeing the truth. It has been proved to us by experience that if we would have pure knowledge of anything we must be quit of the body—the soul in herself must behold things in themselves. . . . In this present life, I reckon that we make the nearest approach to knowledge when we have the least possible intercourse or communion with the body, and are not surfeited with the bodily nature, but keep ourselves pure until the hour when God himself is pleased to release us. And thus having got rid of the foolishness of the body we shall be pure and hold converse with the pure, and know of ourselves the clear light everywhere, which is no other than the light of truth.[7]

Although the Greek philosophers did not counsel the hastening of such "release" through suicide, they did not condemn it. Judaism viewed suicide, except under the most unusual and extreme circumstances, as a crime against God.

The ethico-philosophic school of Cynicism was ascetic in the extreme. One might say it was rancorously and fractiously so. It renounced the world. It was contemptuous of the human body. The human spirit, to be free, must be entirely independent of all desire, even the most innocent, and of all external things. All intellectual pleasures must be foresworn, including the study of philosophy itself. The family, the state, and society are of no account and are sore impediments to the spirit of man.

Stoicism, a far nobler and high-minded system of thought, which for centuries counted many devotees in the ancient world among the lowest and highest, was much less extreme than Cynicism, but nonetheless closely related to it. It advocated renunciation.

Many parallels have been traced between the ideas of leading Stoics such as Seneca and Marcus Aurelius with those of some of their Rabbinic contemporaries.[8] The coincidence of thought on many ethical themes is indeed striking. They may have influenced one another, or their ideas may have derived from a common reservoir of thought included in universal human experi-

ences. But it is clear that the total ethical ensemble of Stoicism
and of Rabbinic Judaism are quite different and distinct.

The brave but melancholy austerity of the Stoics, their *ascesis*,
their complete exemption from all emotion (*apathia*), their lack
of social consciousness or faith in human progress, the little room
allowed in their compact system for the affections of the human
heart, for love and pity and above all for repentance—are elements alien to Judaism. To endure life bravely and to get through
with it is all the special wisdom which they derived from their
conviction that Nature is governed by a rational purpose.

Remember that you ought to behave in life as you would at a
banquet. As something is being passed around and it comes to you,
stretch out your hand and take a portion of it politely. It passes on,
do not detain it. Or it has not come to you yet, do not project your
desire to meet it, but wait until it comes in front of you. So act
toward children, so toward a wife, so toward office, so toward
wealth; and then some day you will be worthy of the banquets of
the gods. But if you do not take these things even when they are set
before you, but despise them, then you will not only share the
banquet of the gods, but share also their rule.[9]

Neo-Pythagoreanism (1 c. B.C.), grounded in absolute dualism,
was a further development of the philosophy of Pythagoras and
of Platonism, including their asceticism. It approved of celibacy.
Apollonius of Tyana (1 c.) was typical of this school. He was a
celibate, walked barefoot, ate no animal food, and practiced other
austerities.

Neoplatonism, the last important school of pagan philosophy,
was also based on the tragedy of the soul which is chained to
the body and the senses, and the desperate need to free it from
all enslavement to the physical world. Plotinus (3 c.), the genius
of Neoplatonism, saw no purpose in actively participating in the
affairs of the world. Porphyry, his disciple, was an extreme
ascetic and celibate. Mithraism, which originated in Persia, made
great inroads in the Roman world and it too preached abstinence
and extolled the celibate. In the first centuries of the common era

various Gnostic religious philosophies were in vogue in the Mediterannean world. They were all redemptionist in outlook. Gnosticism, a blending of Greek religious and philosophic speculation with Oriental thought and mythology, greatly influenced Christianity. At the root of this philosophy or theosophy is the sharp dualism of matter and spirit, and the conviction that the material world is altogether evil. This world, according to some Gnostic speculation, is not even the handiwork of the true God, but of some inferior deity. Man should therefore escape from the fetters of this bodily existence to the world of the spirit, which is the world of the true and supreme spiritual God. The way of escape is through the right gnosis—illumination and renunciation.

Christianity in its early centuries was overwhelmingly ascetic in outlook, and came increasingly to extol self-denial, poverty, and celibacy. There were reasons for it. In the first place, it was firmly rooted in the doctrine of duality which was borrowed from non-Jewish sources. Having accepted dualism as central to its theology, asceticism was the logical consequence.

In the second place, it was dominated by the belief in the swiftly approaching end of the world and the imminence of the Parousia, which would usher in a new order into which only the utterly pure and righteous would be privileged to enter. Accordingly, men were urged to disencumber themselves of all things that were likely to keep their minds and their souls entangled in the affairs of this perishing world. Penance and renunciation were the indicated way.

Even marriage was disapproved of in the early Church. In fact, among the great religions of mankind, it is in Christianity and in Buddhism that celibacy received its highest endorsement. At best marriage was tolerated as a concession to human frailty. Paul declared:

It is well for a man not to touch a woman. But because of the temptation to immorality, each man should have his own wife and each woman her own husband. . . . I say this by way of concession, not of command. I wish that all were as I myself am [unmarried]. . . . To the unmarried and the widows I say that it is well for them to 'remain single as I do. But if they cannot exercise self-control, they should marry. For it is better to marry than to be aflame with passion [I Cor. 7:1ff.].

There were those who did not make any such concession to the flesh, who advocated celibacy as the only correct way for all faithful Christians. The Encratites preached against marriage. Tatian (2 c.), their leader, declared marriage to be nothing else than corruption and fornication.[10] Saturninus (2 c.) and his followers believed that marriage and generation are from Satan.[11] The Montanists (2 c.)—whose founder Montanus was a converted pagan priest, an ecstatic who won over the majority of the Phrygian Christians to his creed and whose doctrine spread far and wide—were given to celibacy, fasts, and other ascetic practices. Tertullian (2–3 c.), who was converted to Montanism, is the most extreme spokesman of its views. Origen (2–3 c.), one of the most influential of Christian theologians, declared that three sacrifices are pleasing to God—a martyr death, voluntary celibacy, and abstinence from sexual intercourse on the part of married persons.

The Manichees were numerically impressive for centuries, both in the East and in the West. Their strong center and the origin of their movement was in Mesopotamia where their founder Mani (3 c.), a Persian, was probably influenced by Indian ideas. His religion was thoroughly dualistic in doctrine. The regimen he prescribed, especially for the elect, was built on self-denial. They were not to marry, nor acquire property, nor eat meat nor drink wine. They were to fast frequently.

Marcion (2 c.), whose extreme Gnostic views made great inroads in the early Church and at times threatened to submerge it completely, was an extreme ascetic. His dualism was extravagant, and therefore his violent anti-Judaistic emphasis—the more dualistic the more anti-Judaistic. He could find no confirmation for dualism in the Old Testament, and consequently rejected the latter and developed a Christian theology which was divorced from it, as well as from the God of the Old Testament and from a Jewish background generally. He expurgated from the Chris-

tian Gospel all references to Jesus' Jewish antecedents and genealogy. The God of whom the Old Testament speaks is not the
Father of Jesus Christ. Jesus was not the promised Messiah of the
Jews. This Messiah is yet to come. Jesus was the revelation of
the good God—the superior God of love and pure benevolence—
who entered history in the fifteenth year of the reign of Tiberius
Caesar to redeem mankind from the domination of the God Who
had created the world, an essentially evil world which could not
have been made by a good God. The Cosmocrator of the Old
Testament, an inferior Demiurge of stern justice and law, himself evil or almost so, was the God of this world. The good God,
revealed in Jesus modalistically—not in the flesh, but in an appearance of the flesh, in a phantom (for all flesh is material and
therefore evil and could not be the dwelling place of God)—was
not the God of this world, but of another, a spiritual world. He
came to destroy the power of the Creator-God and all His works
and to redeem and save men for eternal life.

Marcion of course condemned marriage and insisted upon
complete celibacy. To bring children into being was only to
perpetuate a sinful world. A holy man disregards all family and
earthly ties, becomes a recluse from human society, and practices severe austerities to purify his soul.

Some leaders of the Church, such as Irenaeus and Clement of
Alexandria, combated such excessive ascetic tendencies, especially
those expressed in hostility to marriage. But the general attitude
of abstinence was fully accepted even by them. The Catholic
Church extolled chastity and esteemed the virgin and the celibate
as especially holy and blessed. Synods, councils, and popes from
time to time prescribed absolute chastity for the clergy. Following the Reformation, and as a reaction to it, the Catholic Church
elevated the rule of clerical celibacy to the position of a dogma.

These ideas and practices, stimulated by similar concepts and
behavior in the pagan world where they were particularly rife in
the early centuries of the Christian era, captivated many minds
and gave rise among Christians to numerous institutions which
were foreign to Judaism—hermitages, monasteries, nunneries, re-

ligious orders; itinerant beggars; saints who lived in caves, in cemeteries, in deserts or on solitary mountains and pillars (*Sty-lites*) or in trees (*Dendrites*), or who lived loaded down with chains (*Catenati*), or ate grass like cattle, or took food only once a week from Monday to Saturday (*Hebdomadarii*), and who indulged in many other strange practices of bodily mortification and ascetic extravagance.

Another reason for the widespread acceptance of asceticism in the primitive Church is to be found in the idea of suffering as a means of salvation. Jesus himself, it was held, died upon the cross to atone by his suffering for the Original Sin of mankind, and by so doing he saved the world from its primal guilt and curse. True believers, according to Paul, must suffer with Jesus, the Christ, in order that they too might be glorified with him (Rom. 8:17). Suffering and martyrdom were especially stressed among the Donatists in North Africa and the Novatianists in Asia Minor. They looked upon persecution and martyrdom as of the very essence of the Christian way of life, and they welcomed suffering and death for the faith.

The leaders of the Reformation stressed justification by faith only. They relegated all good works—and this in their eyes included all ascetic religious practices and all piously motivated cloistered seclusion—to a secondary, or even negligible position. Monasticism, compulsory celibacy of the clergy, and other simi-lar classic Christian institutions and practices were denounced. Luther called them the work of the devil. The Augsburg Confes-sion (1530) condemned them. This attitude toward monasticism, however, did not carry along with it any general reconciliation with life and its innocent pleasures and enjoyments. The dour and renunciatory mood was not banished by the Reformation, and it asserted itself dominantly, time and again, in various Prot-estant sects.

Foremost among the modern exponents of unqualified Pauline Christology and its asceticism is Sören Kierkegaard. He rebelled violently against the humanistic trend which he found among Protestant theologians of his day, a trend which has had its noble exponents in many Protestant circles to the present. He was contemptuous of all efforts at social reform. His theology, as we pointed out previously, is dominated by a tormented sense of guilt and sin, dread and catastrophe; by a tragic view of life, of man's utter helplessness to improve himself, of an unbridgeable gulf which separates man from God; and by the conviction that suffering represents the highest expression of the inner life of man. He shared with Meister Eckhart the conviction that "the secret way lies inward . . . the swiftest steed to bear you to your goal is suffering; none shall ever taste eternal bliss but those who stand with Christ in depths of bitterness." [12] Kierkegaard renounced the state of marriage. Man should seek out isolation and solitude. Above all, he should suffer. Dr. Walter Lowrie, in his comprehensive life of Kierkegaard, writes that for a year and a half Kierkegaard had practiced the ascetic life—"to see how much I could bear" is the expression he used. The monastic life in particular had a strong fascination for him. "Back to the cloister," he was ready to cry; "there is only one thing higher, and that is martyrdom." [13]

It was as a result largely of Christian and Buddhist influences that ascetic doctrines and practices came to play such an important rôle in Islam almost from its inception. It has been suggested by Goldziher that Mohammed himself had "the highest regard for true asceticism, praying brotherhoods, penance and fasting—with one exception perhaps—celibacy," [14] and that the spirit of Islam in its beginnings was ascetic.

Mohammed was not, however, a consistent advocate of the ascetic life, although he viewed this present life as "only a toy and a vain amusement; and worldly pomp and the affectation of glory among you and the multiplying of riches and children, are as the plants nourished by the rain, the springing up whereof delighteth the husbandmen; afterwards they wither so that thou seest the same turned yellow, and at length they become dry stubble." [15] His attitude changed later on. His own personal life was not characterized by any noticeable abstemiousness; and the practical considerations of a warring and conquering faith, many of whose followers were attracted to its wars by the prospect of booty and spoils, soon crowded the ascetic otherworldly motifs to the background. His later utterances include outright opposition to asceticism. "O, true believers, forbid not the good things which God hath allowed you . . . and eat of what God hath given you for food that which is lawful and good." [16] He did not approve of the monastic state,[17] and did not prescribe it for Islam.

But as Islam spread from the Arabian peninsula into Egypt, Syria, and Iraq, and further East into Persia, it came in contact with the extensive and long-established ascetic movements and institutions of both Christianity and Buddhism. Many of the true believers, in dread of the Day of Judgment and the torments which would be visited upon them for their sins after resurrection—upon which the Koran dwells at great length—were moved to adopt the way of life of the ascetics whom they saw around them. These adopted the traditional dress and regimen of self-denial—the coarse garment, fasting, and poverty. As with the early Christians, marriage was regarded as a concession, and many advocated outright celibacy. Others became hermits and dwelt in caves, deserts, and cemeteries.

The mystic movement of Islam, which came to be known as Sufism (*Sufi*—"clad in wool"), originated in the eighth century at a time of bitter political and religious strife. It first made its appearance in the cities of Kufa and Basra in Iraq where Buddhist as well as Christian mysticism had long been felt. From there it spread to Khurasan, long a flourishing center of Buddhism. It was also at that disturbed time and in the same place that Karaism, likewise strongly mystic and ascetic, arose among the Jews. "Self-abandonment, vigorous self-mortification, fervid piety, and quietism carried to the verge of apathy form the main features of their (*Sufi*) creed," notes Dr. Nicholson.[18] Shaqi, one of the early Sufis, declared: "Nine-tenths of devotion consist in flight from mankind, the remaining tenth in silence." [19] Love of God spelled hatred of the world.

By 800 C.E. Sufi monasteries began to make their appearance, and by the eleventh century they were numerous, and expanding rapidly. The twelfth century witnessed the rise of the great Dervish orders.

Thus in nearly all the great religions of mankind—Hinduism, Buddhism, Christianity, and Islam—and in the major religious theosophies of the ancient world, we discover not only an attitude of pessimism toward earthly existence but a recurrent emphasis on escaping the trammels and tribulations of life through the mortification of the flesh. Judaism's main characteristics are not related to such attitudes. Its faith is suffused with optimism which derived not from extended national prosperity or political power or prolonged security—rare phenomena indeed in Jewish history, but from a rejection of all dualism and from an unshaken belief in a Guardian God of goodness and justice.

Judaism has no relish for the "scourgings, macerations, mortifyings, fasts, disciplines that clear the spiritual eye and break the soul from earth." [20] It does not regard them as the way to holiness or spiritual freedom. Freedom cannot be acquired through the mortification of the flesh any more than through its indulgence. Only that which is *harut*, engraved on the tablet of the Law (Ex. 32:16), can give man *herut*, true freedom.[21] To become holy and free one need do no more than observe faithfully the clear commandments of the Torah: "That you may remember and do all My commandments and be holy unto your God" (Nu. 15:40). Judaism's aim was not to make men morosely penitent but joyfully active in moral enterprise. It did not seek to curb the impulses and desires of the human heart but to direct them toward the "wholeness" and harmony of living.

Not a single one of the 613 positive and negative commandments of the Torah defining the orthodox norm of Jewish life as developed by the Rabbis enjoins any form of asceticism or mortification upon man. There is but one public fast day ordained in the Pentateuch—Yom Kippur, the Day of Atonement—a solemn day of searching one's soul. The Prophet Isaiah defines the purpose of such a fast day:

Is it to bow down his head like a rush, and to spread sackcloth and ashes under him? . . . Is not this the fast that I choose: to loose the bands of wickedness, to undo the thongs of the yoke, to let the oppressed go free, and to break every yoke? Is it not to share your bread with the hungry, and bring the homeless poor into your house; when you see the naked, to cover him, and not to hide yourself from your own flesh? [Is. 58:5–7].

In sad commemoration of the fall of Jerusalem and the first destruction of the Temple (586 B.C.), four other public fast days were later instituted. They were national memorial days. The prophet Zechariah holds out the promise that these fast days will at the appointed time of reconciliation be converted into "seasons of joy and gladness, and cheerful feasts" (Zech. 8:19). From time to time other semi-fast days (sunrise to sunset), mostly commemorative of historic misfortunes, were instituted. Their observance was neither obligatory nor uniform. A Babylonian Amora of the third century declared: "There are no public fasts in Babylonia except the Fast of the Ninth of Ab." [22]

Public fasting was decreed for special intercession in times of national emergency or in times of prolonged drought or plague.[23] Occasional fasting was prescribed for individuals as penance, and it was looked upon as tantamount to a sin-offering brought to the Temple.[24] The psychological and disciplinary value of fasting was not ignored. But the excessive indulgence in it and the sole reliance upon it for the attainment of purification and holiness were condemned.[25] Self-affliction in itself is no atonement and bestows no sanctity on man. The noted R. Samuel said: "Whosoever fasts [for the sake of self-affliction] is termed a sinner." [26] Mar Zuṭra (4 c.) declared: "The merit of a fast day lies in the charity dispensed." [27]

A man should not tax himself beyond reasonable endurance,[28] and repentance is possible without fasting. Isaac Aboab (14 c.) asserts: "Judaism's way of repentance is easier than that of other faiths who prescribe bodily self-affliction. Our Torah did not ordain any bodily self-afflictions. Repentance is through the prayer of the lips and the meditations of the heart." [29]

The Destruction of 70 c.e. and the Exile cast a pall over the life of the people. Large numbers in Israel became ascetics,[30] fasted and refused to partake of wine or of meat. R. Johanan said in the name of R. Simeon b. Yohai (2 c.): "It is forbidden to a man to fill his mouth with laughter in these days." [31] People no longer decorated or painted their homes. The playing of musical instruments or the singing of songs was discouraged. But it is characteristic that R. Joshua (1–2 c.) offered these words of moderation to his disciples in those dread hours of national calamity and grief: "My sons, come and listen to me. Not to mourn at all is impossible because the blow has fallen. To mourn overmuch is also impossible because we do not impose on the community a hardship which the majority cannot endure." [32]

We do not overlook the fact that there were Nazirites in ancient Israel, men or women who engaged themselves to abstain from wine and strong drink for the purposes of attaining to a higher level of holiness, or of acquiring special occult power, or as penance and intercession. During the period of their vow, the Nazirites denied themselves wine, let their hair grow long, and did not go near a dead body. Their vows were as a rule taken for a fixed period of time (Num. 6:13), the minimum, according to the Talmud, being thirty days. In some instances it was a lifetime pledge (e.g., Samson, Jud. 13:5 and 16:17). For such men, Naziriteship was a career, and they belonged to a distinctive group (Amos 2:11–12).

The Rechabites (8–6 c. b.c.) were also a distinct group whose members abstained from wine. They did not build houses, choosing to dwell in tents, and they did not sow fields or plant vineyards. The way of life they adopted seems to have been motivated by a desire to cling to the early nomadic traditions of Israel and to disassociate themselves from the Canaanitish way of life, which in their eyes was corrupting the pure faith.

But it is significant that nowhere are men and women in Israel commanded or urged to become Nazirites or to adopt the practices of the Rechabites, which were neither standard nor on all scores held to be irrreproachable. As a professional group their numbers were always small. As for laymen, the practice of making even short-term vows of abstinence could not have been extensive, for the expense of the sacrifices required to be brought to the Temple upon the completion of such vows—a burnt offering, a sin-offering and a peace-offering (Nu. 6:15–17)—was heavy enough to discourage the average person from making them. Some of those who did make such vows had to be assisted in order to buy the prescribed sacrificial animals and get themselves clear of their pledges.[33]

The Pharisaic teachers discouraged the making of these and all other vows. It is reported in the Talmud that the High Priest, Simon the Just (2 c. B.C.), was so averse to Nazirite vows that he refused to eat of their atonement offerings except in one rare instance.[34] R. Nathan (2 c.) declared: "If a man makes a vow, it is as if he had built an altar of his own on a high place, and if he fulfills it [does not have it dissolved by an expert Sage], it is as if he had offered up a sacrifice upon it." [35] The general attitude may be said to have been summed up by R. Dimi (4 c.), speaking in the name of R. Isaac: "Are not the prohibitions of the Torah sufficient for you, that you must look for additional prohibitions?" [36]

A feeling prevailed among some of the Rabbis that there was actually an element of sin in the practices of the Nazirite, because he denied himself wine. The Nazirite, according to Scriptures, had to have an atonement made for him "because he had sinned by reason of his soul" (Nu. 6:11). Against whose soul did he sin? asked a Rabbi. Against his own soul, for he denied himself wine. "If this man who denied himself wine only is termed a sinner, how much more so is he who denies himself the enjoyment of everything in life." [37]

The practice of Nazirite vows was limited by law to Palestine, and with the fall of the Temple and the abolition of the sacrificial cult it was abandoned altogether, since no sacrifices could be brought to the Temple to terminate such vows.[38]

It is to be noted that the Nazirites were not pledged to celibacy. The renunciation of normal sex life was never regarded as a virtue in Judaism. This is one of the marked differences which distinguishes Judaism from most of the classic religions of mankind. It differentiates even Jewish ascetic groups from their counterparts among other religions throughout the ages. Speaking of the Ḥasidic ascetics in medieval Germany, Professor Scholem notes:

There is, however, one important respect in which Ḥasidism differs from its Christian contemporaries: it does not enjoin sexual askesis; on the contrary, the greatest importance is assigned in the *Sefer Ḥasidim* to the establishment and maintenance of a normal and reasonable marital life. Nowhere is penitence extended to sexual abstinence in marital relations.[39]

Again, "At no time was sexual asceticism accorded the dignity of a religious value, and the mystics made no exception." [40]

To marry and to beget children in order to preserve the race is a divine command in Judaism. "Be fruitful and multiply" (Gen. 1:28) is the first commandment of the Bible. "Any man who has no wife is not a complete man, for it is said: Male and female created He them and called their name Adam." [41] He who does not contribute to the propagation of the race is as though he sheds blood and diminishes the Divine Image.[42]

The prophet Isaiah was sent to King Hezekiah with a message: "Thus says the Lord: Set your house in order; for you shall die, you shall not live" (Is. 38:1). What is the meaning of "you shall die, you shall not live?" ask the Rabbis; and they reply: You shall die in this world and not live in the world to come. Hezekiah said to him: Why a decree so harsh? Isaiah replied: Because you did not try to have children. The King said: It was because I saw by the Holy Spirit that the children issuing from me would not be virtuous. Isaiah said to him: "What have you to do with the secrets of the All-Merciful? You should have done what you were commanded, and let the Holy One, blessed be He, do that which pleases Him." [43]

"Did you fulfill your duty with respect to establishing a family?" is among the principal questions which, the Rabbis held, will be asked of a man on the Day of Judgment.[44] No one has discharged this obligation to life and society until he has been the father of at least two children. By the age of twenty a man should be married. If one has to study the Torah and to marry, the Halachah is, according to Rab Judah: "A man marries first, and then studies." [45] No High Priest could officiate in the Temple unless he was married.[46] Talmudic literature seems to know of only one celibate Rabbi who remained a bachelor out of love for the study of the Torah—Ben Azzai (2 c.).[47]

The Essenes are said by Philo to have rejected marriage, for they looked upon sexual intercourse as a form of defilement. He also states that there were no youths among them, but that they were all adult men, already declining toward old age. Josephus' account seems to suggest that there were two orders or disciplines among them. Some Essenes "neglect wedlock but choose out other persons' children while they are pliable and fit for learning, and esteem them to be of their kindred and form them according to their own manners. They do not absolutely deny the fitness of marriage, and the succession of mankind thereby continued." [48] Another order of Essenes "agree with the rest as to their way of living, and customs and laws, but differ from them on the point of marriage, as thinking that by not marrying, they cut off the principal part of human life, which is the prospect of succession, nay rather, that if all men should be of the same opinion, the whole race of mankind would fail." [49]

Very little that is undebatable is known about the Essenes, even their name. The recently discovered Hebrew scrolls in the caves of Khirbet Qumran near the Dead Sea brought to light a Manual of Discipline of a Jewish sect made up of priests and laymen, which in many ways closely resembles the doctrines and practices of the Essenes. A near-by monastery whose ruins have been excavated seems to have belonged to this sect. Its members lived together and shared all things communally. There is no historic evidence, however, that the Essenes represented any more than a very small group in Israel—Philo suggests the figure of six thousand in a population estimated to have been over two million—or that they exercised any marked influence upon the life and religious development of the people.

There are scattered references in Rabbinic literature to other groups whose names suggest a mystic character and possibly also ascetic leanings, for example, the Humble Ones (*'Anavim*), the Silent Ones (*Hashaim*), the Chaste Ones (*Zenuim*), but nothing definite is known of their way of life.

The spiritual leaders of Israel lived, worked, and moved among their fellow men. They did not isolate themselves and shun the pressing daily tasks and social responsibilities. The cloistered virtues or the conventual life made no appeal to them. They were not mendicants and friars, going about with staff and bowl, begging alms to sustain themselves while attending to the purification of their souls through feats of abstinence. They did not run away from life out of fear of its temptations and its social stresses—this would be tantamount to deserting the only battlefield where the victories of the spirit can be won. They did not look down upon men who were doing the work of the world. Simeon b. Yohai and his son were rebuked for deprecating physical human labor. They had fled from the Roman authorities and had hid in a cave for twelve years, devoting themselves to prayer and study. When the emperor died they emerged from the cave and, seeing a man plowing and sowing, they exclaimed, "They forsake life eternal and engage in life temporal!" Whatever they cast their eyes upon was immediately burned up (so consuming and ruthless was their sanctity). Thereupon a *Bat Kol* (Heavenly Voice) cried out: "Have you emerged to destroy My world? Return to your cave!" [50]

The guiding principle of the Rabbis was enunciated by the great Hillel: "Do not separate yourself from the community." [51] A man should participate in the life of the community and should not shirk any responsibilities of office. "If a man [summoned to be a judge] says, 'What have I to do with the concerns of the community, what have I to do with their suits, why do I have to listen to their talk? Peace to thee, O my soul!'—such a man destroys the world."⁵² Under all circumstances a man should remain and share in the fate of his community.⁵³ When times are out of joint, there is an especial challenge to a man of faith to remain with his fellow men and try to set things right.⁵⁴

Here and there in the Talmud one finds a Rabbi with marked ascetic tendencies. R. Eleazar (2 c.) believed that fasting is more efficacious than charity, because one is performed with a man's money, the other with his body.⁵⁵ Occasionally, too, a reference is made in what is clearly a hyperbole to a Rabbi like R. Joshua (2 c.), who fasted so long to atone for the sin of having slighted a colleague that his teeth became blackened.⁵⁶ Feats of prodigious fasting are reported of R. Zera (3 c.). But these are rare exceptions. Of more than three thousand Tannaim and Amoraim, known by name in the Talmud, the number of those who are reported to have subjected themselves to severe austerities is insignificant.

Religiously motivated self-torture and self-mutilation are of course strictly prohibited in the Torah, and are regarded as abominable and idolatrous practices. "You are the sons of the Lord your God; you shall not cut yourselves or make any baldness on your foreheads for the dead" (Dt. 14:1) or any manner of tattooing on your bodies (Lev. 19:28). "No one is permitted to injure himself." ⁵⁷ Self-mutilation such as was practiced by the priests of certain religions of antiquity and ceremonies of religious castration, such as those of the Galli, in honor of gods or goddesses were viewed by Judaism as gross heathen abominations. The statement attributed to Jesus in Matthew 19:12: "There are eunuchs who have made themselves eunuchs for the sake of the Kingdom of Heaven. He who is able to receive this, let him receive it," would be utterly inadmissible in Judaism, as would Origen's act of self-emasculation out of motives of piety. Justin points with pride to the Christian who presented a petition to the Governor of Alexandria craving that permission be given to a surgeon to make him a eunuch.⁵⁸ No eunuch could be an officiating priest in the Temple (Lev. 21.20), nor, for that matter, could a man with any physical blemish or mutilation. "He shall not come near the veil or approach the altar, because he has a blemish; that he may not profane My sanctuary."

The body is the Temple of the soul. It should not be desecrated by disfigurement. It should be carefully tended. Once Hillel, when he concluded his studies with his disciples, walked a distance with them. They asked him, "Master, whither are you bound?" He answered, "To perform a religious duty." "What is the religious duty?" they asked. He said to them, "To bathe." Said they, "Is this a religious duty?" "Yes," he replied, "if the statues of kings in theaters and circuses are scoured and washed by the man who is appointed to look after them . . . how much more should I bathe my body which is fashioned in the image and likeness of God, as it is written, 'For in the image of God made He man.' " [59]

Under Islamic mystic influence, and spurred by intense Messianic expectations, asceticism gained in favor among certain Jewish groups in Babylonia and Persia in the centuries following the Arab conquest. The Iswaites and Yudghanites (7–8 c.) abstained from meat and wine and fasted frequently. The Karaites were much given to austerities as acts of mourning for the destruction of the Temple and for the exile and as an intercession for the coming of the Messiah. Among them, the *Abele Zion* (Mourners for Zion), of the Karaite community in Jerusalem, were the most intense in their fasting and prayer.

From this time onward many Rabbinic authorities on law, ethics, and philosophy felt constrained to dwell at some length on the subject of asceticism. Evidently, the number of adherents among the Jewish people had become quite considerable. [60]

Saadia (9–10 c.), Gaon of Sura, the foremost Rabbinic authority of his day, in his monumental work *The Book of Beliefs and Opinions* devotes the tenth and last treatise to an analysis of the principal types of human ambition and how men should control them in order to maintain a proper balance in life. In this discus-

sion he considers also those "one-sided" Jews among whom
ascetic practices had spread in the wake of the fervent Messianic
hopes of his day.[61]

Saadia's approach is one of marked sobriety and is determined
by the clear prescriptions of the Law. While he acknowledged
that abstinence is commendable within measure,[62] he is opposed
to those scholars "who maintain that there exists nothing which
an individual ought to occupy himself with in this world, except
the quest of knowledge" [63] and the worship of God—that is to
say, "fast by day and arise at night in order to praise and glorify
God, abandoning all mundane cares in the belief that God will
provide for his sustenance, medicaments and all his other
needs." [64] The true service of God consists in the fulfillment of
the precepts of the Torah. The hermit who isolates himself from
his fellow men cannot fulfill these commandments. It is true that
a person should rely on God for the needs of life, but God has
provided man with ways of acquiring the means of satisfying
them. Man must make the effort to earn his own livelihood. He
should not rely on miracles.

In the main, Saadia's position is that of the Rabbis of the
Talmud, though somewhat more somber and austere, colored as
it is by the prevalent mystic mood of his day. The basic personal
and social needs and amenities are not spurned; worldly occupations are not scorned. No halo is placed around the head of the
hermit, the saint in the wilderness, the "weeper." Nevertheless,
"the righteous servant of God loves the life of this world merely
because it serves as a stepladder by means of which he may reach
and ascend to the next world—not for its own sake." [65]

There were those who were to go much further along the
road of otherworldliness and self-denial.

Bahya (11 c.), whose *Duties of the Heart* became the most
popular and beloved ethico-philosophic book among the Jewish
people, was one of these. Still strictly correct as far as the letter
of the law was concerned, still seeking to maintain the balance
which Saadia counseled (Bahya was greatly under Saadia's influence, and acknowledged his indebtedness to him), he neverthe-

less moves appreciably nearer to the standard ascetic complex. Bahya's mood and concepts are closely akin to those of the moderate Sufis of Islam. Many of his key terms and forms of expression are technical Sufi clichés.

God's purpose in putting man on this earth is, he says, to test and purge man's soul in order that it might become purified like that of the holy angels. The testing ground is man's corporal body with its physical needs and desires. But man's passions frequently overwhelm his reason and lead him to excesses which are harmful to him and undermine his physical constitution. Hence, the need for deliberate withdrawal from the world's pleasures and enjoyments to the point where the balance is restored and sound health assured.

Inasmuch as the entire human species is in need of this general type of corrective abstinence, Bahya believes it is right that there should be in the world some thoroughgoing ascetics who are completely removed from the affairs of this world, and who can serve as models and examples for the rest of mankind. All men may then learn from them whatever they need to correct and restore the symmetry of their lives. This acceptance of different levels of piety, one for the spiritually élite and another for the masses, is a new departure in Jewish ethical thought.

It is not necessary that all men should belong to the class of ascetics—this would bring about the end of society; but the ascetics are needed as doctors for the souls of men.[66] But even for the rank and file Bahya recommends not only moderation and temperance, but abstemiousness as well. All men should forego worldly occupation short of becoming a burden on others; they should limit their speech, put under restraint the roving eye, the avid ear, the hungry palate; they should be satisfied with one frugal meal a day, and eat it not for pleasure but as if it were medicine—perhaps a few olives, dates, and grapes which they do not have to bother about much in preparing; they should fast one day a week.[67]

Bahya thus urges every possible form of asceticism short of transgressing the specific laws of Judaism which did not countenance celibacy, self-torture, and solitary retirement from society.

There were those who were to go even further than Baḥya.

One finds them among the Jews of Germany in the twelfth and thirteenth centuries. Under the impact of the disasters wrought by the Crusades, and the darkening of their lives in the persecutions of the Middle Ages, the plaintive, mournful mood deepened among the people. In his Code, *Arb'a Ṭurim*, Jacob b. Asher (13–14 c.) suggests that it is especially meritorious for men to rise during the three watches of the night and pray to God to redeem Israel from the fearful exile and to restore Jerusalem and the Holy Sanctuary. His father and mentor, R. Asher b. Jeḥiel (Rosh), had taught him that these hours were especially propitious for divine intercession because the Holy One Himself during these watches of the night laments over His children's exile and their suffering.[68] Jacob b. Asher also declares that a man who indulges in fasts when he is physically able to do so is a *Kadosh*—a holy man.[69]

Messianic hopes were rife among the Jewish communities of the Rhineland during the period of the Crusades.[70] In the Christian world, too, chiliastic hopes were in the air; and intense religious emotionalism, occasionally bordering on hysteria, incited by the Crusades frequently expressed itself in wild penitential acts of self-mortification and flagellation. In this spiritual milieu Jewish mystic and ascetic tendencies found great nourishment. The principal textbook of this movement is the *Sefer Ḥasidim*, in the main the work of Judah the Pious (12–13 c.).

Its dominant theme is renunciation and penitence. Its mood is one of depression and despondency. The love of life is not in it, nor any interest in the enterprises of social existence. It is the weary vigil of lonely souls in the desolate antechamber of Death.

The way of the Ḥasid—the truly pious—is to forsake the world. He should reduce to a minimum his conversation with men, young and old, even with his wife.[71] He should not even take a walk for pleasure.[72] The Ḥasid should assume stricter obligations and burdens than those prescribed by the Torah.[78] In all matters where some Rabbinic authorities favor a more lenient, and others a stricter, interpretation the Ḥasid should follow the latter.[74] He should engage in the most rigorous forms of penitential acts, for they confer great merit.[75]

To sit in the snow or in the ice for an hour daily in winter, or to expose one's body to ants and bees in the summer was judged a common practice among those who followed the new call. It is a far cry from the Talmudic conception of penitence to these novel ideas and practices.[76]

This new note in Jewish religious thought was also sounded elsewhere. In Spain the eminent Talmudist Jonah Gerondi (12–13 c.) wrote penitential tracts which were very influential, in which the ascetic motif is strongly accented. He defines twenty requirements or degrees in repentance, comprising a severe regimen in which great emphasis is laid on the element of sorrow and grief, fasting and weeping, shame and self-humiliation. One should keep his sins as well as the thought of death constantly before him.[77]

There is still another time in medieval Jewish history which is remarkable by virtue of its ascetic pietism. It is the period following the expulsions of the Jews from Spain and Portugal at the close of the fifteenth century. The hundreds of thousands of exiles suffered harrowing experiences before they reestablished themselves in other lands, and these experiences left deep scars on their souls. Homelessness, persecution, a shattered pride, and a sense of guilt induced by the expulsion, which many looked upon as divine punishment for the sins of Spanish-Portuguese Jewry, all contributed to a mood of depression.

The learned among them turned to the mystic lore of cabala as to a well of salvation. They became especially attached to a passionate study of the Zohar (13 c.). Through its mysterious landscapes they moved toward wild shores of fantasy and rapture. In it was to be found the key to the mystery of the exact time of the Messiah's coming. The mere study of the Zohar was of such merit as to hasten his coming.

Common people took to midnight vigils of devotion and prayer and to penitential disciplines and fasting as ways of expiation and propitiation.

The most dramatic center of this austerity at the time of Jewry's sixteenth century diaspora was the city of Safed in Palestine. There a community of a thousand families, composed principally of refugees from Spain and Portugal, came to constitute "a revival camp in permanence." [78] It is to be noted that mass revivalism as a technique for "conversion" is not congenial to the spirit of Judaism, and was a rare phenomenon in Jewish life except in times of Messianic expectations. In Safed were concentrated many of the foremost Talmudic scholars of the age and its most famous mystics. Scholar and mystic alike united in an ascetic exercise unprecedented for intensity in all Jewish history save among the medieval Ḥasidim. The life of the community was steeped in the occult and the thaumaturgic. Men trained themselves in purification to ride through successive stations of ascent (*darga*; among the Sufis of Islam, *maqām*) to a spiritual eminence where they would be privileged to receive the Holy Spirit, a visit from some heavenly mentor (*Maggid*) or perhaps even from Elijah himself.

A formula for the degrees of such ascent into ideality is already suggested in the Talmud and is attributed to R. Phineas b. Yair: "Torah leads to watchfulness, watchfulness to zeal, zeal to cleanness, cleanness to abstinence [*Perishut*], abstinence to purity, purity to saintliness [*Ḥasidut*], saintliness to humility, humility to the fear of sin, and the fear of sin to holiness." [79]

Men organized themselves into coteries in order to encourage one another in saintly living, in ascetic practices, and in confessing their sins one to another—the latter also a novel and unorthodox practice among Jews. They arose while it was yet night to study and pray. Sitting on the bare ground, and dressed in black, they mourned for the destruction of the Temple and for their sins and for the sins of the world which delay the hour of redemption. They fasted long and frequently. Some fasted continuously for three days at each turn of the four seasons of the year. Others fasted every day of the week from sunrise to sundown, and in sackcloth and ashes recited their *Minḥa* (afternoon) prayers—a most propitious time for supplication [80]—accompanied by flagellation. Others fasted twice a week, day and night, and still others three times a week.[81]

In this and similar ways did Safed's "men of action" (*Anshe Ma'ase*—Wonder Workers) storm the gates of heaven. They were deeply earnest men in the grip of the urgency of an ominous hour. In prayer shawls and phylacteries men visited the graves of famous Rabbis and prayed for the redemption of Israel.[82] They prayed for martyrdom, that their sins might be burned away and that they would be found pure and cleansed when the Great Day dawned. This yearning for martyrdom was quite an alien and unsanctioned note in Judaism. R. Jacob Berab (d. 1545) undertook to reestablish the institution of Ordination (*Smichah*) which is a necessary step leading to the reorganization of the Sanhedrin, in preparation for the coming of the Messiah.

The spirit of Safed pervaded other Jewish communities in the sixteenth and seventeenth centuries. The mystic literature of the Luria group found its way into the lands of the diaspora and influenced the works of many popular writers on religion and ethics.

The most eloquent and artistic literary expression of this spirit of the age is to be found in *Mesillat Yesharim* (The Path of the Upright), one of the most popular ethical treatises in all Jewish literature and one of the most beautiful and exalted. It is the work of a rare genius, a mystic and poet—Moses Ḥayim Luzzatto of Padua (1707–1746). In structure, it follows the formula for the degrees of spiritual self improvement of R. Phineas b. Yair referred to above.

Luzzatto first sets forth what a man must do to be righteous, and then proceeds to set forth what a man should do to be holy.[83] "True abstinence means making use only of those things that some natural demand has rendered indispensable." [84] It is true that our sages have prescribed only such laws as the majority of the people can obey, and the majority of the people cannot be saints. It is enough that they are pious. The few, however, who desire to earn the privilege of being near to God, and by their own merit to impute merit to the mass of the people spiritually dependent upon them, must live by that saintly code to which the average person cannot be expected to conform.[85]

Here Luzzatto follows Baḥya. He urges upon the spiritual aristocracy who wish to cultivate abstinence "to keep away not only from anything which is definitely forbidden but also from everything that is under the least suspicion of being forbidden."[86] A man should keep aloof from society, and "not look beyond his four cubits."[87] He will thus come to ignore and disdain all the pleasures of life.[88] Solitude is the best method of acquiring the trait of utter abstinence.[89] A man should always seek to do more than is required of him by the Law. "We can always devise new ways of giving joy to our Creator if we consider what we should do under similar circumstances for a person whom we love."[90] "A lover welcomes every opportunity to prove to his beloved the ardor of his devotion."[91]

But the reaction against these tendencies toward varieties of asceticism among Jews was bound to set in, for they were not, at heart, native or intrinsically Jewish. Bruised spirits in dark hours might give way to them. The life-loving and optimistic spirit of Judaism was certain to resist them. From occasional straying into alien ways, the people always returned to its own classic highway—the strong affirmation of life, and the ideal of moderation in all things which nourish and sustain it.

A new conception of the mystic's quest for holiness came with the later Ḥasidic movement which was founded by Israel Ba'al Shem Ṭov (the *Ba'al Shem* or *Besht*) in eastern Europe in the early part of the eighteenth century. Here the emphasis was on ecstasy of another kind—the *joyous* service of God. "Serve the Lord with gladness; come before Him with singing" (Ps. 100:2). This, to be sure, was not a new note in Judaism; it was in fact a dominant keynote. But in exile many Jews in the bitterness of their lives had forgotten it. In Ḥasidism it was stressed more assertively and more deliberately in worship and in daily life than ever before. The Ḥasidim often referred to the Biblical verse: "Because you did not serve the Lord your God with joyfulness and gladness of heart . . . therefore you shall serve your enemies" (Dt. 28:47). The true service of God must be one of joy and gladness. It must glow like a flame.

The mood of the Ḥasidim was not that of guilt-haunted men obsessed with a conviction of sin, tortured with contrition, awaiting dread judgment when their probationary days on this melancholy earth would be ended. Rather was it the mood of happy pilgrims who, along the many paths of the festive heart, were approaching their God, Whose glory and goodness fill every corner of the universe. To them the promise had been given: "You shall have a song as in the night when a holy feast is kept; and gladness of heart, as when one sets out to the sound of the flute to go to the mountain of the Lord, to the Rock of Israel" (Is. 30:29).

When Ba'al Shem learned that his pupil and disciple Jacob Joseph Ha-Kohen was given to excessive fasting and self-mortification because of his absorption in Lurianic doctrine and practice, he wrote to him and admonished him to desist forthwith. Such practices must lead to melancholy and sadness. He reminded him of what had been frequently taught,[92] that the *Shechinah* (the Divine Presence) does not rest upon a man when he is depressed, but only when he is in a joyous mood consequent upon the performance of a *mizvah* (a commandment).[93] "Do not hide yourself from your own flesh" (Is. 58:7), he counseled him, employing a bold and neat play on words.

"Joy atones for the sins of men for it comes from the World on High," declared R. Phineas Shapiro of Koretz [94]—a startling contrast to the well known Rabbinic dictum: "Suffering atones for the sins of men." R. Moses Leib of Sassov said: "Joy is of a higher degree than tears. Since the destruction of the Temple, according to the Rabbis, all the gates of heaven are closed except the gates of tears. But joy breaks through all gates and all partitions." [95]

R. Baruch of Mezebob, the grandson of the Ba'al Shem, records the answer given by his grandfather to the question which was put to him on fasting as a way of serving God:

I am come into the world to show another way. A man should take into his heart three things: the love of God, the love of Israel, and the love of the Torah. He does not need to engage in ascetic practices. It is sufficient for the average man to understand that in all things, physical and material, there is holiness.[96]

Sadness is not a sin, R. Aaron of Karlin declared; but the greatest of sins cannot cause as much deadening of the heart as sadness. A Jew who is not at all times happy in the fact that he is a Jew is guilty of ingratitude towards God.[97]

The Ḥasidim were not religious dissenters. They were not reformers of faith, doctrine, or law. They were not opponents of Rabbinism, though they often found themselves in conflict with Rabbinic authorities. They did not, as some have maintained, revolt against the overlordship of autocratic community leaders, lay or cleric. They did not aim to correct any widespread moral laxity among the people. They were mystic enthusiasts who walked the "Path of the Upright," who climbed the stations of Phineas b. Yair to higher levels, not dejectedly as if to some solemn obsequies, but exaltedly, with song and dance, as if to a banqueting hall. They accepted without question all the laws and disciplines of the Torah and the Talmud, but their chief concern was with inwardness, the inner life, the inner light, the intuitions of the heart. "God puts in requisition the heart of man." They did not deprecate—nay, they held in high esteem— Talmudic study and scholarship. Some of their own leaders were themselves noted scholars and Talmudic authorities, but they emphasized worship, devout and ecstatic prayer, wherein the soul of man is exercised and stirred to its profoundest depths, and by means of which, man rises to higher transcendental consciousness, to ineffable eminence in a world of unknown dimensions wherein is the radiance of the Divine.

The Messianic motif is, of course, present in the doctrine of Ḥasidism, but it is not as overwhelming as it was with the earlier

Ḥasidim of medieval Germany. This may, in a measure, account for its attitude toward asceticism which always attends climactic Messianic expectations. The Ḥasidim were all cabalistically minded, but here again the study of the cabala was secondary to the way of joyous piety which they pursued.

The Ḥasidic circles which were grouped around a preceptor, a Ẓaddik, were very much like the mystic circles and fraternities of Safed or those which Luzzatto and others founded. But their way of life was not the latter's sunless and lugubrious one. Their brotherhood was welded close together by the personality of the Ẓaddik, by the communion meal which the members were privileged to share with their saintly leader, and by the joy of group dancing and singing of glad and gladdening hearts in a rhapsody of fellowship and faith.

Ḥasidism captivated and attracted large sections of the people. For a time it embraced the majority of the Jews of eastern Europe. Its appeal was especially powerful among the humble and nameless, among whom such movements commonly arise. The message of its leaders was, in many instances, deliberately pitched at a lower level and used great simplicity of thought and expression, in order to reach the mind and heart of the common man. Though not deliberately intended as a "revivalist" movement, it had that kind of powerful impact upon the masses. In a shattered and depressed Jewish world, which was just recovering from the horrible Chmielnicki-led Cossack massacres, the Russian war in Poland, and the Swedish invasion, and in the wake of the spiritual desolation left by the appalling Shabbetai Ẓevi Messianic fiasco, Ḥasidism summoned men to a resurgence of faith and hope. Its confident call to an outpouring of love for God and man, for Torah and Israel, to song and ecstasy in a new blossoming springtime of miracle and grace, came as a draught of cool, refreshing water to parched souls.

As in all such movements, the original impulse spent itself after a time and the fresh waters in many places became stagnant in obscurantism and imposture, in miracle mongering, in the apotheosis of the Ẓaddik and in dynastic rivalries. But its original inspiration never quite disappeared.

Ḥasidism succeeded in banishing the mood of joyless asceticism which had characterized some earlier mystic movements and
which had pervaded sections of world Jewry. In so doing it
exercised a salutary, corrective influence in Jewish religious life.

Broadly surveying the field of ascetic trends in Jewish history,
one is justified in concluding that though they were certainly not
absent, especially in periods of stress, despair, and Messianic
expectancy, they were never major trends and did not prove
decisive for Judaism. The over-all and dominant position of
Judaism on the subject was that which Maimonides summed up
in his great Code:

Perhaps a man will say: inasmuch as jealousy, passion, love of
honor, and similar desires are evil and bring about a man's downfall,
therefore I will remove myself from them to the other extreme
where I will refrain from eating meat or drinking wine or marrying
or living in a pleasant dwelling place or wearing an attractive garment—nothing but sackcloth and coarse wool—just as the Gentile
priests do. This is an evil way and is forbidden! He who follows
these practices is called a sinner! . . . Concerning all these and similar matters, Solomon declared: "Be not righteous over much and do
not make thyself over-wise—why shouldest thou destroy thyself?" [98]

In his Introduction to Abot, Chapter 4, Maimonides discusses
extensively the subject of asceticism. He contends that the Torah
has already prescribed sufficient rules to curb men's appetites and
that no more are required, except in those rare cases where
drastic psychic medicine is called for. He characterizes as per-
fectly wonderful the statement of R. Dimi quoted elsewhere:
"Are not the prohibitions of the Torah sufficient for you, that
you must look for additional prohibitions?" Maimonides suggests that the ascetic trends among Jews were imitations of
non-Jews.
In his *Guide* Maimonides maintains that the Torah is reasonable, and makes no excessive demands on man:

The statutes of the Law do not impose burdens or excesses such as
are implied in the service of a hermit or pilgrim, and the like. . . .

There are persons who believe that the Law commands much exertion and great pain, but due consideration will show them their error.[99]

In a similar vein and somewhat earlier did the foremost Hebrew poet of the Middle Ages, Judah Halevi (11–12 c.), who was not a rationalist like Maimonides, define the position of Judaism on the subject of asceticism. The Rabbi (Ḥaber) who is the spokesman of traditional Judaism before the King of the Khazars is under the necessity of drawing a clear distinction between his own faith and that of Christianity and Islam, and of defending it against hostile philosophies, as well as against Jewish sectaries. In the course of his presentation, the Rabbi had contended that Israel among the nations was like the heart among the organs of the body, the most sensitive to illness and at the same time the most healthy. The diseases are the sins to which Israel is exposed because of its inclination to imitate the Gentiles. Health is restored through repentance and God's forgiveness. Israel is now suffering in exile, while the rest of the world is at rest, in order that it might be purged of its dross, purified, so that the whole world might ultimately, through it, come to enjoy the Divine Essence.

Well, argues the King, we should then be seeing among you more hermits and those who practice asceticism than among other people! No, replies the Rabbi. Man cannot approach God except through the performance of the commandments ordained by Him.

The divine law imposes no asceticism on us. It rather desires that we should keep the equipoise, and grant every mental and physical faculty its due, as much as it can bear, without ever burdening one faculty at the expense of another. . . . Prolonged fasting is not an act of piety. . . . Neither is diminution of wealth an act of piety, if it is gained in a lawful way, and if its acquisition does not interfere with study and good works, especially for him who has a household and children. He may spend part of it in almsgiving, which would not be displeasing to God. . . . Your contrition on a fast day does not bring you nearer to God than your joy on the Sabbath and holy days, if it is the outcome of a devout heart.[100]

The King of the Khazars is evidently convinced. "A religion of this kind can do without ascetics or monastic retirement."[101]

While it refused to build its religious edifice upon the sadness and futility of life, Judaism fully understood the rôle of pain and suffering in the unfoldment of human life and, at times, in the development of character. It did not shut its eyes to the widespread suffering, physical and spiritual, in the world, or declare it to be an illusion. But it maintained that the suffering encountered in life can be made a spiritual discipline and a source of increased power. Suffering should not be sought out as something desirable, but when it is inexorable it should be accepted, whether merited or unmerited, without resentment, bitterness, or rebellion. It should be confronted with courage and dignity.[102] "I found trouble and sorrow, but I called upon the name of the Lord" (Ps. 116:3-4). There is no human life without suffering. No one enjoys a lifelong wayfaring of unbroken serenity. But suffering need not destroy a man. It may help to build his character and exalt him. If accepted, it may prove to be "God's chastenings of love" (*yesurim shel ahabah*) and an altar of atonement.[103] "Him whom God loves, He chastises as a father the son in whom he delights" (Pr. 3:12). "Whatsoever is brought upon you take cheerfully, and be patient when you are changed to a low estate. For gold is tried by fire, and acceptable men in the furnace of adversity" (Ecclus. 2:4-5). Suffering can purge the human soul of pride and teach man compassion and humility. In this sense, "suffering is precious" (*habibim yesurim*).[104]

But suffering is not a virtue in itself. It is not the key to the mystery of life. To court poverty and persecution is frequently the sign of a neurosis. If at the behest of a great devotion, a man, knowing suffering and sacrifice to be unavoidable, nevertheless does not abandon his cause, his merit is very great. But in such a drama of the human soul it is character that is exalted in its invincibility, not suffering. The man whose life is free from undue suffering and whose heart has few grievous loads to bear is, however, blessed. One can become a Ẓaddiḳ, a righteous man, a Ḥasid, a pious man, even a Ḳadosh, a saintly man, without being rent and riven by pain and tragedy. They are not prerequisites of greatness.

The martyr in Judaism was highly revered because "he sanctified the Name." One need not, however, be put to death in order to be accorded the honor of being included among those who sanctify the Name. By a life of nobility and selfless service of God one can merit this title. He who avoids sin, wrote Maimonides, and performs the commandments from no ulterior motive, nor out of fear or cowardice, nor for the sake of glory, but solely for the sake of God, sanctifies the name of God. The man whose dealings with all his fellow men are honorable, who is amiable and friendly, whose speech is kindly, who tolerates an offense against himself rather than offend others, who is respectful of those who are discourteous to him, who does not insist on the strict letter of the law in his claim upon his fellowmen, who pursues his studies out of love and devotion, without isolating himself from his fellow man, he, too, is among those who sanctify the name of God, and of him it is said, "You are My servant, Israel, in whom I will be glorified" (Is. 49:3).[105]

Pain is not the only soil in which human adequacy or greatness can grow. For many people suffering is a shattering and undermining experience. It does not strengthen, it weakens their moral fiber. One need not be broken and tortured to discover the goodness and love of God. R. Johanan b. Napaha (3 c.), in the midst of great suffering, was comforted by his colleagues with the words, "Precious is suffering for its rewards are many." He replied, "We would rather get along without the suffering and without its rewards." [106] One should not force the crown of martyrdom. Greater by far than holiness achieved through one's own suffering is responsiveness to the suffering of other men. That is compassion, one of the profoundest and noblest teachings of Judaism. To share suffering and by so doing to lessen and alleviate it—to be "hurt . . . for the hurt of the daughter of my people" (Jer. 8:21)—that is the ultimate stadium in man's spiritual progress.

Judaism views poverty as it views suffering. It is not to be sought voluntarily for the salvation of one's soul or to please

God. But if a man is poor, he need not be crushed by that fact. Some of the greatest teachers of the Talmud—Hillel, R. Joshua and R. Judah—rose from extreme poverty to the highest positions of leadership among their people. In order to obtain proficiency in the study of the Torah students are counseled to be content with a morsel of bread, a measure of water, to sleep on the ground, and to endure privation.[107] But poverty, like suffering, is not desirable for its own sake, and man should not knowingly invite it. It is not necessary to reduce life to rude and savage simplicity in order to acquire either wisdom or happiness or "salvation." The shoddy cloak, the wallet and stick are not the true symbols of the good life of nobility and quest. Wealth in itself is not evil. "You will find that there are riches that harm certain people while other people are benefited by them." [108] Poverty as a social evil must be eradicated. This is a prophetic summons. No great civilization has ever been reared on the foundations of penury and want.

It is, of course, easier for the man who is free from an overwhelming absorption in material pursuits, from the fever of hoarding and amassing excessive wealth, to reach the higher levels of mind and spirit. But it is not easier for the man who is burdened with a crushing load of dependence, privation and care for himself and for his loved ones. Wealth may cause a man to forget God. "Take heed lest, when you have eaten and are full, and have built goodly houses and live in them and when your herds and flocks multiply and your silver and gold is multiplied, and all that you have is multiplied, that your heart be lifted up, and you forget the Lord your God . . ." (Dt. 8:11–14). It is not wise for a man to spend himself and consume his life in pursuit of wealth. "Do not weary yourself to acquire wealth; be wise enough to desist" (Pr. 23:4). There are greater goods in life—the greatest of them is the nearness of God (Ps. 73:25) and the delight in His statutes (Ps. 119:14). Wealth indeed has its pitfalls, but so has poverty. Sordid poverty, too, can coarsen a man. Want and spiritual independence are by no means synonymous. The poor man is not always free; the rich man is not always the slave. "Poverty in a man's home is worse than fifty plagues." [109] Crushing poverty is one of the three things which deprive man of his senses and of a knowledge of his Creator. Such a man will never see the face of Gehenna, since he has already had his on earth. [110]

Wise and noble is the prayer of Agur: "Give me neither poverty nor riches; feed me with the food that is needful to me, lest I be full and deny Thee and say, 'Who is the Lord?', or lest I be poor and steal, and profane the name of my God" (Pr. 30:8–9).

Life is good and a gracious gift of God. Man should enjoy it in all ways which do not transgress the moral law and which do not impair his spiritual growth. The highest joy is the *simḥa shel mizvah*—the joy of a good deed.

The Zohar declares: "When the High Priest was to appear before God in the Sanctuary, he was to enter that holy place with joy, and all things about him were to express joy—for in God's service there is no room for sadness." [111]

One should not experience any sense of guilt in the legitimate enjoyments of life. They are of God. Man can worship God with his total being—with body, mind, and soul.

Basing himself on the wording of the Creation story in Genesis I, R. Naḥman, the son of R. Samuel, commented: "Behold, it was very good," refers to the good desire or natural impulse (*Yezer Ha-Ṭob*); and "Behold, it was very good," to the evil desire (*Yezer Ha-R'a*). Can then the evil desire be very good? But for the evil desire, no man would build a house, take a wife, and beget children. [112] "To love the Lord with all your heart" (Dt. 6:5) means to love Him with both your inclinations, the good and the evil. [113]

This thought too is developed in the Zohar:

When God came to create the world and reveal what was hidden in the depths and disclose light out of darkness, they were all wrapped in one another, and therefore, light emerged from darkness, and from the impenetrable came forth the profound. So, too, from good issues evil and from mercy issues judgment, and all are intertwined, the good impulse and the evil impulse, right and left, Israel and other peoples, white and black—all depend on one another.[114]

Body and soul depend on each other. The body is not to be charged with all sin and the soul credited with all virtue.

To what may this be compared? To a king who owned a beautiful orchard which contained splendid figs. Now he appointed two watchmen therein, one lame and the other blind. One day the lame man said to the blind: I see beautiful figs in the orchard. Come and take me upon your shoulder, that we may both eat them. Some time after, the owner of the orchard came and inquired of them: Where are those beautiful figs? The lame man replied: Have I then feet to walk with? The blind man replied: Have I then eyes to see with? What did the owner do? He placed the lame upon the blind and judged them both together.[115]

In the basic thought of Judaism, good and evil are not cosmic forces in eternal conflict, wherein one must destroy the other. They are complementary attributes of God's creation, which are reconciled in the wisdom of God.[116]

Man should avail himself of every opportunity for enjoyment and happiness. One need not and should not renounce what is lawful. Food and drink are given by God to man to sustain life. "Thou preparest a table before me, Thou anointest my head with oil, my cup runneth over" (Ps. 23:5). It was with the gifts of the good earth that Isaac blessed his son Jacob: "May God give you of the dew of heaven, and of the fatness of the earth, and plenty of grain and wine" (Gen. 27:28). One should partake of the gifts of God in gladness and bless Him for His bounty. "Blessed art Thou, O Lord," a man should recite, for bread and wine, for fruit and oil, for spices and fragrant plants, and on seeing a beautiful tree or a rainbow, and for all the goodness and beauty and joy that are in the world. The last of the joyous blessings pronounced at every wedding ceremony rings with exultation: "Blessed art Thou, O Lord our God, King of the Universe Who hast created joy and gladness, bridegroom and bride, mirth and exultation, pleasure and delight, love, brotherliness, peace and friendliness. . . ."

God's world is unutterably beautiful. "The heavens declare the glory of God and the firmament proclaims His handiwork" (Ps. 19:1). R. Judah declared:

In the spring when a man goes forth and sees beautiful trees swaying in the air, he should stop and offer a prayer: "Blessed is the Lord for having created a world in which nothing is wanting and for having fashioned living things and beautiful trees and plants to delight the heart of man." [117]

No literature of any people of antiquity is so rich in the awareness and appreciation of the majestic grandeur of nature as the literature of Israel. One is aware of a strange dearth of exalted nature poetry among the ancients, even among the Greeks. Greek culture was a product of city life. Architecture, sculpture, drama, and philosophy were its supreme expressions. The Greeks saw many things clearly. They looked deep into the troubled heart of man. They speculated much about the true way to human happiness. They thought profoundly about the structure of their city states and the obligations of citizenship. In their literature they celebrated the great deeds of heroes, gods, and men. Somehow, the Greeks did not lift up their eyes to the mountains—the mountains which were all around them. They worshiped many nature deities, sky and earth, sun and moon, river and sea, and the elemental forces of nature. But these were powerful and without mercy and not at all interested in the aspiring life of man. They did not nurture man's optimism. The Greeks thought much about nature, but they had in mind the operation of nature's inexorable laws, not the lyric beauty of a world which "day to day pours forth speech, and night to night declares knowledge" (Ps. 19:2), a world where "all the trees, as it were, converse with each other. They converse with mankind. All the trees were created for the enjoyment of man." [118]

The Greeks never really ceased to fear nature. They never transcended an attitude of sacramental awe toward it. Their poetry was thought contemplating nature, not life eagerly embracing it in the ecstasy of confidence and joy. The ancients, remarked Santayana, in writing of Lucretius, were not particularly poets of landscape. "Still nature is rarely presented to our view" in the Iliad of Homer, writes George Soutar:

In Greek poetry we find no forest-sentiment. Hesiod did not treat of trees. Homer has little flower sense. Homer does not indulge in mountain descriptions or in mountain sentiment. . . . Of the belief in the power of nature to comfort the heart, to subdue the passions, and to speak peace to the souls of men we find no trace in Greek poetry.[119]

Professor Butcher calls attention to the gradual change which took place in later times, especially in the Alexandrian Age, as the belief in the old mythology began to crumble away and "the human form no longer projected itself across the whole field of vision." [120] He believes that the first cause "which prepared the way for a new view of nature was the dissolution of the ancient polytheistic creed." [121]

The Greeks told a story with deep probing and insight. They never sang a faith exultingly. They could not sing: "O Lord, how manifold are Thy works! In wisdom hast Thou made them all; the earth is full of Thy handiwork" (Ps. 104:24). In Judaism's vision, behind all nature and in all nature there was a living, loving God, and in the Temple of His world all of nature's voices could be raised in one exalted rhapsody: "Let the sea roar and the fulness thereof, the earth and those who dwell in it! Let the floods clap their hands; let the hills sing for joy together, before the Lord, for He comes to rule the earth" (Ps. 98:7–9). It may well be that only a fervid monotheistic faith in a personal God of goodness can yield great lyrical nature poetry, the majestic orchestration of a doxology to God the Creator of all. Nowhere in ancient literature does one find anything comparable to the enraptured contemplation of creation which one finds in the Bible, in the Book of Job (Chaps. 38–41), for example, or in the exalted nature Psalms,[122] or the exquisite nature vignettes of the Song of Songs, or Ben Sira's descriptions of the beauty of the world (Ecclus. 43), or the exultant Benedicite of *The Song of the Three Children*.[123] The Jewish spirit was enthralled with the pageant of life, with the breathless panorama of nature, in whose glowing splendor Judaism saw God Who created all beauty to gladden the heart of man, so that the human heart could cry out: "I will sing to the Lord as long as I live" (Ps. 104:33).

Worship in Israel was song. The darkness of life was of course there too, and the shadow of death, the vast sorrows and tribulations, the tears, the wrongs, the anguish, and the many broken hopes of mortal man. But the spirit of man was taught not to be utterly cast down. "Hope in God!" (Ps. 42:6). The human heart should deeply feel that God will at last wipe away all tears. "Weeping may tarry for the night but joy comes in the morning" (Ps. 30:6).

Let man therefore enjoy his life on earth.

The wise physician of the body and soul, Ben Sira (3 c. B.C.), writes: "Defraud not thyself of the good day, and let not the part of a good desire pass thee by, for there is no seeking of the dainties in the grave" (Ecclus. 14:14).

Rab, who together with Samuel established the leading academies in Babylonia and made it a center of Rabbinic studies, is quoted as saying: "A man will some day have to give an account to God for all the good things which his eyes beheld and of which he refused to partake." [124] He also said to his disciple R. Hamuna, "My son, according to your ability do good to yourself, for there is no enjoyment in the netherworld, nor will death be long in coming." [125] It was Rab too who composed the beautiful prayer which is incorporated in the Prayer Book and is recited on the Sabbaths ushering in the new months:

May it be Thy will, O Lord our God, and God of our fathers, to renew unto us this coming month for good and for blessing. O grant unto us long life, a life of peace, of good, of blessing, of bodily vigor, a life marked by the reverence of God and the fear of sin, a life free from shame and reproach, a life of prosperity and honor, a life in which the love of the Law and the fear of Heaven shall cleave to us, a life in which the desires of our heart shall be fulfilled for good. Amen.

⊸(XII)⊷

THAT MEN ARE NOT EQUAL

The truths which the Founding Fathers of the American Republic held to be "self-evident"—"that all men are created equal and that they are endowed by their Creator with certain unalienable rights"—were never really self-evident to any important section of mankind at any time. On the contrary—they always appeared as supremely unorthodox and radical ideas which had to fight their way in the world against deeply rooted religious and metaphysical conceptions, against vested interests and powers, against pseudoscientific biologic theories, and against all forms of rationalization.

Many of the peoples of antiquity constituted completely stratified societies, though the "racialism" which the Western World of the nineteenth and twentieth centuries came to know, whose radiational "fall-out" led to gas chambers and genocide, was not as homicidally articulated among them. The caste system of India is ancient—nearly three thousand years old. It probably began when the Aryan invaders conquered India and subjugated the indigenous population, reducing it to slavery. Conqueror and conquered belonged to different races. The conqueror asserted the superiority of his race, and the conquered had to accept the status of an inferior race. Religion soon sanctioned this distinction and declared these differences to be divinely ordained, irrevocable and eternal. Caste thus became religious custom and law.

India developed the caste system in its most detailed and comprehensive form. From a basic four-caste system of priests, nobles, cultivators-artisans, and serfs, it soon proceeded by a process of fission to subdivide itself into some eight hundred castes. The higher castes were composed, of course, of the élite, the privileged, the "twice born." The lowest castes were composed of the contaminated, the "untouchables." A low-caste man dared not even approach the Brahman. The chasms which separated men were impassable. To break the bonds of caste was accounted as the unpardonable sin.

Buddhism, which arose in India in the sixth century before the common era, opposed this caste system, and taught a gospel of human equality; but the caste system has survived among the hundreds of millions of Hindus to this day, and Buddhism lost its foothold among them. It is only in recent years that a real beginning has been made to eradicate caste demarcations in India.

Ancient Rome divided its population into patricians, plebeians, and slaves. Organized for war and continuously engaged in war, Rome needed a large slave population to provide food and to do the work of its own citizens who were away fighting, or who preferred a life of ease at home. It has been estimated that in the beginning of the common era there were probably twenty million slaves in the Roman Empire, three slaves to every free inhabitant.

Citizenship in the Roman Empire was restricted. It was not until the days of Caracalla in the third century of the common era that the right of citizenship was extended to all free men in the Empire.

In the Middle Ages there was the widespread serfdom under feudalism, and a classified, rigidly stratified society in which nobleman and priest possessed privileges which were denied to peasants and serfs.

With the emergence of the middle class in Europe in the seventeenth and eighteenth centuries, the need was felt for a theory to justify its claims to equality with the privileged estates, and to free it from feudal, clerical, and monarchical

restrictions. This was found in what has come to be known as
"Natural Rights," a theory ably propounded by the Englishman
John Locke, and by the Frenchman Jean Jacques Rousseau.
According to this view, no class possesses rights on the basis of
status. Human rights are rooted in the very nature of man. All
men are equal. There is no hierarchy of political privilege. These
ideas played a powerful rôle in the American and French revolu-
tions.

In addition to the rigid systems of caste and class which they
applied to their own societies, many peoples of the ancient world
also entertained notions of natural or racial superiority vis-à-vis
other peoples. Greece, at its classical summit, in the fifth and
fourth centuries before the common era, was racially sharply
exclusive. The Greeks regarded themselves superior to all other
peoples, whom they called "barbarians."

The theory of the inferiority of the barbarians became accentuated
during and after the Persian Wars. In the fourth century it was a
dogma that was accepted throughout the Greek world and one
which was firmly held by men like Aristotle and Isocrates. In the
eyes of the Greeks the barbarians were not only foreigners, but inferior beings; between Greek and barbarian, says Isocrates, there is
no less difference than between man and beast.[1]

This in spite of the fact that in another connection, in praising
Athens for the cultivation of the art of speech, Isocrates eloquently declared that "she has brought it about that the name
'Hellenes' suggests no longer a race but an intelligence, and that
the title 'Hellenes' is applied rather to those who share our culture than to those who share a common blood." [2] This was de-
clamatory rhetoric. Isocrates almost invariably characterizes the
non-Hellene as a barbarian and speaks of him with contempt.[3]
Because they felt themselves superior, they claimed rights over
other peoples. Thus the great Greek dramatist Euripides declared: "It accords with the fitness of things that barbarians
should be subject to Greeks, for Greeks are free men and
barbarians are slaves by nature." [4]

It was only later in the Hellenistic age, when it became necessary to integrate and maintain a widely diffused Greco-Oriental empire, that it was deemed wise to blend as far as possible the many races and peoples in the new Asiatic and African *Lebensraum* of the Greek and Macedonian colonists and to create a common culture. It was then that Greek exclusiveness slowly gave way to a broader and more tolerant view, to a wider cosmopolitan outlook, and to the conception of the unity of mankind. Zeno (4–3 c. B.C.), founder of Stoicism, himself a Hellenistic Semite, is an outstanding forerunner of this new cosmopolitanism.

The Athenians had a fierce pride of race. They held themselves not alone superior to the barbarians who were "their natural enemies," but boasted superiority over all other Greeks because of their unadulterated blood. In *Menexenus*, ascribed to Plato, Socrates delivers himself of the following panegyric on Athens and its citizens:

Such was the natural nobility of this city, so sound and healthy was the spirit of freedom among us, and the instinctive dislike of the barbarian, because we are pure Hellenes, having no admixture of barbarism in us. For we are not like many others, descendants of Pelops or Cadmus or Egyptus or Danaus, who are by nature barbarians, and yet pass for Hellenes, and dwell in the midst of us; but we are pure Hellenes, uncontaminated by any foreign element.[5]

Judaism rejected all the caste and race ideologies of the ancient world. Hierarchy has been called an Aryan concept. It is certainly not a Jewish concept. Judaism defied all notions of inherent racial and national superiorities. The prophet Amos made it unmistakably clear to his people: "Are you not like the Ethiopians to me, O people of Israel? says the Lord. Did I not bring up Israel from the land of Egypt and the Philistines from Caphtor and the Syrians from Kir?" (Amos 9:7.) The implications of this verse can be fully grasped only if we recall that the Philistines and Syrians were the traditional enemies of Israel, and the Ethiopians were universally despised. Nevertheless the prophet tells his nation that Yahweh is also the God of those nations, that He guides their destinies as well, and in His sight they and Israel are alike. In the day of the universal healing of the nations, "Israel will be the third with Egypt and Assyria, a blessing in the midst of the earth, whom the Lord of hosts has blessed, saying, 'Blessed be Egypt *My people*, and Assyria *the work of My hands*, and Israel My heritage" (Is. 19:24-25). Here again it should be recalled that Egypt had been the "iron cauldron" of Israel's servitude for centuries, and Assyria had destroyed the Northern Kingdom of Israel. As regards the origin of Israel, the prophet Ezekiel sharply reminds his people: "Your origin and your birth are of the land of the Canaanites; your father was an Amorite and your mother a Hittite" (Ezek. 16:3).

Israel entertained no pride of blood. Israel was "chosen" not because of any "natural nobility" or purity of stock. The people of Israel were not descended from the gods; they were not of celestial origin—a common conceit of many of the nations of antiquity. When an Israelite brought his basket of first fruits to the sanctuary of God as an offering, he began his prayer with the humble confession that his father was "a wandering Aramean" (Dt. 26:5).

In creating Adam, reads one of the legends of the Rabbis, God took dust from the four corners of the earth, and the dust was of various colors—red and black and white—to indicate the essential unity of all mankind.[6]

Judaism regarded Israel as a "chosen people," a "holy people," not because every member was assumed to be holy and morally immaculate, or because the race itself was regarded as divine—as Shintoism conceives of the Japanese race, or as the Teutonic racialists from Fichte to Hitler conceived of their race. Judaism opposed the race myth even as it opposed the nature myth. It tolerated no doctrine of racial superiority or exclusiveness. Its teachers were interested in keeping pure not their race but their religion. Israel was a "holy people" in respect to the object which it was to serve—to increase holiness in the world—and in the sense of being "separate" and "distinct" from heathen peoples and their heathen ways. Concerning the Biblical exhortation, "And ye shall be holy men unto Me" (Ex. 22:30), R. Ishmael (1–2 c.) says: "*If you are holy then you are Mine.*" [7]

"Holiness" is not an accolade of self-glorification but a hard discipline of self-purification. It was never assumed that the people of Israel were beyond sin and transgression. God does not effect His purposes through perfect men or perfect nations. There are none. The Prophets and Sages denounced Israel again and again for their sins and for their apostasy and backsliding. "Know therefore, that the Lord your God is not giving you this land to possess because of your righteousness; for you are a stubborn people" (Dt. 9:6). How often they provoked the Lord! "You have been rebellious against the Lord from the day that I knew you," Moses chided them (Dt. 9:24), and he feared that they would be even more rebellious after his death (Dt. 31:27). For their sins the people of Israel were severely punished and corrected but never abandoned. "Yet for all that, when they are in the land of their enemies, I will not spurn them, neither will I abhor them so as to destroy them utterly and break my covenant with them" (Lev. 26:44; Jer. 31:35–37). Nor was Israel ever relieved of its assigned mission, or of its obligations under the covenant. "I will make you pass under the rod and I will restore you to the bond of this covenant. And I will purge out from among you the rebels" (Ezek. 20:32, 37–38). Therefore "even though the people have sinned, it is still called Israel. . . . A myrtle, though it stands among the reeds, is still a myrtle, and it is so called." [8]

Christianity challenged the Jewish claim of being the "chosen people," not on the ground that the doctrine of election was in principle invalid, but that Israel, though originally elected, had by its sins forfeited that privilege and its place was now taken by the Church. The Church now claimed to be the true Israel, "Israel after the spirit," the heir of election. The Church came to speak of itself as the "Holy Church," and claimed for its members an especial grace. Its members, having received the Spirit, were frequently referred to as "the sons of God," "the first-born among many brethren" (Rom. 8:14-19; John 1:12), and the "Chosen People." "But you are a chosen race, a royal priesthood, a holy nation, God's own people that you may declare the wonderful deeds of him who called you out of darkness into his marvelous light" (I Pet. 2:9). Paul frequently applies the term "holy" to such true believers. It is only in the sense of consecration to the service of divine purposes that the term "holy" has any validity, whether applied to a people or to a non-national religious community. In any other sense it is an intolerable impertinence.

Judaism recognized differences in individuals and in nations. Men differ in their physical and mental endowments, but not in their essential humanity. Men differ as to their backgrounds, their aptitudes, their opportunities, but not in any organic sense, not with reference to any natural hierarchy of status. Judaism did not envisage any amorphous amalgam of peoples. On the verse "When the Most High gave to the nations their inheritance, when He separated the sons of men He fixed the bounds of the peoples" (Dt. 32:8), a Rabbi commented: "God fixed their boundaries so that they would not become a motley admixture." [9] However, while welcoming differences among nations, Judaism stressed at all times their common origin, their mutual dependence, and the hope of their ultimate reconciliation in peace and brotherhood.

There are no impassable racial barriers in Judaism. We have noted that when the Aryans invaded and conquered Hindustan, fearing a racial admixture with the indigenous population, they excluded them permanently from their community and from their religion. When the Israelites invaded and conquered Canaan, they, too, feared an admixture with the indigenous population, the so-called Seven Nations, but not on racial grounds. The reason was religious—fear of idolatry. "For they will turn away your sons from following Me, to serve other Gods" (Dt. 7:4). Upon abandoning idolatry they, as proselytes, were welcomed into the community of Israel. Even in the case of Ammon and Moab, against whom Israel had a bitter grudge for a great wrong done to it in its hour of dire need, and against whom it was decreed,

"No Ammonite or Moabite shall enter the assembly of the Lord even to the tenth generation" (Dt. 23:3), the prohibition against intermarriage was in time relaxed. Men of Israel married women of Ammon and Moab. R. Joḥanan (3 c.) declared that the daughter of an Ammonite proselyte was eligible to marry a priest.[10]

An Ammonite proselyte came before the Rabbis in the Beth Ha-Midrash and said to them: Am I permitted to enter the assembly? [that is, marry a Jewess] R. Joshua said to him: You are permitted to enter the congregation. Said Rabban Gamaliel to him: Is it not already laid down, an Ammonite or a Moabite shall not enter into the assembly of the Lord? R. Joshua replied: Do Ammon and Moab still reside in their original homes? Sennacherib, King of Assyria, long ago went up and mixed up all the nations.[11]

One law of basic social justice was established for the native born, proselyte, and alien free man. This is repeated time and again in the Torah to emphasize its importance. "There shall be but one law for the native and for the stranger who sojourns among you" (Ex. 12:49; Lev. 24:22; Num. 15:16).

The Bible speaks occasionally of genealogical records and family registers. Ezra kept a registry of all those who went up with him from Babylon (Ezra 8:1). This record included not only the names of the priestly families but of others. It was, of course, important for priests to keep exact family records, attesting to the purity of their Aaronic lineage so as to qualify them to officiate in the Temple. King Herod (73–4 B.C.), an Idumean by descent, in order to cover up his own non-Judaic origin and possibly also for political reasons, ordered the official genealogical tables to be destroyed. The Mishnah enumerates ten genealogical categories which came up from Babylon. These ranged from priests, Levites and Israelites of unmixed stock, through proselytes and freedmen down to foundlings.[12] All, according to Hillel, were permitted to intermarry.[13]

The illusion was at times vigorously fostered by some in the academies in Babylon that all those who had remained behind in Babylon and had not returned with Ezra were of the pure, unimpeachable stock, fit to marry into any Jewish family. "All countries are as dough [mixed flour and water] in comparison with Palestine, and Palestine is as dough in comparison with Babylon." [14] The Babylonians compared themselves to pure fine flour. In their eyes the family pedigrees of the Jews of Palestine who had been subjected to numerous invasions, persecutions, and infiltrations were far less dependable than theirs, since their own fortunes had been far more favorable. The Sages, however, ruled that no country was as dough to any other country. [15]

Still, there were families who prided themselves on their pure descent. R. Ḥama b. R. Ḥanina (3 c.), scion of a wealthy family, who was given to boasting about the noble deeds of his ancestors, [16] declared: "When the Holy One, blessed be He, causes His divine Presence to rest, it is only upon families of pure birth in Israel." [17] But others among the Rabbis made light of the whole matter of pedigrees. They were aware of the great intermingling which had taken place through the generations, and knew that nothing could be done about it. They knew, too, that the greatest men of their time belonged to uncertain categories. [18] Rab (2 c.) declared: "He who declares others unfit, is himself unfit." [19]

One Sage, who had evidently reflected long upon the history of men and nations, addressed himself to one of his colleagues: "Why have you not taken a wife for your son?" "Do I then know whence to take one?" the other replied. He was not sure of the pure descent of anyone. "Do we know whence we are descended?" countered the Sage; "perhaps from those of whom it is written: 'They ravished the women in Zion, the maidens in the cities of Judah'" (Lam. 5:11). He proceeded to give his colleague some sound advice. "Marry your son into a peaceful family. The children of the West [Palestine] have a saying, 'When two quarrel they see which one becomes silent first and then they say, This one is of superior birth!'" [20] Noble origin is revealed in character and privileged birth in inner nobility.

This concept is beautifully illustrated in the Haggadah: Adam —the ancestor of the human race—was created alone in order to avoid sharp family rivalries in the future. As it is, there is too much of it in the world; but how much more would there have been if God, in the beginning, had created two Adams, and men could claim competitively to be descendants of the one Adam who was nobler than the other.[21]

What really occupied the minds of the great teachers of Judaism was not the existence of many races, which they recognized, nor their different psychic endowments, which they acknowledged, nor the factors of heredity and environment of which they were aware, but how to bring about cooperation among all races and peoples for the building of the good society. They were not interested in pure races or master races, but in morally clean and healthy human beings, uncorrupted in mind, unpolluted of heart, purged of coarseness and cruelty. This is the eugenics of Judaism to which so much of its law and discipline is directed.

The mentors of Israel also taught their people that their greatness and national survival lay not in race or blood but in loyalty to their Torah. There have been and there are some who seek the key to Israel's survival in some unique community of blood. Israel's existence is assured, they maintain, not by land, language, custom, or law, but by its own body and blood. Franz Rosenzweig, the saintly philosopher and homilist, probably influenced by the nationalistic romanticism and race mysticism so popular in his native land at the turn of the twentieth century, declared:

And so in the final analysis, it [the Jewish people] is not alive in the sense the nations are alive: in a national life manifest on this earth, in a national language giving voice to the soul of the people, in national territory, solidly based and staked out on the soil. It is alive only in that which guarantees it will endure beyond time, in that which pledges its everlastingness, in drawing its own eternity from sources of the blood.[22]

Buber, too, shares in this emphasis on race which, however, in his hands and in Rosenzweig's, because of inevitable Hebraic qualifications, differs sharply from its Teutonic counterpart.

The devout among the people of Israel believed that God

bestowed eternal life upon Israel by giving it the Torah. After the reading of a section of the Law in the synagogue, the following blessing is recited: "Blessed art Thou, O Lord our God, King of the Universe, Who has given us the Law of truth and has implanted eternal life within us; blessed art Thou, O Lord, Who givest the Law." It was the giving of the Torah at Sinai which imparted immortality to the people of Israel, which made Israel "free from the Angel of Death." [23] Survival depends on loyalty to the faith. The community of blood which the "lost" ten tribes presumably shared with the people of Judaea did not save them from assimilation and extinction. "I have set before you life and death . . . therefore choose life that you and your descendants may live, loving the Lord your God, obeying His voice, and cleaving to Him; for that means life to you and length of days" (Dt. 30:19–20).

The grace of God and the full privilege of religion were likewise not restricted by Judaism to any privileged individuals, groups, or nations. Many of the mystery religions of antiquity were exclusive and esoteric as regards initiation. They were not intended for all men, but for the elect, the chosen. The inner light was reserved for the few, though not restricted to any one people. This is true also of Hīnayana Buddhism and of the doctrine of Election in Christian thought. True faith and the grace of God were not within the reach of all.

Judaism was essentially a democratic faith, a people's religion. The covenant was made with "all the men of Israel, from the hewer of your wood to the drawer of your water" (Dt. 29:11). The Torah was given to all and in the sight of all (Ex. 19). The entire people was summoned to become a "kingdom of priests and a holy nation" (Ex. 19:6). Moses was intolerant of those who would monopolize the gift of prophecy and restrict it to a few only: "Would that all the Lord's people were prophets" (Num. 11:29). On the verse: "You stand this day all of you before the Lord your God; your heads, your tribes, your elders, and your officers, all the men of Israel" (Dt. 29:9), a *midrash* expounds: God says: "Even though I have appointed over you heads and judges, elders and officers, you are all equal in My sight." This is the meaning of "*all* the men of Israel"—all are alike.[24]

Merit, worth, greatness must be earned and may be forfeited. They are not initially bestowed nor forever secured to any nation, race, group, or individual.

Judaism knows no Predestination, such as one finds in the theology of Augustine, Luther, or Calvin. Judaism knows of no doctrine of Election, according to which God, from the beginning of time, chose certain men for everlasting life while condemning others to eternal death. Israel's selection for a special covenant and mission did not consign any other people to moral disability or deprive anyone of status or of any present or future reward. On Israel it bestowed only the privilege and the burden of religious leadership.

In the eyes of some Rabbis, even Israel's selection for its special mission was not entirely a matter of divine grace. It was conditioned on Israel's choice and acceptance of the Torah. "Said R. Johanan: The Holy One, blessed be He, offered the Torah to every nation and every tongue, but none accepted it, until He came to Israel who received it." [25] God did not choose Israel until they had committed themselves, and pledged their children as surety that the Torah would be faithfully preserved.[26] "The one whose actions He perceives to be good, him He chooses and brings near to Himself," concerning which verse R. Nehemiah in the name of R. Samuel b. R. Isaac (3–4 c.) said:

Not every one who is near to God is of necessity permanently near, nor is every one who is far, of necessity permanently far. There are some who are chosen and rejected and then brought near; and there are others who are chosen and cast off and not brought near.[27]

The prophet Jonah thought that his mission to help men find their way to God was intended only for Jews. When God sent him to the most sinful city of the heathen, Nineveh, a city and a people feared and hated by the Jews, with a warning to them to repent so that the city and its inhabitants might be spared, Jonah fled to Tarshish. But God brought him back to his mission and to the insight that six hundred thousand men and women that cannot discern between right and wrong were also God's children, even though they were not Jews. They were not beyond His forgiveness and His love. God is the God of all men; all are equal in their claim upon His compassionate love.

All men, regardless of race or creed, are entitled to respect, fair dealing, and charity. In the interest of peace, the poor among the heathen must be permitted to share in the Gleanings, the Forgotten Sheaf, and the Corner of the Field.[28] "Our Rabbis have taught: We support the poor among the heathen along with the poor of Israel, and visit the sick of the heathen along with the sick of Israel, and bury the dead of the heathen along with the dead of Israel in the interest of peace."[29] The Tosefta adds: "and we eulogize their dead and we comfort their mourners!"[30] For "God is good to all and His tender mercies are over all His creatures" (Ps. 145:9).

In spite of the bitter resentment which the people felt against the oppression, expropriation, and iniquitous taxation which the heathen who ruled over them often practiced against them, the Jews were prohibited from robbing the heathen or circumventing him by subterfuge, or retaining a lost article of his; indeed, they were taught that it is more criminal to rob a heathen than to rob an Israelite, for the former involves the profanation of the Name of God.[31]

At times, in some occasional saying of a Rabbi, we become startlingly aware of some bitter, intolerant judgment clearly struck out of the tense emotions of the hour. We hear the cry wrung out of a hurt and wounded spirit by the cruel wrongs visited upon the people by the oppressors of Israel. These have been preserved as the sad records of a tragic national experience. They are neither precept nor norm.

From their long nomadic history prior to their entrance into Canaan, and their many centuries of later wandering in the wilderness as nomadic tribes wherein no sharp class distinctions existed, the Jews carried over into their settled life in Palestine a love of freedom and equality which survived through all the subsequent centuries. They cherished a tradition which was bound up with the dignity of man fashioned in the image of God, and with his fundamental and inalienable rights. It was that tradition, enshrined in the Bible, which more than any other factor gave sanction and inspiration to the Peasant Rebellions in Germany in the sixteenth century, the Puritan Revolution in England in the seventeenth, and the American Revolution in the eighteenth.

Israel never accepted in silence the despotic, absolute rule which was so characteristic of ancient Asiatic and Egyptian monarchs. Kings in the ancient world were regarded as divine. The Pharaohs of Egypt were unequivocally gods—divine from birth, divine even prenatally. The kings were frequently described as having neither earthly father nor mother.[32] They were worshiped. Sacrifices were offered to them. As gods they were the sole legislators and were themselves above the law. They were above all strictures; to criticize them was an act of impiety, to obey them implicitly a religious duty. The Mesopotamian kings too were divine, whether regarded as descendants of gods, or through deification following their sacred marriage with a goddess.[33] So were the kings of Canaan and of the neighboring peoples. Certain scholars have called the deification theory concerning Mesopotamian rulers into question, or regard the practice as having been "limited and atypical at best." [34] These rulers may have regarded themselves as subservient to the overriding powers of higher deities or "to the tyranny of the omens," but it is clear that many of them boasted of attributes of divinity. From the bronze age through Hellenistic and Roman times, and especially in the latter, the deification of kings and their worship continued.

In Rome the emperor was apotheosized, and his statue, as symbol of the state, was worshiped in the temples of the empire. This was true also of nearly all the religions of the Far East. In Japan the emperor was held to have been descendant from the sun-goddess and until very recently was worshiped as a visible god:

The hallowed Scion of Divine Descent, our Emperor, represents on earth all the celestial virtues, wisdom and might. He comes among us in unruptured lineage from the remotest ancestral Deity, the Heavenly god, who laid the foundation of the empire destined to be so mighty and so lasting. In his veins runs the very blood of the god, and in him we behold the glory and effulgence of the Supreme Being, self-existent and eternal.[35]

Judaism rejected all ideas of king-gods. Kings possessed special rights, to be sure, but no special divine nature. They were not exempt from the operations of the fundamental moral laws of society. King Ahab could not lawfully enforce his will against Naboth who chose not to sell his ancestral vineyard (I Kings: 21). Kings were to receive all honor due to their station. They were to be obeyed, but only when their laws or commands were not in opposition to the laws of the Torah.[36] There were no images of the kings of Israel in the sanctuary, and no images of foreign rulers were ever tolerated. This would have been sacrilege. There was no glorification of the State in Israel. The prophets, on the authority of God, placed themselves above the State, above rulers, and above the official priesthood in demanding allegiance to the supreme moral law. Judaism could never reconcile itself to any form of political absolutism or totalitarianism. It resisted the unification of all authority in any one but God.

Hard was the road which royalty traveled in Israel. Its kings, with rare exceptions, never arrived at that absolutism possessed by the potentates of other ancient oriental kingdoms.[37] When Saul was proclaimed first King of Israel, Samuel, the prophet who anointed him, "told the people the rights and duties of the kingship and he wrote them in a book and laid it up before the Lord" (I Sam. 10:25). What this constitution, defining "the rights and duties" of the king, was may be gathered from Deuteronomy (17:14–20). The king must not multiply horses for himself, or wives. He must write for himself a copy of the Law, and peruse it constantly and keep its statutes "that his heart may not be lifted up above his brethren and that he may not turn aside from the commandments, either to the right hand or to the left."

The Law did not originate with kings; it originated with God. And when the kings failed to abide by it, as they often did, the prophet was always there to admonish them. In the name of a law higher than that of kings, Samuel faced Saul, Nathan denounced David, Shemaiah threatened Rehoboam, Jehu imprecated Baasa, Elijah anathematized Ahab, and Jeremiah pronounced doom upon Zedekiah because he humbled not himself before Jeremiah speaking in the name of the Lord (II Chron. 36:12).[38]

Judaism curbed the power of priests even as it curbed the power of kings. It granted priesthood no preferred moral status. It resisted ecclesiastical dictatorship. The prophets of Israel were as unsparing in their denunciation of the abuses of priestcraft as they were of the sins of kings, princes, or the common people. None was permitted to find shelter from the exactions of the one universal moral law behind the bulwark of special privilege, special sanctity, or special indulgence. The priests were not permitted to monopolize the authority of teaching and of interpreting the Torah. Scribes and Rabbis claimed the same right and insisted on an unrestricted democratic leadership in religion. This was at the heart of the protracted struggle between the Pharisees and the Sadducees. Every Israelite, the former maintained, who was properly trained was qualified to share in the sovereign freedom of teaching and expounding the Law, of discovering its recondite meanings and of applying it to the problems and conditions of his time.[39] The right of teaching the Torah and of interpreting it, both legally and homiletically, was steadily taken over by laymen. Their stronghold was the synagogue and the academy. They proceeded to ordain prayers and to fix the lay ritual. In due time they asserted their authority even over the ritual in the Temple itself. They fixed the Canon of the Bible. They democratized the concept of sanctification. Rabban Gamaliel derived from the Biblical injunction "You shall be holy, for I the Lord your God am holy" (Lev. 19:2), a conclusion which he proceeded to impart to his disciples: "Holiness was not given to the priests exclusively, but to all, Priests, Levites, and Israelites."[40]

Rabbis in Israel never possessed religious privileges which were not shared by all other Jews. All rites and ceremonies in Judaism, other than those assigned to the priests—which to all intents and purposes practically terminated with the destruction of the Temple—may be performed by any qualified Jewish layman. The Rabbi, on the strength of his knowledge of the Law, was authorized to act as teacher and judge in the community and, as a rule, at the latter's own proper invitation and election.

The religious authority of the Rabbis, following the Destruction, was seldom implemented by any arm of enforcement. The heads of the important academies in Palestine and Babylonia exercised great authority for many centuries over Jewish communities throughout the world. Upon the decline of these academies, individual Rabbis in other lands who were noted for their erudition came to enjoy varied degrees of authority. Jews turned to them on all occasions for guidance in matters of faith, law, and ritual. But it was always in the nature of a voluntary submission to what were at all times unenforceable decisions—a spontaneous deference to recognized scholarship and character. It was also an extraordinary display of democratic self-discipline on the part of a scattered people, resolved to safeguard the unity and cohesion of its religious and communal life.

The Rabbis curbed their own temptation to exalt the scholar and elevate him into a privileged category above all others. "Do not make of the Torah a crown wherewith to exalt yourself," declared R. Zadok (1-2 c.). Scholars were admonished to be exceedingly modest, lowly of spirit, and long-suffering.[41] They were not to plume themselves as superior beings on the strength of their erudition.

Some Rabbis were unnecessarily severe and exclusive in their attitude toward the ignorant and the illiterate, and when provoked on occasion by the hostility of the latter they retaliated with bitter invectives. But these occasional outbursts, which are recorded in Rabbinic literature and which probably reflect temporary political incidents, by no means represent the considered judgment and consistent attitude of the Rabbis. All classes were regarded by them as worthy for they were all essential to society, and interdependent. R. Simon b. Lakish (3 c.) said:

This people [Israel] is like unto a vine; its branches are the men of property [Ba'ale Batim], its clusters the scholars, its leaves the common people, its twigs those in Israel who are devoid of learning. This is what was meant when word was sent from there [Palestine]: "Let the clusters pray for the leaves, for were it not for the leaves the clusters could not exist." [42]

A man's love for his fellow men should not be limited to scholars or to their disciples but should include the ignorant as well.[43]

R. Eleazar (3 c.), who entertained a special dislike for the 'Ame Ha-arez,[44] expressed the thought that they will be denied resurrection. Whereupon his teacher, R. Johanan, rebuked him: "It is no satisfaction to their Master [God] that you should speak of them in this manner." [45]

R. Jannai (2–3 c.) was properly rebuked when in the pride of his great learning—he had founded an academy—he insulted a man who was ignorant not alone of Torah and Talmud, but even of the simplest prayers. The man offered the Rabbi, walking on the road, the hospitality of his home. The Rabbi accepted and was entertained with food and drink. During the meal the Rabbi examined his host in the Talmud, Haggadah, the Mishnah, and Scriptures and found that he was ignorant of them all. R. Jannai then said to him: "Take up the wine cup and recite Grace." The man, not knowing how, requested the Rabbi to recite Grace. The Rabbi then said to him: "Are you able to repeat what I say to you?" "Yes," answered the man. "Say, 'A dog has eaten bread with Rabbi Jannai.'" The man rose and caught hold of the Rabbi and said: "You have mine inheritance, which you are withholding from me!" "What inheritance?" cried the Rabbi. "Once when I passed a school," answered the man, "I heard the voices of children reciting: 'The Torah which Moses commanded us is the inheritance of the congregation of Jacob.' (Deut. 33:4). It is not written 'the congregation of R. Jannai' but 'the congregation of Jacob!' " [46]

The Jewish people did not articulate any elaborate theories concerning the democratic state, as did the Greeks, nor any system of direct popular government; but the democratic ideal powerfully influenced every department of life. Autocratic power was curbed. The rights of the individual were not sacrificed to ruler or state. Any unwarranted exercise of authority was certain to encounter the fierce resistance of the people.

Heine, whose poetic insight frequently bordered on the prophetic, wrote of the time to come when "freedom will speak everywhere, and its speech will be Biblical." Hitler, whose hatred of freedom and democracy was surpassed only by his hatred of the Jews, somewhere stated: "Democracy is fundamentally Jewish, not Germanic." Friend and foe alike seem to agree that there is an organic relationship between Judaism and the ideals of human freedom and liberty. It was not accidental that the attack upon human freedom and the rights of man made by the Nazi régime, which alone among all Fascist régimes faced the ultimate ideologic implications of its position in their totality, went hand in hand with a violent attack on the Bible and on the essential teachings of Judaism.

◄(XIII)►

THAT MEN ARE NOT FREE

That man is not free and that his life is governed by fate is, as we have had occasion to show, a central belief in most religions. Man is subject either to the compulsion of impersonal nature, to the influence of the stars and planets, to his own irrevocable past acts, to Original Sin, or to the unaccountable willfulness of some deity.

In denying and rejecting all these beliefs, Judaism gave men the assurance of a God of absolute freedom Who granted them a capacity to exercise their own will as part of their endowment as human beings. It taught men to act as free agents in a world wherein they could build for progress and happiness.

Men were led to fatalism by what they saw and experienced. All around them was the phenomenon of death—inevitable, unpredictable, and awesome. They experienced accidents and calamities which they could not explain. They were baffled by the apparent unrelatedness of man's conduct to his allotted station and condition on earth, by the frequent irrational frustrations of human effort, and by the persistent and obdurate character of evil. They concluded that this world was governed by an unalterable fate or by a God Whose ways were beyond the reach and prayers of men.

In a way, these beliefs were man's way of adjusting himself to conditions which he could not or did not know how to correct. For many it was a way of escape from moral responsibilities—since there was nothing man could do about it, nothing needs to be done to set aright the wrongs in the world. Injustice and evil were predestined from the beginning and cannot be altered.

The predominantly fatalistic character of Oriental thought has figured prominently in this inquiry. Hinduism and Buddhism accepted as dogma that man's conduct and destiny are irrevocably predetermined. There is a universal causal law, karma, which holds sway over men, and there is no escaping the vast carryover from past existences. Man reaps in the present what he has sown in past incarnations of which he is unaware. The causal nexus between sin and redemption is never broken. Man is never morally newborn. To discover the way to break this chain of causation, to escape from the remorselessly rotating wheel of rebirths, from the evil cycle of existence—that is "salvation." This can be done only by nullifying oneself completely, and by passing on to the stage of *An-atta*—Not-Self.

Fatalism and predestination are characteristic also of the religions of China. Confucius was frankly a fatalist, and so was Lao-tse, the founder of Taoism.

We have seen, too, that Gnosticism, the redemptive theosophy which so greatly influenced early Christianity, was fatalistic in outlook and denied free will to man. It maintained that the majority of men will forever be denied redemption regardless of what they do.

Christian theology, with some notable exceptions, leaned heavily toward moral determinism, predestination, and election.

Paul himself was inclined toward these doctrines which stem directly from his conception of mankind's Original Sin. Man's salvation is entirely the work of God's grace; and grace does not assist—it determines man's moral efforts. Paul denied man free choice in charting the course of his own moral life in order to exalt God's unconditioned grace and the gift of the redemptive sacrifice of Jesus. His denial of the efficacy of good works was also in order to exalt the rôle of faith in the risen Christ and his redeeming sacrifice. In his Epistle to the Romans, Paul writes:

So it depends not upon man's will or exertion, but upon God's mercy. . . . So then He has mercy upon whomever He wills and He hardens the heart of whomever He wills. . . . Has the potter no right over the clay, to make out of the same lump one vessel for beauty and another for menial use? [9:16, 18, 21]. For those whom He foreknew He also predestined to be conformed to the image of His Son, in order that he might be the first-born among many brethren. And those whom He predestined He also called; and those whom He called He also justified; and those whom He justified He also glorified [8:29–30].

Paul did not fully confront all the ethical implications of these teachings which in the face of such thoroughgoing divine dictatorship make man's moral endeavors of little moment and, if logically followed through, would utterly paralyze man's moral will.

Some of the Greek Fathers, especially Clement and Origen, were strong proponents of the doctrine of free will. The Latin Fathers, on the other hand, in the main inclined toward predestination and the denial of free will. Augustine supremely represents this point of view. He fought bitterly against the free-will doctrines of his contemporary, the British monk Pelagius, and the latter's denial of Original Sin. Aquinas redefines but hardly deviates from Augustine. The struggle to preserve a measure of free will in man within the framework of salvation through faith was a long, difficult, and unresolved one within Christian theology through the centuries.

The Council of Trent called predestination "a hidden mystery," and it accepted it as Catholic dogma. The Church "regards eternal happiness primarily as the work of God and His grace, but secondarily as the fruit and reward of the meritorious actions of the predestined." [1]

The early Reformers Luther, Calvin, and Zwingli were uncompromising champions of election and predestination. Melanchthon was an outstanding exception. According to the former, some men are predestined to eternal life, and others, by far the majority of mankind, are not. Election, as well as rejection, is not determined by man's ethical conduct. Election does not follow faith, but faith follows election. Some are elected to be saved, others to be damned. Some are predestined to heaven, others to hell. Calvin, the most consistent and thoroughgoing spokesman of predestination, declares:

For the seed of the word of God takes root and brings forth fruit only in those whom the Lord, by His eternal election, has predestined to be children and heirs of the heavenly kingdom. To all the others (who by the same counsel of God are rejected before the foundation of the world) the clear and evident preaching of truth can be nothing but an odor of death unto death. Now, why does the Lord use His mercy toward some and exercise the rigor of His judgment on the others? We have to leave the reason of this to be known by Him alone. For He, with a certainly excellent intention, has willed to keep it hidden from us all. The crudity of our mind could not indeed bear such a great clarity, nor our smallness comprehend such a great wisdom.

Only let us have this resolved in ourselves, that the dispensation of the Lord, although hidden from us, is nevertheless holy and just. For, if He will to ruin all mankind, He has the right to do it, and in those whom He rescues from perdition one can contemplate nothing but His sovereign goodness. We acknowledge therefore, the elect to be recipients of His mercy (as truly they are) and the rejected to be recipients of His wrath, a wrath which is nothing but just.[2]

Centuries after the rise of Christianity, Islam developed a powerful deterministic theology. Mohammed himself was self-contradictory on this subject, but declarations in the Koran such as: "All men would believe, did God so will and none believes but by God's permission"; [3] "God makes whom He will to err and whom He will He guideth and ye shall be called to account for your actions"; [4] and "Whom He pleaseth will He forgive and whom He pleaseth will He punish; for God is all-powerful"; [5] contributed to a rigid doctrine of predestination, which became orthodox for Islam in spite of the valiant efforts of the Kadarites (7 c.), the Kharijites (7 c.), and the Mu'tazilites (8 c.).

Judaism proclaimed the liberating doctrine of moral self-determination and therefore also of moral responsibility. "See, I have set before you this day life and good, death and evil . . . therefore, choose life!" (Dt. 30:15–20). R. Eleazar said: "From the Torah, the Prophets and the Writing, it can be shown that a man is allowed to follow the road he wishes to pursue." [6] God did not fashion man to be a helpless creature of passive receptivity but one capable of selection, decision, and origination. To function as a moral being, man had to be dowered with free will, and consequently also with the capacity to do evil. These are the very conditions of his humanity. In his spiritual life, man has been granted by God the artist's gift and privilege of dominating the material before him; and the more trained and skilled he becomes, the greater his freedom of choice and execution.

The theologic and philosophic dilemmas involved in human freedom were not unknown to the teachers of Judaism, and these men were also not unaware of the difficulties in reconciling man's freedom of choice with God's prescience. An occasional Scriptural passage, such as "God hardened the heart of Pharaoh" (Ex. 7:3), gave them no end of trouble. But the intellectual difficulties they encountered in their efforts to solve these problems did not move them to commit the error of denying free will altogether.

They were faced with a paradox, but the paradox did not cast them down. They acknowledged it as one of the mysteries of the religious life. They did so not to vindicate God's omnipotence but to safeguard man's moral competency. They resigned themselves to the impossibility of solving what appeared to them an inherent contradiction. Akiba declared: "Everything is foreseen, yet free will is given to man." [7] God's foreknowledge cannot contradict man's freedom. God is aware of all possibilities, and yet man is free to determine his moral conduct. A few centuries before Akiba's time, Ben Sira confronted the same problem. He, too, did not see his way to go beyond the same paradox.

Do not say: It is through the Lord that I sin. . . . It is He Who made me err. . . . He has set fire and water before you; put forth your hand unto whichever you choose. . . . Life and death are before man, and whichever he likes will be given him. . . . **Nevertheless, the wisdom of God is boundless. He is omnipotent and He sees all.** . . . He knows every action of man, but He commanded no man to sin [Ecclus. 15:11-20].

The noted Raba puts the defense of determinism in the mouth of Job:

Job sought to exculpate the whole world. He said: "Sovereign of the Universe, Thou hast created the ox with cloven hoofs and Thou hast created the ass with whole hoofs! . . . Thou hast created righteous men and Thou hast created wicked men, and who can prevent Thee?" His companions answered him . . . If God created the evil inclination, He also created the Torah with which to temper it.[8]

By following the Law, man becomes a free agent.

God cooperates with man in his moral life, but does not constrain him. God created a moral universe, and man's freedom is its hallmark. As a created physical being, man's life is determined by fixed biologic laws; as a creative moral being, man to a large degree is self-determining. Human action affects history, and God intended that it should, as part of a design not grasped by man. Even those among the Rabbis who, like R. Ḥanina (3 c.), believed that a man's physical and material destiny is predetermined and that at birth it is decreed whether a man will be strong or weak, wise or foolish, rich or poor, refused to apply determinism to man's moral life—whether he will be wicked or righteous. "Everything is in the hands of God except the fear of God." [9] "Fear of God" (*Yirat Shamayim*) is the Rabbinic equivalent for man's ethical conduct and his religion.

Medieval Jewish philosophers—Saadia, Halevi, Maimonides, Crescas, and others—exerted themselves mightily through philosophic argumentation to harmonize man's free will with God's omniscience. They argued in many subtle and persuasive ways that God's knowledge is not causative, that there are two kinds of contingencies, the general in which the causal chain operates and the particular in which man is free. But they failed to advance the solution appreciably. Baḥya was perhaps wisest when he declared that this problem is "too complicated for human solution." [10]

But by whatever avenue of argumentation they approached it, the goal for the teachers of Judaism was always the same—the stout and unequivocal affirmation of free will. God's knowledge is not of the same kind as man's, declared Maimonides, but totally different from it and admits of no analogy. It is the will of God that man should have power to act according to his own will or choice within the limits of his capacity. A man is free in accordance with his character, and he himself is a decisive factor in the fashioning of that character:

God does not decree that a man should be good or evil. It is only fools and ignoramuses among Gentiles and Jews who maintain that God decrees at a man's birth whether he shall be righteous or wicked. Any man born is free to become as righteous as Moses, as wicked as Jeroboam, a student or an ignoramus, kind or cruel, generous or niggardly. The subject of man's freedom and God's fore-knowledge is profoundly difficult for man to grasp, as difficult as it is for man to understand God. We believe that the actions of man are in God's hands, and yet God does not coerce man or direct him to act one way or another.[11]

The keen critic of Maimonides, Abraham b. David of Posquières (12 c.), wrote that Maimonides had not acted wisely in opening up the subject at all, since he had no satisfactory answers to the questions which he raised, and this might create doubts in the minds of many who might otherwise be left in the unquestioning innocence and simplicity of their faith. He himself, however, attempts an answer which he knows to be only a partial answer. Just as the knowledge of an astrologer enables him to know beforehand what the planetary influence will be in any given contingency, without his being in any way responsible for that influence (nor does that knowledge prevent the individual from freeing himself from the planetary influences by his moral actions), so God's knowledge is not determinative; God Himself created the possibility of alternatives in man's moral decisions, and man in altering the decrees of the celestial bodies is not changing the mind of God.[12]

Before Maimonides, Saadia had asserted that the "Creator does not in any way interfere with the actions of men and that He does not exercise any force upon them either to obey or disobey Him." Saadia resorted mainly to the argument that God's foreknowledge of things is not the cause of their coming into being.[13]

Halevi treats the subject extensively in his *Kuzari*. He begins with experience. Man experiences freedom of choice and action. "If he believed in absolute necessity, he would simply submit, and not equip himself with weapons against his enemy, or with food against his hunger." Freedom of choice is not incompatible with a belief in Divine Providence. The decisions of man precede the knowledge of God. It is through a series or chain of intermediary, secondary causes that man's free will traces itself back to the first cause. "The course is not compulsory, because the whole thing is potential and the mind wavers between an opinion and its opposite, being permitted to turn where it chooses." [14]

Abraham ibn Daud (12 c.) devoted his chief work to this problem of divine omniscience and human freedom. In his desire to establish man's freedom, he is inclined to circumscribe God's absolute prescience. Reason, Scripture, and Rabbinic tradition affirm human freedom, he maintains. Whatever appears to be contradictory to this doctrine in Biblical texts must be interpreted in such a way as to bring it into harmony with this basic tenet. God has Himself created the contingency of man's freedom. God knows what possibilities exist but not the actual outcome, and He has willed it so.[15]

This also is the view of Gersonides (13–14 c.).[16] Crescas, perhaps alone among the medieval Jewish philosophers, constricts the concept of man's free will in order to safeguard God's prescience. He admits only a partial kind of freedom in man.

Because the boundaries between what is free and what is determined are not clearly defined, Judaism urged man to act as if these boundaries did not exist at all as far as his moral initiative was concerned, and not to proceed on the assumption that his actions are foreknown and his future foredoomed. It is man's duty to develop his freedom just as it is his duty to develop his mind and reason, although they too have their limitations.

In nontheologic terms modern man finds this issue restated for him as one between cultural determinism and free will. How can man exercise any choice or moral initiative whatsoever, seeing that his conduct and way of life are coercively conditioned by the society in which he is born and reared and by its economic, political, social, and legal requirements and mores? Within such a straitjacket of social repressions and traditions, how can the individual be sufficiently autonomous to master his own moral career and to be accountable for it?

The best thought of our day has veered away from the doctrine of cultural-social determinism toward a more dynamic conception. Man is able to fashion his own private world within the larger social framework which in itself is not static but subject to change and redirection by man himself.

We can today, I believe, offer a new and fruitful conception of culture and the individual, viewing the individual as no longer a helpless social atom, subject to the operation of vast social forces, nor as a passive member of a culture submitting to the coercion of traditions. Rather we can see the individual as the dynamic agent who, with increasing recognition of his place and rôle in the social order, of his inescapable but potentially creative participation in culture, can make choices, can set goals that will increasingly alter the social order and redirect the culture.[17]

Man's recorded history is a drama of growth and achievement. Biologically and socially man has advanced, and he has demonstrated that he has the capacity to influence his own evolution.

Man must work within definite limitations of environment and heredity. But these are not ironclad, absolute, or unalterable. While man is not all-powerful, he is not powerless either. He is not a mere tool. He is a self-willing and competent agent. He has resources of power within himself to accomplish very much, resources of which he may not even be aware and which are certainly never fully explored.

Whenever mankind has chosen wisely and has been prepared to pay the price for its choice, in labor and struggle and effort, it advanced in knowledge, health, and well-being. Whenever it has not chosen wisely, it has stagnated or retrogressed. Mankind cannot escape its responsibility by unloading all the evil of the world, or all the evil that it commits, on God or on fate. Individuals may often appear to fail, even when they choose wisely and morally. Good men have suffered frustration and defeat; but there is actually no real failure in the pursuit of any noble objective. There is heartache and sorrow, but the grandeur of the individual's life is never dimmed by defeat nor is his cause permanently denied. Because man is free, his life can be heroic or it can be tragic. Without freedom of decision his life could only be fortunate or pathetic.

Until quite recently science gave encouragement to ideas of absolute determinism in physical nature. The universe, it was maintained, was carried on in an ordered sequence of cause and effect, and there was no room in it for any unpredictable novelty, for divergence or dynamic deviation. In the twentieth century scientists seem to be abandoning this mechanistic view of the universe. The law of causation has given way to the law of probability, and the quantum theory has forced a reexamination of classical physics.

How far this new scientific approach can be used in confirming the fact of free will in human experience is not entirely clear. What is clear is that henceforth scientific absolutes can no longer be used to discredit this basic postulate of the spiritual life of man, as Judaism propounded it. The new sciences of psychoanalysis and psychotherapy are based on the theory that man can be helped to change his life, his attitudes, his conduct, and hence his destiny, once he is given new insights and a clearer understanding of himself, his history, and his capacity.

The only fatalist in the Bible, as we have noted previously, is the disillusioned Koheleth, who alone among the writers of the Bible maintains "that what is crooked cannot be made straight," prefers death to life, and asserts that it were better not to have been born at all. In all essential regards Koheleth is the least Jewish in its outlook of all the books of the Bible.

Not only is man able to improve and renew himself but in this enterprise toward newness and regeneration lies the very meaning of his life. Concerning all the things which God created in the first days of the world, the Bible says, "And God saw that it was good." The creation of light, of the firmament, and of the beasts of the earth is characterized as "good" and "very good." But of the creation of man, it is not said it was good. Because, say the Rabbis, man was not created perfect, but perfectible. His destiny is to perfect himself and his world.

It is for continuous newness and aspiration in all realms of life that this religion of unity, freedom, and compassion pleads. It urges men always to go forward to make new covenants with a better life. The danger lies in accepting as inevitable what is inadequate in oneself or in society. Real freedom consists in voluntarily assuming the yoke of the Law. Wilfullness is a form of slavery—the more one assumes the liberty to do what one should not do, the heavier are the chains of his servitude. "No man is a free man save he who occupies himself in the study of the Law." [18] Perfect freedom is to live and to act in such a way as to fulfill the will of God. "The servant of time," Halevi said, "is the slave of slaves; the servant of God, he alone is free."

~⪡ XIV ⪢~

THAT MEN SHOULD NOT
RESIST EVIL

That men should not resist evil is a doctrine widely held by religions and schools of philosophy from earliest times to the present. It had its earliest and fullest expression in India and China. Through Christianity it passed impressively into the Western world, although it had been preached by Stoics and other schools of ethical philosophy long before Jesus proclaimed, "Resist not evil."

The dogmatic pessimism of Buddhism led it to preach an uncompromising doctrine of nonresistance. Because this world is irremediably evil and because there is no possibility of happiness in it, to try to improve it is only to sink deeper and ever deeper into a morass of involvement and attachment.

Hinduism, which Gautama, the Buddha, came to reform, entertained more or less the same attitude toward human existence. Life is emptiness and a mirage. The wise man seeks a way of escape from it, not ways of ameliorating it, although war, as we shall see, is far from being ruled out in Hinduism.

In China, in the sixth century before the common era, Lao-tse, founder of Taoism, taught that the ideal inner state for man is freedom from all desire. Tao, the fathomless source of all things in the universe, acts without acting. "The Tao never does, yet through it everything is done." [1] Man, too, should avoid all action, even if it is devoted toward the suppression of evil.

The devaluation of all effort, striving, and aspiration are at the very core of Taoism. "Attain the utmost in Passivity. Hold firm to the basis of Quietude." [2] The cultivation even of virtues through action is evil. "The world is God's own Vessel, it cannot be made [by human interference]. . . . He who makes it spoils it. . . . Hence the Sage does not shape it, so he does not damage it." [3] "On the decline of the great Tao, the doctrine of 'humanity' and 'justice' arose." [4]

In the West, nonresistance found an able spokesman in Zeno, the founder of Stoicism (4 c. B.C.). Since, as we have observed, neither the Stoics, the Cynics, nor the Epicureans were ever seriously concerned with overcoming or correcting the evils of society, each school worked out for itself an art of living and a pattern by which the individual might confront the unpleasant circumstances of his life. A minimum of effort, involving a minimum of perturbation of spirit or of social innovation, was desirable. Underlying them all was a fundamental pessimism—the exhausted spirit of a brilliant age whose gods had died, whose political ideals had been shattered, and whose social disciplines had fallen apart.

It is not easy to trace the infiltration of these ideas and doctrines into Palestine. Undoubtedly they were in the air everywhere in the eastern Mediterranean world. By the first century B.C. we find them held by small mystic sects of Jews, such as the Essenes.

As far as the Western world is concerned, the doctrine of nonresistance finds its classic expression in the Sermon on the Mount:

You have heard that it was told: "An eye for an eye and a tooth for a tooth!" But I say to you, Do not resist evil (or one who is evil). But if any one strikes you on the right cheek, turn to him the other also; and if anyone would sue you and take your coat, let him have your cloak as well; and if any one forces you to go one mile, go with him two miles. . . . You have heard that it was said, "You

shall love your neighbor and hate your enemy." But I say to you,
Love your enemies and pray for those who persecute you. . . .
[Matt. 5:38–44]

In Jesus' mystical outlook, the world was fast coming to an end
and there was no point in resisting evil. It would automatically
cease with the Millennium and the imminent establishment of
God's Kingdom. Man's chief concern should therefore be not to
fight evil, but to prepare himself for the new age. He should
cleanse and purify himself inwardly as rapidly and as thoroughly
as he can so that he will be spared the inevitable screening and
winnowing of all sinners, and thus will be privileged to enter immediately into the Kingdom of God. Whereas Buddhism's nonresistance grew out of metaphysical conceptions of the evil nature of all life, and Taoism's had a considerable politico-social
motivation, the nonresistance doctrine of primitive Christianity
stemmed from a belief in the impending collapse of the existing
world order and the coming of a new Messianic age which God
by His grace and power was about to usher in.

In keeping with this overwhelming conviction, Jesus also
taught: "Do not be anxious about your life, what you shall eat or
what you shall drink, nor about your body, what you shall put
on. . . . But seek first His Kingdom and His righteousness, and
all these things shall be yours as well" (Matt. 5:25–33).

It has been argued that Jesus' admonition not to resist evil applied only to the evil of the oppressive Roman government of his
day and was directed against those elements in the Jewish population who were determined to oppose the Roman oppressors by
revolution and violence, such as Judah of Galilee and his followers.

It is doubtful, however, whether Jesus had only Rome and
these militant patriots in mind. His ethical counsel was as a rule
addressed to the individual, whom he summoned to quick repentance in view of the approaching End. He was not concerned
with the political struggle against Rome, one way or another. He
had no political interests or program. "Render therefore to Caesar
the things that are Caesar's, and to God the things that are God's"

(Matt. 22:21; also Matt. 17:24–27). The existing order would endure unchanged until it was ended for all time by the approaching cataclysm, which would precede the establishment of the Kingdom of God. Had Jesus a particular party in mind, in speaking about nonresistance, he would have mentioned it by name as he did in the case of the Scribes, the Pharisees, and the Sadducees. Opposition to revolutionary measures against Rome existed in many circles even among the Pharisees and the Sadducees, but this was based on practical and political considerations. It was not rooted, as was the case with Jesus, in a thoroughgoing philosophy of pacifism and nonresistance to evil.

The early Christians followed quite literally the pacifist teachings of their Master. They offered no resistance to their persecutors. They practiced nonviolence. They would under no circumstances bear arms in war. They refused even to hold any civil office in the Roman Empire because that might involve them in coercive practices and in the exercise of police power. Whenever in subsequent centuries there arose sectarian movements whose purpose was to return to the pristine teachings of the primitive Church, or to Gospel text and authority, they were almost invariably strongly pacifist and nonresistant. This was the case with the Albigenses and the Waldenses (11–13 c.), the Lollards (14–15 c.), the Hussites (15 c.), and the Anabaptist sects, the Moravians and the Quakers in the centuries following the Reformation.

When Christianity became the official religion of the Roman Empire in the fourth century, the doctrine of absolute pacifism, already receding, was pushed far into the background. Its periodic reappearance was, as we have noted, among unorthodox sects in Christendom. In the modern world one finds it occasionally in individuals like Tolstoi who seek to recapture the original message of the Church.

Tolstoi's pacifist philosophy came closer to the teachings of Jesus than that of any other man in modern times. He based himself squarely on the Sermon on the Mount: swear not at all, resist not evil, and judge not that ye be not judged. These he regarded as the principal doctrines of Jesus, the key to his life and mission, and the distinctive core of true Christianity, which had been disregarded, he maintained, through the centuries. Following these ideas through to their logical conclusion. Tolstoi rejected all organized political states; the state he saw as a source of evil. He rejected all use of force in the administration of justice. In fact, he rejected all civilization, including its arts and sciences. His philosophy may best be summarized as Christian anarchism.

In the Oriental world, modern pacifism in the person of Gandhi assumed a different character. He believed in resisting evil, but through nonviolent methods. There were other methods—noncooperation with the oppressing government, for example, and civil disobedience.

Such passive resistance was advocated by Thoreau whose essay on "Civil Disobedience" greatly influenced the thinking of Gandhi, and by Shelley, a generation earlier:

> With folded arms and steady eyes,
> And little fear, and less surprise,
> Look upon them as they slay,
> Till their rage has died away.[5]

The aim of passive resistance is to achieve reform. As a technique it may sometimes succeed. This is the strategy of dharma—to sit fasting even unto death at the door of the house of the one from whom redress is sought. In the case of rulers or governments, they may or may not be shamed into yielding by such demonstrations. They may also be encouraged to carry on with even greater ruthlessness, confident that they will not be physically resisted. This could ensure the triumph of injustice in the world. It is not difficult to imagine what the fate of modern India would have been if the oppressors against whom Gandhi's policies were applied had been German Nazis rather than British imperialists.

Judaism rejected all doctrines of nonresistance and all forms of pacifism. It demanded action from its devotees. It taught that there is evil in society and that it is man's duty to overcome it—

if need be, by force, though force is by no means the only way by which evil can be overcome.

It is not enough to improve oneself; one must also seek to improve one's environment. The only refuge from the cruel wrongs of the world is in the effort to set them aright. There is no ethics of resignation in Judaism. There are certain evils which man *cannot* eradicate. He cannot do away with death or the accidental tragedies of life. They are inherent in the very structure of human existence. But man can reduce the incidence of disease and accidents. He can lessen pain and physical suffering. Man can also put an end to moral evils. He can eradicate poverty and war— among the chief sources of human misery and suffering. He can eliminate the evils of illiteracy, of bigotry, of exploitation, of inequality.

The administration of laws and the proper exercise of police power on the part of a just government are not evil. The Torah prescribed a proper organization and administration of social life based on a system of just laws and their effective enforcement.

Judaism believed that righteous laws and sound regulations in behalf of those who are in need are ways of training and developing man and of directing him away from brutality and selfishness toward the good life. Chapter 19 of the Book of Leviticus, one of the noblest chapters of the Torah, instructs man how to attain this good life. It defines the "way"—sharing what one has with those who are in want, and avoiding all forms of oppression and exploitation of other men. The way is that of impartial justice, of just balances and weights, of respecting the rights of the stranger, of reverence for parents and the aged, and of special solicitude for the blind, the deaf, and the otherwise handicapped. The way is that of family purity and the shunning of the perversions, corruptions, and the superstitions of the heathen; of forgiveness and of refraining from vengeance and hate. This is *how* to "love your neighbor as yourself."

These are all possible, though not easy, goals. Judaism believed that they can be reached.

Man must work, toil and fight for the good society. Over and over again the Bible admonishes: "And thou shalt eradicate the evil from your midst" (Dt. 13:6; 17:7; 21:21; 24:7). Evil is something to be *eradicated*, to be resisted!

It is not enough to love what is good; we must hate what is evil—not the evildoer, but the evil. We must never resign ourselves to it. The prophet Amos defined man's tasks: "Hate evil! Love the good! And establish justice in the gate!" (Amos 5:15)

If one sees his neighbor attacked and in danger, he must not stand idly by the blood of his neighbor. He must run to his assistance, even if it means endangering his own life. One dare not say at such a moment: "I do not believe in violence. I believe in nonresistance," and so leave one's neighbor to become a victim of wanton assault and brutality.

> I was eyes to the blind, and feet to the lame,
> I was a father to the poor, and I searched out the
>   cause of him whom I did not know.
> I broke the fangs of the unrighteous, and made him
>   drop his prey from his teeth [Job 29:15–17].

If one lives in a community of poverty, political corruption, crime, and the perversion of justice, one must not accept them as inevitable; or say it is God's problem—in His own good time He will set things right—and in the meantime I will look after my own soul.

"Seek justice," cried the prophet Isaiah, "correct oppression, defend the fatherless, plead for the widow" (Is. 1:17). Tyrants and oppressors must be fought. Insurrection and revolution against tyranny are, under certain conditions, not only justified but mandatory.

We do not solve the world's problems of crime and wickedness by turning the other cheek to the smiter or by giving also our cloak to him who would take our coat. To follow these ideals literally is to turn the world over to the smiter, the thief, the criminal, the men of greed and violence who refuse to abide by the canons of a civilized society. It is to ensure the destruction of decent society.

An individual may decide for himself the degree to which he may wish to practice nonresistance in a matter which involves his own interests and only his own safety. Society and government cannot make such choices. Only as society and government protect all citizens through law and administrative justice against the chaos and anarchy which would ensue if criminals were allowed to carry on their activities unchecked—only then can an individual undertake, if he so desires, the spiritual exercise of nonresistance, secure in the protection of a system of law enforcement which he repudiates.

Along with the duty of resistance is also that of forbearance. "A man should always be willing to forgive an insult or an injury done to him," said the Rabbis. It is sometimes an act of great nobility of spirit to be patient with personal abuse, insult, and wrong. Certainly no one should stoop to personal vengeance. "Say not I will pay back the evil that was done to me," we read in the Book of Proverbs (Pr. 20:22). In the Book of Ecclesiasticus (3 c. B.C.) it is written: "He that taketh vengeance shall find vengeance from the Lord, and God will keep his sins in remembrance. Forgive thy neighbor the hurt that he has done unto thee, so shall thy sins also be forgiven when thou prayest" (Ecclus. 28:1–2). So also in the Book of Enoch (2 c. B.C.): "When you might have vengeance, do not take it, either against your neighbor or your enemy."

It is one thing, however, to be forbearing and forgiving; it is another to submit to evil as a matter of principle, to turn the other cheek to the oppressor. Judaism was the first among the religions of mankind to project the vision of universal peace, when nations would beat their swords into ploughshares and learn war no more. But until that hoped-for time comes to pass, Judaism does not deny nations the right of self-defense. War in self-defense is a dreadful but inescapable necessity, and citizens must take up arms to protect their country or their faith against aggressors who would destroy them. The principle of self-defense in personal life as well as in national life is the same in Jewish law: "If one comes to kill you, kill him first!" [6]

From the stone age to the atomic age, no people has been free of war. The history of Israel is no exception. War was neither a rare occurrence in Israel's history, nor, on occasion, devoid of ferocity. The religious teachers of Israel, however, never extolled war as a national career, never regarded it as a noble pursuit, but sought to humanize it as far as possible and to mitigate its horrors. They were sustained by the divine promise, "I will abolish the bow, the sword, and war from the land" (Hos. 2:18). They held aloft the vision of disarmament and universal peace (Is. 2:1–4). The Deuteronomic Code provides that the inhabitants of a city which capitulates should be spared, and where there is resistance the lives of the noncombatants should be spared. Amos denounced the cruelty practiced by nations at war (Chaps. 1–2).

The *Iliad* is the story of deadly wrath and pride of war and battlefield. The *Aeneid* sings of arms and the warrior. "In the age of classical antiquity . . . war continued, notwithstanding the growing culture, to be regarded as the most honorable and almost the most urgent of human pursuits." [7] Plato and Aristotle justified war. In the eyes of Aristotle it is a legitimate part of acquisition when directed against other peoples, like the barbarians, who are intended by nature to be governed but who will not submit; "for war of such a kind is naturally just." [8]

The spirit of the Vedas is warlike. In many ways it is a paean of glory to the military caste. The 200,000-line epic poem *Mahabharata* is one long-drawn-out battle between two brothers in a war of succession.

The Bhagavad-Gita, the "Song of God" (5–2 c. B.C.) which has been called "the Gospel of India" and "the focus of all Indian religion," may be said to be Hinduism's metaphysical defense of war. This in spite of the fact that it sees life as an illusion, and finds no way of improving it. Before the decisive battle on the plain of Kurukshetra, the hero Arjuna, recognizing in the ranks of the men whom he is about to fight and possibly kill many of his friends and kinsmen, throws aside his bow and arrows and decides not to fight. "Murder most hateful, murder of brothers! Am I indeed so greedy of greatness?" But the incarnate god

THAT MEN SHOULD NOT RESIST EVIL

Krishna chides him for his weakness, calls his scruples despicable, and orders him to do battle. The body is an illusion, declares Krishna, and therefore its destruction in battle is also an illusion. No one is really slain and no one actually slays. Therefore, no one should grieve. "Bodies are said to die, but that which possesses the body is eternal. It cannot be limited or destroyed. Therefore, you must fight."

Arjuna is also told by Krishna that he belongs to the warrior caste, and therefore it is his caste duty to fight: "Die and you win heaven. Conquer, and you enjoy earth. Stand up now, son of Kunti, and resolve to fight." [9]

There is nothing in the laws of Manu to suggest that wars of aggression are unjust, or that there can be a nobler way of life for mankind. Even Buddhism has little to say about the wrongfulness of war, and nowhere envisions a warless society. Islam exhorted men to wage war for the faith.[10] In Christendom, holy wars were preached by priests, and crusades were launched to recover the Holy Sepulcher—although Jesus was not only averse to war, but preached unqualified pacifism.

Peace as a noble ideal and an objective to be pursued by men and nations became at an early stage an essential part of the religious culture of the Jew. Over and over again the burden of the message of Judaism was: "Not by might, nor by force, but by My Spirit" (Zech. 4:6).

Judaism hated war and the shedding of blood. "If one sheds blood it is accounted to him as though he diminished the image of God" (Gen. 9:6).[11] King David was denied the privilege of building the Temple because his hands had spilled much blood (I Chr. 22:8). There is no glorification of war in Judaism; there was never any call to Israel to become a great military power. Military prowess is nowhere extolled as the noblest of virtues. That the Jews fought when necessary, and with extraordinary valor and heroism, the legions of Rome, the armies of Antiochus, and the hosts who faced Joshua and the chieftains of Israel could well testify. But Israel did not emphasize its military achievements. Israel's hope for the future was bound up with the hope of universal disarmament, with an international society banded in brotherhood, united in the law of God for justice and freedom.

Judaism was convinced that the good society is possible, but that it will not come about through inaction, abdication, or despair. It summoned men to resist all evil—the evil in themselves and the evil in society—to hasten the day "when man shall live each under his vine and under his fig tree, with none to make him afraid" (Micah 4:4).

THAT DEATH IS BETTER THAN LIFE

Death overshadows the thought of nearly all the religions of antiquity. It was also at the core of the most important ethical-philosophic systems. The sad and hopeless quest of immortality is the central theme not only of the Sumerian epic of Gilgamesh, but also of the myth of Adapa, and of many others. The religions of Egypt concerned themselves to the point of obsession with death and the Hereafter. Even the finest philosophic minds of ancient Greece could not escape its dark and dread enchantment. The calmest and most scientific of the Greeks, Aristotle, declared: "Not to be born is the best thing and death is better than life!" And Sophocles' Chorus chants in *Oedipus at Colonus*: "Not to be born is, past all prizing, best, but when a man hath seen the light, this is next best by far, that with all speed he should go thither, whence he hath come." [1]

Judaism alone was primarily preoccupied with life, with man's life here on earth. The Torah is called *Torat Hayim*, a Torah for life, not for "eternal" life but simply for this life, not even for "eternal life" in the fabricated sense of some modern theologians —the "eternal" moment in the passing experience. The Torah uses terms far more simply and therefore far more profoundly.

The laws of the Torah are a preparation for life—the full life of the affections and senses, as well as of the mind and the spirit— "which, if a man do, he shall live by them" (Lev. 18:5). "The commandments were given for no other purpose than to help men to live because of them, and not to die" [2] The Torah shows no interest in the career of the soul after death. "Death is a matter of comparative indifference and seldom a subject of profound reflection in the Old Testament. Life goes on, and death cannot seriously retard its progress through the centuries of history." [3]

It is remarkable to note the extraordinary reticence of the Bible and the Mishnah on the subjects of death, resurrection, immortality, the Hereafter, the Judgment Day in the afterlife, Heaven and Hell, and the Messiah—subjects which occupied so large a place in the religions of the Near East, the Greco-Roman world, and Christianity. Resurrection is mentioned once in the Mishnah, when it is announced as a dogma; [4] again when it is stated that "we make mention of the Power of Rain in the second of Eighteen Benedictions—the Resurrection of the Dead"; [5] and once again in the statement of R. Phineas b. Yair that the Holy Spirit leads to the resurrection of the dead and that the latter will come through Elijah. [6] There are no descriptions of the world to come in the Mishnah, and none of the symbolic trivia characteristic of an apocalypse. The "Days of the Messiah" is mentioned once in connection with an interpretation of a verse in the Bible ("all the days of your life" [Dt. 16:3] is to include the Days of the Messiah). [7] It is also stated that in the days of the Messiah vast disorders and social anarchy will occur [8]—and that is all!

The strong-willed faith of a robust, life-loving people, directed toward a full and creative human existence, could not have been centered in death. The supreme privilege of the faithful was "to walk before God and to see the goodness of God in the land of the living" (Ps. 116:9; 27:13). In a bold homily on the verse in Ecclesiastes, "for a living dog is better than a dead lion" (9:4), the Rabbis pointed up the priority which must be accorded to life. When King David died, Solomon, his son, "sent an inquiry to the Bet Hamidrash: 'My father is dead and lying in the sun; and the dogs of my father's house are hungry; what shall I do?' They sent back word: feed the dogs first and then attend to your dead father." ⁹ The living dogs took precedence over the dead king!

King Hezekiah, sick and at the point of death, prays: "O restore me to health and make me live! . . . For Sheol cannot thank Thee, death cannot praise Thee; those who go down to the pit cannot hope for Thy faithfulness. The living, the living, he thanks Thee, as I do this day!" (Is. 38:16, 18–19). The same thought is echoed in Psalm 115:16–18. "The heavens are the Lord's heavens, but the earth He has given to the sons of men. The dead do not praise the Lord, nor do any that go down into silence. But we will bless the Lord from this time forth and evermore." (See also Ps. 6:6, and Ps. 88:10–12.) So also Ben Sira: "Who can praise God in the grave? . . . Thanksgiving is not with the dead; the living, the living he alone can praise God" (Ecclus. 17:27–28).

All these expressions seem as if they were deliberately aimed at the Egyptian notion concerning the rôle of the dead in the netherworld. The dominant note in all the Pyramid Texts "is an insistent, a passionate protest against the reality of death." ¹⁰ The Bible, on the other hand, wishes man to accept the finality of death, and to become reconciled to it: "We must all die, we are like water spilt on the ground, which cannot be gathered up again" (II Sam. 14:14).

Judaism made a determined effort to direct the attentions of men away from the realm of the dead, away from necrolatry and necromancy to the enterprise of life and to the faithful observance of God's statutes and ordinances "all the days that you live upon the earth" (Dt. 12:1). Isaiah scorns those who consult the dead in behalf of the living and who seek "the ghosts and the familiar spirits that chirp and mutter" (Is. 8:19–20). In the eyes of the Deuteronomist, necromancy is one of the abominations of the heathen because of which they are being driven out. "But as for you, the Lord your God has not allowed you so to do" (Dt. 18:11–14). Leviticus looks upon those who seek the ghosts and the familiar spirits as having defiled themselves. "I will set my face against that person, and will cut him off from among his people" (Lev. 19:31; 20:6). In the days of Saul mediums who consulted the dead were put to death (I Sam. 28:9).

The Rabbis advised men not to speculate too much about the future life, not to try to penetrate beyond the boundaries of this world, but to concentrate on this world and how it can be made a good place for men to dwell in.

"Whosoever speculates upon four things, it were better for him if he had never been born: what is above, what is below, and what was before [creation] and what will be after." [11] Nothing is known about the future life. It may be a life of perfect happiness for the righteous, but "better is one hour of repentance and good works in this world than the whole life of the world to come." [12] The general approach is laid down in Scriptures: "The secret things belong to the Lord our God, but the things that are revealed belong to us and to our children that we may do all the words of this law" (Dt. 29:28; see also Ecclus. 3:21–23).

The Kingdom of God—which mankind with the help of God is to build—is in Judaism's view definitely of this world, and all of man's tasks are centered here. In Judaism, the Kingdom of God means the Good Society. In Christianity, it means the Future World—the Hereafter.

When Jesus declared, "My Kingdom is not of this world" (John 18:36), he correctly defined the nature of his gospel. But Judaism's Kingdom of God referred to the reign of the one true God on earth, to the conversion of all peoples to faith in Him alone, and to the establishment of universal justice and peace. It saw Jerusalem as the spiritual center of a united and reformed humanity. "It shall come to pass in the end of days that the mountain of the house of the Lord shall be established as the highest of the mountains . . . and peoples shall flow to it, and many nations shall come and say: Come, let us go up to the mountain of the Lord . . . that He may teach us of His ways and we may walk in His paths" (Is. 2:2–3; Mic. 4:1–2).

When the ideas of resurrection and other eschatological notions gained headway among the Jewish people toward the beginning of the common era, an otherworldly interpretation was given to the concept of the Kingdom of God. In it were included also the resurrected dead. It is from the apocalypses and their Iranian and Hellenistic sources that these beliefs, which proved dominant in the New Testament, derive. But eschatology never displaced the original prophetic element in Judaism's vision of the Kingdom of God.

Among the Rabbis, the term Kingdom of God was also used metaphorically for "the true religion," the belief in the one true God. A convert to Judaism accepted "the yoke of the Kingdom of Heaven," which was symbolized by his recitation of "Hear, O Israel, the Lord our God, the Lord is One."

No prayers to or for the dead are ordained in the Bible, no sacrifices to the dead, no ancestor worship, and no prescribed rites of sepulture. There are no mortuary incantations and talismanic formulae, such as abound in the Pyramid Texts of the Egyptians. No public games were held in honor of the dead, as was the case with the Greeks, no equestrian contests and no musical festivals. Judaism opposed the cult of the dead even as it opposed the cult of nature. Nowhere in the Pentateuch is there the promise of reward and punishment in a future life, or of a Judgment after death, or any information about Heaven or Purgatory or Hell. The fact that no spiritual promises for the future world are mentioned in the Torah in the same way as are the material promises in *this* world caused—to quote the Jewish philosopher Joseph Albo (15 c.)—"no end of difficulty to the ancients as well as to the moderns." He himself devotes two chapters in his *Book of Roots* to an attempt to explain it.[18]

The Judaism of the Bible does not rest upon the dogmas of resurrection and immortality, though an occasional late reference to resurrection may be found in it (Is. 26:19; I Sam. 2:6; Dan. 12:2). They are not key ideas with the Hebrew prophets. For a thousand years throughout Judaism's greatest creative period, these beliefs were not regarded as essential doctrines, though they were undoubtedly entertained by some, principally in the latter days of the Second Commonwealth, and more particularly by Jews living amidst powerful alien influences beyond the borders of Judaea. Dr. Zeitlin calls attention to the fact that the only book of the Second Commonwealth that argues for the doctrine of resurrection and speaks of praying for the dead is the Second Book of Maccabees, which was written outside Judaea around the beginning of the common era.[14]

It is only with the Book of Daniel—the only apocalyptic work admitted to the Canon of the Bible—which reflects in its second part the desperate plight of the faithful during the unprecedented religious persecutions of Antiochus, and the bitter Maccabean struggle for the preservation of Judaism, that the promise of reward for the righteous and punishment for the faithless after death comes into prominence. This belief was accepted in the circle of the Ḥasidim. It became a characteristic feature of subsequent apocalyptic writings which were modeled after the Book of Daniel. With these writings there came into vogue many other mystic concepts and symbols—which, if not altogether new, were in their number and emphasis a sharp deviation from normal Jewish standards. "It is increasingly clear," writes Professor Albright,

that indirect pagan influences entered mainly through the compositions of eschatologists who swarmed in Jewry during the period which began with Daniel and Enoch and which ended with the Apocalypse and IV Esdras. . . . Through the eschatologists innumerable elements of pagan imagery and even entire myths entered into the literature of Judaism and Christianity.[15]

These apocalypses were very popular and they had their value. They voiced the patriotic sentiments of the people, their need for comfort and vindication. But they had their dangers, too, and these were not fully recognized and confronted by the Rabbis until after the spread of Gnosticism and the rise of Christianity. In the second century the Rabbis placed a ban upon the whole apocalyptic literature, exclusive of the Book of Daniel.[16] "Those who read them will have no portion in the world to come."[17]

The late and desultory reference to resurrection and immortality in Jewish literature is not due to the fact that the Jews before the second century B.C. were either unaware of these ideas or had not reached a level of spiritual development where they could entertain them. Belief in resurrection and immortality in one form or another was well nigh universal.

Even among some of the most primitive peoples of antiquity one finds the widespread beliefs that "the dead do not wholly die," that they survive in body or soul or both, either in or near their place of entombment or in some separate spirit world, that they are possessed of some form of consciousness and may sometimes, as earth-spirits, intervene in the destiny of the living. Belief in resurrection, based on the analogy of the annual regeneration cycle of vegetation, was common. Even higher conceptions of the soul of man, as having its source in a supreme deity and returning at death to its original home, were not unknown in the ancient world.

These prevailing beliefs could not have been unknown to the teachers of Judaism. The Jews in Babylonia, who came in such close contact with the religious ideas and institutions of that country, could not have been uninfluenced by them. Nor could the Jews of the Persian Empire have been unaware of the cardinal ideas in the highly developed eschatological system of Zoroastrianism. This must have been especially true of the Jews of Egypt who lived among a people who "never ceased to contemplate death," and whose religions and funerary art began "with the strangest collective madness in history." [18]

The inference is clear. The teachers of Judaism knew about these ideas and for a long time resisted them deliberately, refusing to give them official sanction. Their uncompromising monotheism could not be reconciled to a concept of resurrection which was everywhere linked up with ancestor-worship or necromancy. Nor could they incorporate into Judaism a doctrine of immortality which in many minds endowed the soul with some form of divine status. In the ancient world disembodied souls were either regarded as gods and worshiped as such, or they were closely identified with the deity. Recounting the sins of Israel in the wilderness, the Psalmist says: "They attached themselves to Baal Peor, and ate the sacrifices offered to the dead" (Ps. 106:28). In the Book of Jubilees, Abraham admonishes Jacob, "Separate thyself from the nations, and eat not with them, for they offer their sacrifices to the dead, and they worship evil spirits, and they eat over the graves." [19] King Saul, who had demanded of the medium of Endor that she bring up to him the prophet Samuel from the netherworld, said to her, "What do you see?" And the woman said to Saul, "I see a god coming up out of the earth" (I Sam. 28:13).

This was the case with the rituals of Osiris in Egypt:

> In every funeral inscription known to us from the Pyramid Texts down to the roughly written prayers upon the coffins of the Roman period, what is done for Osiris is done also for the deceased, the state and condition of Osiris are the state and condition of the deceased; in a word the deceased is identified with Osiris. If Osiris liveth forever, the deceased will live forever; if Osiris dieth, then will the deceased perish.[20]

Similar ideas dominate the Greek Orphic and Eleusinian mysteries. Immortality, to the Greek mind, was what distinguished gods from men. To ascribe immortality to the soul meant ascribing divinity to it.

Professor Guthrie correctly observes: "Gods may have other characteristics, but primarily and essentially they are the immortals, and it is their immortality which differentiates them from men. . . . It follows that to believe the soul to be immortal is to believe it to be divine. If man is immortal, then he is god." [21]

Such a notion was intolerable to Judaism. Man's destiny and God's are not identical. Man does not become one with God through ecstasy in life or when death overtakes him. Just as Judaism established levels between man and the beast, below which he must never sink, so it set boundaries between man and the divine above which he must not aspire. Man has his own large and sufficient domain. To "cling to God," to "seek His nearness"—*hitdabkut*—even in their most intensive modes among the Jewish mystics, never involved a crossing of the barriers separating mortal man from immortal God. To emphasize this thought some Rabbis, like R. Jose, pupil of Akiba (2 c.), declared categorically: "The Shechinah [Presence of God] never descended to earth, and Moses and Elijah never ascended to Heaven, as it is written, 'The heavens are the heavens of the Lord, but the earth He gave to the sons of men.' " [22]

Clearly, therefore, it was not any spiritual evolution in Judaism which, toward the beginning of the common era, brought the doctrine of resurrection and immortality within the framework of authoritative Judaism, but, quite simply, the inability of its leaders further to withstand popular pressure. The belief was finally sanctioned because it could no longer be ignored or minimized. It had gained the upper hand. The final sanction was made easier by the fact that the dangers to monotheism among the Jewish people and the fear of their relapse into idolatry had greatly diminished during the Second Commonwealth, especially after the Maccabean victory. The Pharisaic leaders of Judaism were accordingly less inhospitable to these popular longings.

Even Anan and most of the Karaites in later times, who in their doctrines and practices resembled so closely the Sadducees, departed sharply from them on the issues of resurrection and immortality, and adopted the position of the Rabbis. These beliefs had become too much a part of the religion of the Jewish people to be challenged, even though the Karaite leaders realized full well that there was no authority for them in Scriptures.

The popular imagination, once let loose in the eschatological wonderland, ranged far afield in the realms of Heaven and Hell, in the mansions of the blessed and the dread abodes of the doomed, concerning which Scriptures and prophets had been so remarkably reticent. Secret and wondrous things were reported about these domains which had now become places of reward and felicity for the good and punishment and torment for the wicked. Sheol, which had formerly been viewed only as a land of silence and a realm of shades, and not as a place of torment, is now "a waste and horrible place." [23] *Ge Hinnom,* the Valley of Hinnom, the place of refuse outside Jerusalem where aforetime Moloch had been worshiped with human sacrifices, now, in the hands of the Apocalyptic writers, became the Place of Judgment, the bottomless and fiery pit where sinners are punished.[24]

In *The Sibylline Oracles, The Assumption of Moses, Baruch,* and elsewhere in the Apocalypses, changes are rung on the theme of the rewards of the righteous in the Hereafter, in Heaven, in Paradise, and the punishments of the wicked in Sheol, in the Abyss, in Gehenna, according to the taste of the respective authors as to what is most exquisite in pleasure or pain.

Many tales and expressions of an apocalyptic nature are to be found in Rabbinic literature, but always only as Haggadah. They never became dogma or theology. Dr. Kohler pertinently observes in his study *Heaven and Hell*:

Still, there is an essential difference between the rabbinic eschatology and that of the New Testament, in that the latter has been fastened into a firm, dogmatic creed, allowing no dissension, whereas the former was regarded simply as the free expression of individuals allowing for a wide diversity of opinion.[25]

Eternal punishment for the wicked finds no official acceptance in Judaism. There were few Rabbis indeed who entertained the violent views of the Apocalypses on this subject. There were those who spoke of the sudden and total annihilation of the utterly wicked after a limited period of punishment, but not of their interminable suffering. The Mishnah, which contains only scant reference to Gehenna, limits the punishment of the wicked to twelve months. In the opinion of the famed Halachist R. Johanan b. Nuri (1 c.), it is limited to seven weeks.[26] No one under twenty is subject to punishment in the Hereafter,[27] and no Rabbi speaks of punishment for infants. Some teachers, like Maimonides, regarded Gehenna as a state or condition, rather than a place, and did not take it literally.

Even after the ideas of resurrection and immortality gained acceptance, despite tremendous and prolonged opposition, the feeling persisted that they represented a deviation from the classic position of the Torah. Resurrection was for generations the chief doctrinal point of contention between the Pharisees and the Sadducees. The Sadducees denied it entirely on the ground that it had no basis in Scriptures. The Pharisees were hard put to locate such a doctrine in the Pentateuch.[28] As late as the first and second centuries of the common era, Rabbis, in their polemics with the Christians—who found their principal authority for the belief in resurrection in the miracle of the risen Jesus—were still casting about to find adequate Scriptural authority for their own belief in an afterlife. Opposition to the doctrine among Jews continued well into the third century c.e., long after the Sadducees had ceased to exist as a party in Israel. Rabbis like Simon b. Lakish (3 c.) were still under the necessity of marshaling arguments in its defense.

Centuries before, in the Book of Job (4 c. b.c.), the belief in resurrection had been weighed and rejected as a possible solution to the problem of the suffering of the innocent. "As the cloud fades and vanishes, so he who goes down to Sheol does not come up" (Job 7–9). On the basis of this verse Raba (3–4 c.), head of the academy at Maḥoza, declared that Job denied the resurrection of the dead.[29] It was "while in the flesh," that Job wished to be vindicated by God in his righteousness (Job 19:25–26).

The Book of Ecclesiastes (4–3 c. b.c.) is thoroughly skeptical regarding the whole subject:

For the fate of the sons of men and the fate of the beasts is the same; as one dies, so dies the other. . . . All go to one place; all are from the dust, and all turn to dust again. Who knows whether the spirit of man goes upward and the spirit of the beast goes down to the earth? [3:19–21]

A similarly categoric denial of an afterlife—though without Koheleth's defeatist attitude—is to be found in the writings of Ben Sira (3 c. b.c.). He who speaks with such deep pathos of human suffering, and instructs men how bravely and patiently to face life's predicaments, pain, bereavement, and death, cannot offer the consolation of resurrection or immortality to man. Death is part of God's plan for the human race, and as such should be accepted with fortitude and resignation:

Fear not the sentence of death, remember them that have been before you, and that come after; for this is the sentence of the Lord over all flesh. And why are you against the pleasure of the most High? There is no inquisition in the grave, whether you have lived ten, or a hundred or a thousand years.[30]

But there is a blessed immortality in the echoing renown of one's life *on earth*. "A good life hath but few days; but a good name endures forever." [31] The life of the individual ends in extinction, but not the life of his people, nor the good things which a man has built, nor the noble causes which he has served, nor his memory or influence. To live esteemed of men, to die in peace and to abide in grateful remembrance is a hope not unworthy of noble men and may for them be ample and serene fulfillment. No man should be deterred or discouraged from maximum idealism or self-fulfillment in life by the thought of death. Death should make life more precious, and the brevity of man's days on earth should give to his tasks the spur of urgency.

I Maccabees (100 B.C.), which records the heroic struggles of the Jews for faith and freedom and their persecutions and martyrdom, offers no promise of reward in an afterlife to the faithful. Men should give their lives for the Law because the Law is precious and it is the way to do honor to the ancient covenant of their fathers (2:50). Nor does the Book of Baruch (200 B.C.) encourage any such expectations (2:17). Its promise is one of deliverance from exile, of restoration and joy to the whole people of Israel.

One cannot escape the impression that the deviation toward eschatology represented a sharp departure from classical Judaism. Whether due to alien mystic influences which proved irresistible, or to the weakening of the sense of group solidarity wherein the individual could formerly find complete fulfillment and could merge his destiny with the imperishable life of his people, it was now apparently necessary to comfort the individual with promises of a happy dénouement to the drama of his earthly existence, not only in time but in eternity, not only here but in the hereafter. This was a radical departure from what the prophets had promised—a happy consummation to the unrequited labors, sorrows, and frustrated hopes of Israel "at the end of days," but here on earth and in historic time.

Nevertheless the doctrine of resurrection, and its associated eschatological elements to which the Jews added nothing original, gained ground rapidly from the period of the Hasmonean struggle onward, and came to be firmly established in Rabbinic Judaism.

Probably under Greek influence, the doctrine of the immortality of the soul also came to be widely accepted. For the Sages of Israel, however, the doctrine of immortality was not, as with Socrates and Plato, a metaphysical necessity or a solution for the dualism of matter and form, of body and soul, since in this material world it was not possible for man to know full truth. The Rabbis presented it as a moral necessity. It was a solution for the problem of unmerited human suffering on earth, an answer to the bitter plaint: "This is the Torah, and this is the reward?" It was to justify the ways of God to man.

This is dramatized in the story of Elisha b. Abuyah. Why did he become a heretic? ask the Rabbis. He once saw a man climb to the top of a palm tree on the Sabbath, take the mother-bird with the young (both acts in violation of the Law), and descend in safety. At the termination of the Sabbath he saw a man climb to the top of a palm tree and take the young but let the mother-bird go free (both acts in keeping with the Law), and as he descended a snake bit him and he died. Elisha exclaimed, "It is written: 'You shall let the mother go, but the young you may take to yourself; that it may go well with you, and that you may live long' [Dt. 22:7]. Where is the well-being of this man, and where is the prolonging of his days!" He was unaware of how R.

Akiba explained it: " 'That it may be well with you' in the world [to come] which is wholly good, 'And that you may live long' in the world which is unending!"[32]

It is noteworthy, however, that centuries later orthodox Jewish philosophers, like Ḥasdai Crescas (15 c.) and his pupil Joseph Albo, still refused to include resurrection among the basic principles of Judaism, but regarded it only as a secondary, derivative "belief accepted by the nations."

Crescas, in opposition to the views of Maimonides, does not include resurrection and immortality among his basic principles of Judaism.[33] And Maimonides, while accepting resurrection as an article of faith and while including it in his Thirteen Principles, makes no menton of it in his *Guide,* and does not find place for it in his philosophic system.

Albo, who participated in the religious disputations at Tortosa (1413), writes in his *Book of Roots*:

But it [Resurrection] is not itself either a fundamental or a derivative principle of divine law in general or of the Law of Moses in particular, for they can be conceived without it. As long as one believes in reward and punishment generally, whether corporeal, in this word, or spiritual, in the world to come, he does not deny a principle of the Law of Moses if he disbelieves in resurrection. Nevertheless it is a dogma accepted by our nation, and everyone professing the Law of Moses is obliged to believe it. . . .[34] Belief in the Messiah and in the resurrection of the dead are principles peculiar to Christianity which cannot be conceived without them. But resurrection and the Messiah [in Judaism] are like branches issuing from the principles of Reward and Punishment and are not root principles in themselves.[35]

Albo is correct in drawing attention to the relative importance which the doctrine of resurrection has for Christianity in contrast to Judaism. With Christianity it is the *sine qua non*—the chief cornerstone of the entire edifice of its faith. Paul made that point unmistakably clear. "But if there is no resurrection of the dead, then Christ has not been raised; if Christ has not been raised, then

our preaching is in vain and your faith is in vain" (I. Cor.
15:13f.).

A man should serve His God, the teachers of Judaism maintained, regardless of reward, and should endure his share of unavoidable suffering in brave and quiet resignation, not blaming
God but relying upon His justice and wisdom. Men could live
contentedly in such a faith, and die exultingly in its defense. The
Jews produced the first martyrs for religion in history at a time
when the belief in personal immortality was not part of their
authoritative faith. In the period of the frightful religious persecutions of Antiochus, Jews laid down their lives for their faith in
large numbers. In his *Jerusalem Under the High Priests*, Edwyn
Bevan writes:

And when we reckon up our debt to Israel, we must remember that
it is this crisis which opens the roll of martyrs. There were many in
that day of agony who endured everything, the several forms of
torture and death, rather than disobey the Law of their God. . . . In
a way the Jewish martyrs of this type were more sorely tried than
their Christian successors. The Christians were prepared for persecution; in connection with the whole scheme of things, with the certain
future blessedness, it was at worst only a transitory moment of
pain. . . . But the Jewish martyrs were the pioneers on this road;
to them this affliction was an appalling surprise; death, remember,
had not been to their thinking the gate into life, but a darkness which
God, in the case of His faithful servants, held back till they had
enjoyed their full measure of days.[36]

The Jews had been prepared to accept the rôle of martyrdom
by a faith which was tested in the fires of several earlier experiences of national disaster and suffering, such as the Babylonian
exile, and the tragedies which occurred in later generations.
They loved their faith and clung to it with sacrificial devotion
regardless of life's bitter trials and vicissitudes. They did not require the promise of rewards in some future life to validate their
sacrifices. How else could the Psalmist sing: "The snares of death
encompass me; the pangs of Sheol laid hold of me; I suffered dis-

tress and anguish. . . . I have kept my faith, even when I said, I am greatly afflicted. . . . Precious in the sight of the Lord is the death of his saints" (Ps. 116:3, 10, 15). They believed that "the righteous shall be requited on earth" (Pr. 11:31); but even where experience ran contrary to this faith, they nevertheless continued to trust the hidden wisdom of their God, Who was the consolation of Israel and his high hope.

It was enough in those times for the faithful Jew to know that God is in the world and that in His own good time goodness and righteousness will triumph. The faithful Buddhist did not wish to survive. The Orphic, the Platonist, and the Christian wished to survive eternally. The Jew of the Bible and until late in the period of the Second Commonwealth was content to fulfill himself in this life, and in the continuing life of his people. "The life of a mortal man is of numbered days, but the life of Jeshurun [Israel] is of days without number" (Ecclus. 37:25). He found sustenance in the knowledge that a divine promise and covenant ensured the eternity of Israel, that he belonged to a people whose work in the world was God's work. To be so privileged, if only for the duration of one's finite life, was sufficient—nay, was abundantly generous.

Homer's heroic folk, too, faced life and death in some such manner. They had no faith in personal immortality. Beyond the grave was a somber shadow-land, "a dim world where men are bloodless and impotent ghosts." [87] Yet they fought and died bravely for honor and duty, for pride of family and native land. They lacked, however, the glowing faith in a personal God of justice and love which the Hebrews had, a God Who had chosen Israel as His beloved instrument. Hence the underlying spiritual pessimism of the Homeric heroes and the sadness of their world.

Some writers have treated the ethics of the Torah rather condescendingly and have dwelt with distaste upon the earthly rewards of prosperity and peace which are promised to those who obey the Law. They point rather vaguely to a conception of higher and selfless ethics in the New Testament. It is difficult to understand why the expectation of rewards for a good life in this world is any more mercenary than the expectation of eternal rewards in the next world. If anything, the former expectation appears to be a far more modest and reasonable return on a relatively limited investment.

Actually, the Old Testament dwells abundantly on the so-called higher ethics as well. The virtue and nobility of disinterested piety is the very core of the ethical message of Job, and the theme is eloquently restated time and again in the Psalms: "Whom have I in heaven but Thee and there is nothing upon earth that I desire besides Thee. Though my flesh and my heart fail, God is my rock and my portion forever. . . . My highest good is to be near God" (Ps. 73:25-26, 29). The singer of Psalm 17 does not envy the prosperity of the wicked, the men who are interested only in the material things of this world—how to fill their bellies with plenty and how to leave a rich material heritage to their children. "As for me, I shall behold Thy face in righteousness; when I awake, I shall be satisfied with beholding Thy form" (v. 15).

Normally, it was held that good will follow the good—and evil will result in evil. Were this not so, no social order could exist. Law would have no meaning and ethical conduct would have no basis whatsoever in the life of man. There may be "pure sciences" unrelated to utilitarian needs, but there is certainly no "pure ethics" and no "pure faith." But the rule of compensation in human terms is not unfailing, and the reasons for the deviations are beyond man's ken. Man should not look for or expect automatic compensations for his meritorious conduct, or automatic punishment for his evil conduct. "Be not like servants who serve their master for the sake of receiving a reward; but be like servants who serve their master without any expectation of reward." [38] This position of Antigonus is enthusiastically endorsed by R. Eleazer (perhaps R. Eleazar b. Zadok), who explains the verse, "Blessed is the man who fears the Lord, who greatly delights in His commandments" (Ps. 112:1) by saying: "In His commandments, but not in the reward of His commandments." [39] R. Eleazar b. Zadok said: "Do good deeds for their own sake." [40]

R. Eleazar's father is the author of the following saying: "Make not the works of the Law a crown wherewith to magnify yourself or a spade wherewith to dig." [41] This was also the view of Hillel.[42] On the verse: "to love the Lord, your God" (Dt. 11:13), the interpretation is given: A man should not say, I will study the Torah in order that I might become a scholar, or rich, or that I might receive a reward in the next world. One should serve God out of love.[43] Certainly no self-serving morality here!

Maimonides maintains that all the promises of reward were intended to encourage the young and the immature who had not yet reached the correct understanding of the nature of the good and the true, and who have not yet learned the deep satisfactions which may be derived from pursuing them for their own sake.

The sole object of seeking wisdom is to know more. The sole object of seeking truth is to know truth. Torah is truth; the sole object of studying the Torah is to do what is prescribed therein. . . . It is forbidden to a man of mature mind to ask what reward will I receive for doing good or refraining from doing evil. This is the way of a child who needs to be enticed to do what he should do, by the promise of sweets, nuts or figs. There is nothing wrong about these beliefs which the Sages "permitted" the masses, in their spiritual immaturity, to entertain; for from performing the commandments not for their own sake, they might ultimately come to perform them for their own sake.[44]

"The reward of a good deed is another good deed, and the punishment of sin is another sin." [45]

Of the great in the Bible—the Patriarchs, Moses, David, the later prophets—nothing is reported of their deaths except that they died and were gathered to their fathers. Their story is not continued by some epic in an afterlife.

To learn about the religion of the Egyptians one must go to the Pyramid tombs and to the mastaba shrines of the royal burial places, to which so much of the art, labor, and wealth of ancient Egypt was devoted.

In Judaism the dead body is the gravest of all defilements (Nu.

19:11; Lev. 22:4–6). Priests were not permitted to contaminate themselves by coming in contact with the dead except for the nearest of kin. The High Priest was not to go near the dead body even of his own father and mother (Lev. 21:1, 10–11). A mourner was barred from the Temple Mount during the first two or three days of mourning,[46] and a man who had contact with the dead was excluded from the Ḥel, the Rampart which surrounded the inner precincts of the Temple.[47]

The dead were often buried within Christian churches, but never in a synagogue. There was no apotheosis of martyrs in Judaism, no worship of saints and their relics, though veneration was shown to the graves of the patriarchs, prophets, and other worthies, and prayers were offered at their tombs. There are no special Saints' Days in Judaism, and no saint as such is commemorated in the calendar of the Synagogue. No one was ever officially canonized as a saint. There is remarkable little *passiones* or *acta martyrum* in Jewish literature. Jews were chary of hagiology, although martyrs were held in supreme reverence by the people of Israel: "Those martyred by the State—no man can stand within their exalted station." [48] It is an understatement to say: "The significance of the martyr, of his relics and grave, the anniversary of his death as well as the belief in his great interceding powers played an incomparably greater rôle in the Church." [49] Emperor Julian chided the Christians of his day: "You have filled the whole world with tombs and sepulchers, and yet in your scriptures it is nowhere said that you must grovel among tombs and pay them honour." [50]

Food and drink and furnishing were provided the departed among many ancient peoples. Wives and servants were often immolated to accompany the dead. Widow burying and self-immolation (suttee) persisted in India to very recent times. Sensual enjoyment and houris in Paradise were promised to the faithful by the founder of a religion as late and as severely monotheistic as Islam.[51] Judaism spurned all such ideas. In the face of all such appetitive wish fulfillments for the next world, not unknown among some of his own people, Rab declared: "In the future world there is no eating nor drinking nor propagation nor baseness nor jealousy nor hatred nor competition, but the righteous sit with their crowns on their heads feasting on the brightness of the divine presence." [52]

The fact of inevitable death did not determine for Judaism either its creed, its ritual, or its way of life. The crisis in human existence is not the fact of death or the awareness of man's insurmountable finiteness. Whatever is inherent, universal, and inevitable in the race of man does not constitute a crisis. It is the avoidable evils which men do, singly and collectively, to themselves or to others which bring crisis and tragedy into their lives. It is the needless and profligate waste of their limited years, the unassayed tasks, the locked opportunities, the talents withering in disuse, and all the summoning but untrodden ways of mind and soul which give rise to men's spiritual malaise and the deep-rooted and undefined sorrows of their lives.

Judaism counseled men not to be afraid of death nor mourn too long for their dear departed. "Weep not for the dead in excess, neither bemoan him beyond measure." [53] Men should not indulge in sorrow as in a luxury and dwell in the shadow-land of sad and never ending remembrance. Implied in prolonged mourning is a reproach against God. Men should not build monuments for the dead; the words and the deeds of the righteous are their true memorials.[54]

~(XVI)~

DIFFERENCES AND UNDERLYING UNITY

We have dwelt on the great new insights of Judaism which are easily recognizable at all stages of its development and which gave it a distinctive stamp and character: that God is One—Spiritual, Creator and Ruler of the universe, indwelling all nature, and yet transcending it; near to man in all his needs, and yet beyond man's full comprehension. That man, while fashioned out of the earth, is nevertheless made in the spiritual image of God. That while he is bound by his physical and mental limitations, he is boundless in his moral aspirations and is free to determine his own spiritual progress through his own efforts assisted by the grace of God. That both body and soul are of God, and that the whole of man—body, mind, and soul—is sacred. That all men are equal in their essential humanity and in the sight of God. That there is but one moral law for prince and pauper, ruler and subject, native born and stranger. That life is good and a gracious gift of God. That the moral ills which exist in the world can be overcome, and that in overcoming them lies the true meaning and the adventure of human life. That an age of universal justice, brotherhood, and peace awaits the human race and can be hastened by the efforts of the human race. That there is divine retribution in ways and forms not always clear to man. That man's concern should be with life this side of the grave.

These are the basic and the enduring ideas of Judaism. Some of the other great religions of mankind possess one or more of them. Some adopted them directly from Judaism. But Judaism wove them all into a single and unique pattern, integrated and correlated them in a religious idealism and an ethical code which have powerfully influenced civilizations in the past and which will continue to mold them in the future.

These great insights are found in the Bible, which has been called the epic of the world, the book of the ages, which is inextricably bound up with the culture, ethics, history, art, and literature of half the world. It has nourished the hearts and minds of countless generations of men, and has guided, challenged, and inspired the humble and the great, the idealist, the social reformer, the advocate of peace, the champion of freedom and democracy, the dreamers of mankind's great dreams. The truths of the Bible are inexhaustible and deathless, and, in freshness and relevancy, unaging.

But while the crown jewels of Judaism are found in the Bible, its spiritual treasures are not limited to it. Subsequent ages also produced Sages, Seers, and Rabbis, whose wisdom is embodied in later Jewish writings—in the Apocrypha, the Talmud, the Midrash, and the individual works of scholars, poets, and philosophers which have continued to this day. Their teachings constitute an integral part of the endlessly replenished religious literature of Judaism.

Along with a unique religious literature, Judaism created also a unique type of worship and a unique religious institution which is called the synagogue. The eminent Christian scholar and historian of religion, Robert Herford, wrote: "With the synagogue began a new type of worship in the history of humanity, the type of congregational worship. In all their long history the Jewish people have done scarcely anything more wonderful than to create the synagogue. No human institution has a longer continuous history and none has done more for the uplifting of the human race." And Professor Moore wrote:

The consequences of the establishment of such a rational worship for the whole subsequent history of Judaism was immeasurable. Its persistent character, and, it is not too much to say, the very preservation of its existence through all the vicissitudes of its fortunes, it owes more than anything else to the synagogue. Nor is it for Judaism alone that it had this importance. It determined the type of Christian worship, which in the Greek and Roman world of the day might otherwise easily have taken the form of a mere mystery; and, in part directly, in part through the church, it furnished the model to Mohammed. Thus Judaism gave to the world not only the fundamental ideas of these great monotheistic religions but the institutional forms in which they have perpetuated and propagated themselves.[1]

It is not argued in these chapters that in all matters in which Judaism differed from other systems of religious belief it was superior to them. In many ways, indeed, Judaism was superior, and as pioneer in the field of ethical religion, Israel did merit the Biblical designation of "first-born" (Ex. 4:22). But qualitative differences are not necessarily competitive assessments. All rivers run to the sea, but their courses and channels differ widely. Each system of thought has its own texture and pattern, and each faith its own perspectives. There are radically divergent views, for example, between Judaism and Buddhism—a faith which in all probability was in no way influenced by Judaism—in regard to basic perspectives of life and human destiny; yet both created noble patterns of life for their followers and inspired generations of men. Both Christianity and Islam, which did inherit much from Judaism, but deviated from it in certain essential regards, molded great civilizations and produced men of noblest character and idealism. Differences should not obscure the underlying unity of the human race or the common needs of human life which all institutions and beliefs of mankind aim to serve, or the urgency for their close cooperation to achieve their common purposes.

To draw attention to priorities or to certain superior levels of religious, intellectual, artistic, or technological evolution attained by this or that people is simply to indicate stages in the progress of the human race, which never advances in any fixed, regular, or uniform procession for all peoples alike. No one people has a monopoly on all fields of progress. Excellence in one field may be counterpoised by deficiencies in others. The span of creative achievement of any people is neither unlimited or uninterrupted. Nor are the contributions of any one people sufficient for the encompassing life of humanity. Whatever is finally achieved by any people by way of enduring truth, beauty, or utility becomes in the end the grateful possession of all.

No religious body has warrant for complacency, and none should live abstracted from the realities of the present hour and its unfinished tasks, bemused by thoughts of former triumphs and trophies. The humbling thought for all religions is the realization that none has fulfilled its promise and its mission in the world. "We look for justice but there is none; for deliverance but it is far from us" (Is. 59:11). Mankind has come a long way, to be sure. It has indeed perceptibly advanced through the long centuries, but how slowly! And how dark and perilous still are our times! How many pay homage only with their lips to the faith they profess, and how often are the fires of these faiths quenched in dank formalism and ecclesiasticism and made the instruments of bigotry and fanaticism. How often are their cups of blessing turned into cups of staggering, turbid with the dregs of hate!

The one universal God does not require one universal church in which to be worshiped, but one universal devotion. In the realms of ascertainable facts, uniformity can be looked for. In the realms of art and philosophy there can be only sincerity of quest and expression—only dedication. Religion is the supreme art of humanity.

Judaism developed through the ages its own characteristic style, as it were, its own view of life, its code and forms of worship. It possesses its own traditions based on Torah and covenant.

Its adherents today find inspiration and spiritual contentment in it, as did their fathers before them, and wish to continue its historic identity within the configuration of other religious cultures. Other religions, too, developed their characteristic ways based on their unique traditions and experiences. There is much which all religions have in common and much which differentiates them. Their common purpose in the world will not be advanced by merger or amalgamation. Were all arts, philosophies, and religions cast into one mold, mankind would be the poorer for it. Unwillingness to recognize differences in religions is no evidence of broadmindedness. To ignore these differences is to overlook the deep cleavages which existed in the past and to assume a similarity of doctrine and outlook which does not exist in the present. The attempt to gloss over these differences as a gesture of goodwill is a superficial act which serves neither the purposes of scholarship nor the realities of the situation. It is far better and more practical to look for ways of working together on the basis of a forthright recognition of dissimilarities rather than on a fictitious assumption of identity. Indifference to one's own faith is no proof of tolerance. Loyalty to one's own is part of a larger loyalty to faith generally.

There are great areas of common interests in which all religions can cooperate in mutual helpfulness and respect, influencing one another and learning from one another.

Judaism, which differed and continues to differ from other religions in significant matters of belief and practice, has sought and seeks opportunities of friendly cooperation with them in all things which may contribute to the building of the good society, firm in its own convictions, reverent of theirs, hoping for the great day of universal reconciliation of all peoples, when "they shall not hurt nor destroy in all My holy mountain, and the earth shall be full of the knowledge of God as the waters cover the sea."

NOTES

INTRODUCTION

[1] Maimonides, *The Guide for the Perplexed*, III, 54, trans. M. Friedländer (1919), p. 394.
[2] The daily *'Amidah*, the Eighteen Benedictions of the Prayer Book.
[3] *Letter of Aristeas*, par. 235.
[4] A. N. Whitehead, "Nature and Life," in *Modes of Thought* (1938), p. 232.
[5] The Prayer Book, the second benediction preceding the Shm'a.

CHAPTER I. ONE AND THE SAME

[1] Naḥman Krochmal, *Moreh Nebuche Ha-Zeman*, ed. S. Rawidowicz (1924), Chaps. 8-11.
[2] Jerusalem Talmud, Sanhedrin 10:5.
[3] Maimonides, *Responsa*, ed. A. Freimann (1934), p. 310.

CHAPTER II. A PATTERN IN HISTORY

[1] See Paul Schubert, in *The Idea of History in the Ancient Near East*, ed. R. C. Dentan (1955), p. 342.
[2] San. 98a.
[3] *Mechilta D'Rabbi Ishmael*, ed. J. Z. Lauterbach (1949), II, 198.
[4] Yebamot 48b.
[5] Shabbat 31a.
[6] Tosefta San. 13:2.
[7] Megillah 13a.
[8] Ḳiddushin 40a.
[9] Pesaḥim 87b.
[10] See also Richard Broxton Onians, *The Origin of European Thought* (1951), p. 189, note 2.
[11] Augustine, *City of God*, Bk. XVIII, 45-46.

CHAPTER III. ON BEING RECEPTIVE

[1] Abot 1:1.
[2] Mo'ed Ḳatan 5a, Yeb. 21a, based on Lev. 18:30 and 22:9.

[3] 'Abodah Zarah 15b.
[4] S. Angus, *The Mystery Religions and Christianity* (1925), pp. 277f.
[5] Ignaz Golziher, *Mythology Among the Hebrews* (1877), p. 317.
[6] Berachot 8b. See I. H. Weiss, *Dor Dor Ve-Doreshav* (1924), pp. 14f.
[7] Ber. 58a.
[8] Baba Kama 82b.
[9] Sotah 9:14.
[10] See Saul Lieberman, *Hellenism in Jewish Palestine* (1950), pp. 100f.
[11] Meg. 1:8.
[12] *Ibid.*, 9b.
[13] Ludwig Blau, "Early Christian Epigraphy," in *Hebrew Union College Annual* (hereafter *H.U.C. Annual*) *I* (1924), p. 225.
[14] Shab. 75a.
[15] Menahot 99b. See also Sifre, ed. Friedmann (1864), p. 74a,b.
[16] Isaac Husik, *Philosophical Essays* (1952), pp. 11–12.
[17] See Thorleif Boman, *Das Hebräische Denken in Vergleich mit dem Griechischen* (1952), pp. 166f.
[18] Madariaga, *Essays with a Purpose* (1954), pp. 134f.
[19] See Cyrus H. Gordon, "Homer and Bible," in the *H.U.C. Annual XXVI,* pp. 43–108.
[20] See Joseph Klausner, "Judaea and Greece—Two Opposites?" (in Hebrew), in *Festschrift Armand Kaminka* (1937), pp. 49–58.
[21] *Mishneh Torah, Hilchot Yosede Ha-Torah,* 4:13.
[22] Hagigah 11:1.
[23] See the interesting decision of the noted cabalist Jacob Israel ben Raphael Finzi, Rabbi of Pesaro, 1540–1560, published by Simcha Asaf in *Sinai,* Vol. V, and included in his volume *Mekorot U-Mehkarim Be-Toledot Yisrael,* pp. 238ff.
[24] San. 29a.
[25] J. Shab. 3c.
[26] *Ibid.*
[27] See S. Zeitlin, "Les Dix-Huit Mesures," *Revue des Études Juives,* Vol. 68 (1914), pp. 22f.; *Jewish Quarterly Review* (hereafter *J.Q.R.*), XVI, p. 387; also A. Büchler, "The Levitical Impurity of the Gentile in Palestine Before the Year 70," *J.Q.R.*, XIII, pp. 39f.
[28] Hag. 15a.
[29] San. 99a.

CHAPTER IV. ON BEING DIFFERENT

[1] J. B. Pritchard, *Ancient Near Eastern Texts Relating to the Old Testament* (Princeton, 1950).
[2] W. F. Albright, *From the Stone Age to Christianity* (1940), p. 214. See also Adolphe Lods, *Israel* (1932), p. 148.
[3] Plutarch, *Lycurgus.*
[4] *Lives of Eminent Philosophers,* VI, 72; VII, 33 and 131.
[5] Fragment 15 in *Epictetus,* Loeb Class. Lib., II, 461.
[6] *Stromata,* Bk. III, 2.
[7] Yeb. 20a.
[8] Pesikta Rabbati, ed. M. Friedman, p. 185b.
[9] Nedarim 20a.
[10] Lev. Rabba 10:21.

[11] John J. I. Döllinger, *The Gentile and the Jew* (1906), II, 252.

[12] *Ibid.*, II, 289.

[13] Ḳid. 82a.

[14] Shab. 33a.

[15] *The Legacy of Egypt* (1942), p. 184.

[16] Ḳid. 49b.

[17] Frederick C. Grant, ed., *Hellenistic Religions* (1953), Intro., xxv.

[18] San. 10:1.

[19] Shab. 75a.

[20] E. R. Goodenough, *Jewish Symbols in the Greco-Roman Period* (1953), II, 160.

[21] Albright, *op. cit.*, p. 263.

[22] Shab. 156a,b.

[23] Ned. 32a. Gen. R. 44:14.

[24] 'Ab. Zar. 11b.

[25] Par. 181.

[26] Par. 200.

[27] Par. 201.

[28] Par. 202.

[29] Par. 204.

[30] Par. 203.

[31] Pars. 209–210.

[32] Par. 212.

[33] Pars. 15–16.

[34] Par. 8.

[35] From *The Book of the Dead*. See Pritchard, *op. cit.*, p. 36.

[36] J. M. Powis Smith, *The Origin and History of Hebrew Law* (1931), p. 37.

[37] Hyman E. Goldin, *Hebrew Criminal Law and Procedure* (1952), p. 54.

[38] B.Ḳ. 83b. Solomon Zeitlin, "The Pharisees and the Gospel" in *Essays and Studies* in Memory of Linda R. Miller (1938), pp. 240f.

[39] *Laws*, Bk. IX, 868.

[40] *Politics*, I, 3, 5, 8.

[41] *The Babylonian Laws*, by G. R. Driver and Sir John Charles Miles, (1952), p. 223.

[42] See Isaac Mendelsohn, *Slavery in the Ancient Near East* (1949), pp. 95–98.

[43] *Ibid.*, p. 123.

[44] 'Arakin 30 b.

[45] *Mechilta D'Rabbi Ishmael*, III, 5–6.

[45a] Ḳid. 22b.

[46] Giṭṭin 42b.

[47] Ḳid. 25a.

[48] Ketubot 68a.

[49] Baba Batra 8b.

[50] *Hilch. Mattenot 'Aniyim* 9:3.

[51] Ḥag. 5a.

[52] Yalḳuṭ, on I K. 7, par. 186.

[53] Maimonides, *Hilch. Mattenot 'Aniyim* 10:7–13; *Shulḥan 'Aruch, Yore De'ah, Hilch. Ẓedakah*, 249:6.

[54] B.B. 9b.

[55] Herodotus, *History*, II, 167.

[56] Cicero, *De Officiis*, I, 42.

[57] Tosef. Ber. 7:8.

[58] Tanḥuma, ed. Wilna, 52b.
[59] Pes. 118a.
[60] B.B. 110; Pes. 113a.
[61] *Midrash Ne'elam*, ed. Venice (1663), p. 7c.
[62] Ned. 49b.
[63] Abot 2:2.
[64] H. D. Griswold, *The Religion of the Rigveda* (1923), pp. 9, 20.
[65] *Republic*, V, 460.
[66] *First Apology*, Chaps. 27 and 29.
[67] Koran, Sura 6:150.
[68] *History*, I, 5.
[69] Jer. Peah., 15d.
[70] Bezah 32b. See also Yeb. 79a.
[71] Baba Mezi'a 4:10.
[72] *Ibid.*, 58b.
[73] See Cecil Roth, *The Jewish Contribution to Civilization* (1943), pp. 343f.
[74] Shab. 128b.
[75] See Com. of ibn-Ezra *ad. loc.*
[76] Ber. 40a.
[77] B.M. 85a. An interesting Responsum of Sherira Gaon (10 c.) on this subject is given in Franz Kohler's *A Treasury of Jewish Letters* (1953), I, 119–121.
[78] Makkot 1:10.
[79] *Ibid.*
[80] Josephus, *Antiquities*, XIII, 10:6; XX, 9:1.
[81] *The Legacy of Egypt* (1942), p. 206.
[82] Josephus, *The Jewish War*, I, 30:2f.
[83] Semaḥot. 2:9; San. 43a.
[84] San. 6:5. The court procedure is described in the Mishna Sanhedrin, Chaps. 4–6.
[85] Canticles Rabba 1:6; *Mechilta*, I, 8–9.
[86] Midrash Shoḥar Ṭob. on Ps. 4.
[87] *History*, V, 1f.
[88] Ex. R. 36:1.

CHAPTER V. ON CLINGING TO EMINENCE

[1] Arnold J. Toynbee, *A Study of History* (1939), IV, 262–263.
[2] *Ibid.*, V, 658.
[3] George Foot Moore, *Judaism*, I, 348–349.
[4] Vincent M. Scramuzza in "The Policy of the Early Roman Emperors Towards Judaism," Note XXV to F. J. Foakes Jackson and Kirsopp Lake's *The Beginnings of Christianity*, V, pp. 277–296.
[5] Toynbee, *op. cit.*, IV, 308.
[6] Friedrich Nietzsche, *The Birth of Tragedy*, in The Modern Library, p. 1027.
[7] Toynbee, *op. cit.*, I, 35, 90.
[8] Aurel Kolnai, *The War Against the West* (1938), pp. 509, 511.
[9] Shab. 128a.
[10] Sifre Dt. 33:26, ed. L. Finkelstein (1939), p. 422.

[11] Yoma 9b.
[12] Quoted from Louis Finkelstein's review of Johannes von Hempel's *Gott und Mensch im Alten Testament* in *J.Q.R.*, XXI, 329.
[13] *The Lives of the Caesars*, Bk. IV, *Gaius Caligula*, V–VI.
[14] Moore, *op. cit.*, I, 21.

CHAPTER VI. ON REJECTING TREASURES

[1] Otto J. Baab, *The Theology of the Old Testament* (1949), p. 270.
[2] F. J. Foakes Jackson and Kirsopp Lake, *The Beginnings of Christianity*, I, 288–289.
[3] *Test. of Joseph* 18:2 (2 c. B.C.).
[4] Abot 1:12.
[5] Tosef. Demai II, 18.
[6] *Ibid.*, II, 5, 16, 17.
[7] Tosef. 'Ab. Zar. III, 10.
[8] Demai 1:9.
[9] Tosef. Demai 2:3, 5; Bakorot 30b.
[10] Josephus, *Antiquities*, XIII, 11:5.
[11] *Ibid.*, XVIII, 1:3.
[12] *Ibid.*, XVIII, 4.
[13] Ed. Schechter, p. 82.
[14] See the author's essay "The 'Am Ha-areẓ in Soferic and Tannaitic Times," *Hebrew Union College Monthly*, Dec. 1914, Jan. 1915, Feb. 1915.
[15] Yoma 85b.
[16] J. Yoma 8:5.
[17] Josephus, *op. cit.*, XII, 8:3.
[18] Giṭ. 36a.
[19] Ḥag. 1:8.
[20] San. 71a.
[21] Sotah 9:9.
[22] Shab. 10b.
[23] From the Sabbath Day Ritual in the Prayer Book.
[24] A. Marmorstein, *Studies in Jewish Theology* (1950), p. 224.
[25] Maimonides, *Hilch. Yesode Ha-Torah*, 9:3; San. 90a.
[26] Jackson and Lake, *op. cit.*, I, Prologomena I (1939), Preface, p. vii.
[27] See the author's *Messianic Speculation in Israel* (1927), pp. 6, 16f.
[28] Abraham I. Katsh, *Judaism in Islam* (1954), p. xvi.
[29] *Against Heresies*, I, 26.
[30] *To the Magnesians*, X, 3.
[31] See Marmorstein, *op. cit.*, pp. 197f.
[32] *Mechilta*, III, 15.
[33] Gen. R. 44:1.
[34] Mak. 3:16.
[35] From the Prayer Book—a prayer composed probably before the common era.
[36] *Baruch*, 77, 13–16, ed. R. H. Charles.
[37] Gilbert Murray, in *The History of Christianity in the Light of Modern Knowledge* (1929), pp. 77–78.
[38] *Mishneh Torah, Hilch. Melachim*, Chap. 11 (ed. Rome, c. 1480).

CHAPTER VII. ON AVOIDING ALTERNATIVES

[1] Gen. R. 12:15.

[2] Ahad Ha-'Am, "Essays," in *Philosophia Judaica*, trans. Leon Simon, East and West Library (1946), pp. 128f.

[3] Sifra on Lev. 19:18.

[4] *Hilch. Abel* 14:1. See Isaac Herzog, "Maimonides as Halachist," in *Moses Maimonides VIIIth Memorial Volume* (1935), p. 149, note I.

[5] Ahad Ha-'Am, *op. cit.*, pp. 132–133.

[6] Abot 5:10.

[7] Sotah 14a.

[8] Eccl. R. 7:4.

[9] Sukkah 49b.

[10] B.M. 30b.

[11] Reinhold Niebuhr, *The Nature and Destiny of Man* (1948), p. 141.

[12] San. 4:5.

[13] Karl Barth, *Die Theologie und die Kirche* (1928), p. 354.

[14] Abot 4:15.

[15] *Ibid.*, 3:16.

[16] San. 11:2.

[17] *Jewish Encyclopedia*, VI, 353.

[18] 'Ab. Zar. 26b.

[19] San. 10:1f.; Maimonides, *Hilch. Teshubah* 3:6f.

[20] See Louis Finkelstein, *The Pharisees* (1938), pp. 78f.

[21] *A Study of History*, V, 387.

[22] *War and Civilization* (1950), Preface, p. xi.

[23] *'Ikkarim*, Chap. 42.

[24] San. 99a.

[25] Ber. 34b.

[26] San. 97b.

[27] See Israel Abrahams, *Some Permanent Values in Judaism* (1924), pp. 41–42.

[28] *Clement of Alexandria*, Loeb Class. Lib., pp. 291–299.

[29] San. 99b–100a.

[30] Ber. 9:5.

[31] Abot 5:22.

[32] San. 34a.

[33] Yeb. 11b; 24a.

[34] Ber. 7b.

[35] Sotah 47b; San. 58b.

[36] See Jacob Z. Lauterbach, "The Ancient Jewish Allegories in Talmud and Midrash," *J.Q.R.*, I, 281–333; 503–531.

[37] See Z. H. Chajes, *The Student's Guide Through the Talmud*, trans. Jacob Schecter (1952), pp. 233f.

[38] Abraham Halevi of Barcelona, *Sefer-Ha-Ḥinuch*, ed. Ḥayim Dov Shevel (1952), p. 639.

[39] Sotah 40.

[40] Cant. R. 2:14.

[41] Giṭ. 60a.

[42] J. Ma'asarot, III, 10.

[43] B.K. 2b; Hag. 10b.
[44] 'Ab. Zar. 19b.
[45] *The Kuzari*, III, 73.
[46] Yoma 9b.
[47] See Saul Lieberman, *Hellenism in Jewish Palestine* (1950), App. I, on "Bath Kol," p. 194.
[48] Yoma 21b.
[49] B.B. 12b.
[50] *Ibid.*
[51] B.B. 12a.
[52] B.M. 59b; Pes. 114a.
[53] Hag. 13a.
[54] See Esther R. 7:24: "The prophecy of the Gentiles is ambiguous. . . . The prophecy of the Jews is clear."

CHAPTER VIII. ON BEING REASONABLE

[1] B.B. 16a.
[2] Abot 3:18.
[3] *Ibid.*, 2:16.
[4] *IV Ezra* 9:15.
[5] Edwyn Bevan, *Stoics and Sceptics* (1913), p. 71.
[6] *The Book of Beliefs and Opinions*, IV, 3.
[7] Ber. 25b.
[8] Sotah 3:4.
[9] *Ibid.* 22b.
[10] 'Arak 8:4.
[11] Ket. 50.
[12] *Ibid.*, 50a.
[13] B.B. 11a.
[14] San. 106b.
[15] Ber. 6a.
[16] Pes. 50b.
[17] *Ibid.*
[18] Pes. 114b.
[19] Ber. 16b–17a.
[20] Kid. 39b.
[21] 'Ab. Zar. 10b, 17a, 18a.
[22] J. Ta'anit 1:4.
[23] *Hilch. De'ot* 1:6 and 2:3.
[24] *Ibid.*, 1:5.
[25] *Guide*, III, 54, pp. 396–397.
[26] *Ahad Ha-'Am*, ed. Leon Simon (1946), p. 148.
[27] Ber. 61b.
[28] *A Treasury of Jewish Letters*, ed. Franz Kohler, I, 186.
[29] San. 74a.
[30] *Ibid.*
[31] B.B. 60b.
[32] San. 74a.
[33] San. 74a,b. See note 6, p. 503, in Soncino ed; also Tosef. Sab. 15:17.
[34] Gen. R. 82:8.

[35] *To the Romans,* Chaps. 5–7.
[36] J. Shekalim 6:1.
[37] Bezah 25b.

CHAPTER IX. ON SOCIAL PROGRESS

[1] S. H. Butcher, *Some Aspects of the Greek Genius* (1929), pp. 133f.
[2] *Ibid.,* p. 165.
[3] *Politics,* VII, 10:1329b. 7.
[4] *Laws,* Bk. III, 676–677.
[5] Marcus Aurelius, *Meditations,* XI, 1; IV, 32.
[6] Thomas Whittaker, *The Neo-Platonists* (1928), p. 93.
[7] Ber. 17a.
[8] Kid. 40b.
[9] Aurelius, *op. cit.,* IV, 26.
[10] Theos Bernard, *Hindu Philosophy* (1947), p. 13.
[11] *The Shepherd of Hermas* (2 c.), Sim. I, Loeb Class. Lib., Apostolic Fathers, II, 139.
[12] Philo, *On Husbandry,* p. 65.
[13] Abot 4:16.
[14] Didache 10:6.
[15] Erich Dinkler, "Earliest Christianity," in *The Idea of History in the Ancient Near East* (1955), p. 210.
[16] *Medieval Islam* (1946), p. 239.
[17] Shab. 119b.
[18] *Ibid.,* 54b; 'Ab Zar. 18a.
[19] Lev. R. 28:1.
[20] Meg. 7a.
[21] Shab. 30b.

CHAPTER X. THAT MEN NEED TO BE SAVED

[1] Thomas Aquinas, *Basic Writings,* II, 655ff.
[2] *The Book of Beliefs and Opinions,* Yale Judaica Series, trans. Samuel Rosenblatt (1948), pp. 259ff.
[3] J. Ta'an. II, 1; Pesikta D'Rab Kahana 191a, ed. S. Buber (1868).
[4] Abot 4:13.
[5] *Ancient Near Eastern Texts,* Tablets VI–XI, p. 50.
[6] *Encyclopedia of Religion and Ethics,* IX, 562.
[7] W. R. Inge, in *The Legacy of Greece* (1922), p. 53.
[8] *IV Ezra* 7:118. See also 3:20; 4:30–31.
[9] *II Baruch* 54:15–19.
[10] W. B. Davis, *Paul and Rabbinic Judaism* (1938), p. 34.
[11] Cant. R. 5:2.
[12] Reinhold Niebuhr, *The Nature and Destiny of Man,* p. 145.
[13] A. Cohen, *The Psalms* (1945), p. 162.
[14] San. 104a; Sifre, Ha-azinu, Piska 329.
[15] Shab. 55a.
[16] Gen. R. 1–4.
[17] Ruth R. 6:4.

[18] *Ibid.*
[19] See H. A. Wolfson, *Philo*, II, 252b.
[20] Ber. 34b.
[21] Ambrose, *On Penitence*, II, 10.
[22] Tertullian, *On Repentance*, Chap. VII.
[23] *Ibid.*
[24] Ex. R. 19; Lam. R. 3.
[25] Ta'an 16a. See also Ecclus. 34:25-26.
[26] Ber. 60b. This is included in the Prayer Book.
[27] Niddah 30b.
[28] B.M. 107a.
[29] Harry M. Orlinsky, *Ancient Israel* (1954), pp. 161-162.
[30] Yoma 8:9.
[31] J. Ber. 9:1.
[32] Ta'an. 16a.
[33] *Mechilta*, ed. Lauterbach (1949), I, 34.
[34] *Ibid.*, I, 96.
[35] *Ibid.*, I, 252. Here one finds a noble apostrophe to faith which recalls Chap. 11 of Hebrews, in the New Testament.
[36] T. W. Arnold and Alfred Guillaume, *The Legacy of Islam*, p. 114.
[37] Bk. VII, 13:13.
[38] *Piers Plowman*, "The Vision of the Holy Church."
[39] Peah 1:1.
[40] San. 59.
[41] 'Ab. Zar. 17b.
[42] Lev. R. 37:7.
[43] Abot 1:17; Num. R. 14:10.
[44] Maimonides, *Guide*, III, 54, pp. 396-397. See I. Epstein, "Maimonides' Conceptions of the Law and the Ethical Trend of His Halachah," in *Moses Maimonides VIIIth Centenary Volume* (1935), pp. 62f.
[45] J. Ḥag. 1:7.
[46] The Prayer Book.
[47] Abot 3:16.
[48] *Ibid.* 2:16.

CHAPTER XI. THAT MEN SHOULD NOT ENJOY LIFE

[1] See the *Laws of Manu*, Chap. 6:42ff.
[2] See Clifford Herschel Moore, "Greek and Roman Ascetic Tendencies," in *Harvard Essays on Classical Subjects* (1912), p. 136.
[3] Ll. 74-76.
[4] W. K. C. Guthrie, *Orpheus and Greek Religion* (1935), p. 16.
[5] *Ibid.*, p. 156.
[6] *Laws*, Bk. X, 891.
[7] *Phaedo*, 66, 67, trans. B. Jowett.
[8] See A. Kaminka, "Les Rapports entre le Rabbinism et la Philosophie Stoicienne," in *Revue des Études Juives* (1926), pp. 233-252; and his article in *Keneset*, IV, 345-364.
[9] *Manual*, in Loeb Class. Lib. *Epictetus*, II, 495.
[10] Irenaeus, *Against Heresies*, XXVIII, 1.
[11] *Ibid.*, XXIV, 2.

[12] Melville Chaning-Pearce, "Sören Kierkegaard" in *Modern Christian Revolutionaries*, ed. D. Attwater (1947), Chap. 4.

[13] Walter Lowrie, *Kierkegaard* (1938), pp. 499–450.

[14] Ignaz Goldziher, *Mohammed and Islam* (1917), p. 155.

[15] Koran, Sura LVII, 19f.

[16] *Ibid.*, Sura V, 89:10.

[17] *Ibid.*, Sura LVII, 27.

[18] R. A. Nicholson, *A Literary History of the Arabs* (1930), p. 231.

[19] *Ibid.*, p. 233.

[20] Tennyson, *Becket*, Act V, Scene 1.

[21] Abot 6:2.

[22] Ta'an. 11b.

[23] *Ibid.*, 22b.

[24] Ber. 17a.

[25] Ta'an. 2:1.

[26] *Ibid.*, 11a.

[27] Ber. 6b.

[28] Ta'an. 11b. See *Shul. 'Aruch, Orah Hayim, Hilchot Ta'aniyot.* 57:1.

[29] See Isaac Aboab, *Menorat Ha-Maor*, Krotoschin (1848), III, 127; also p. 172.

[30] B.B. 60b.

[31] Ber. 31a.

[32] B.B. 60b.

[33] Josephus, *Antiquities*, Bk. XIX, Chap. 6; B.R. 91; Ber. 8; J. Ber. 7:2.

[34] Tos. Naz. 4; Ned. 9b.

[35] Yeb. 109b.

[36] J. Ned. IX:1.

[37] Ta'an. 11a.

[38] Maimonides, Mishneh Torah, *Hilch. Nezirut* 2:20.

[39] Gershom G. Scholem, *Major Trends in Jewish Mysticism* (1941), pp. 105–106.

[40] *Ibid.*, p. 230.

[41] Yeb. 63a.

[42] *Ibid.*, 63b.

[43] Ber. 10a.

[44] Shab. 31a.

[45] Kid. 20b.

[46] Yoma 1:1.

[47] Yeb. 63b.

[48] *War of the Jews*, Bk. II, Chap. 8:2.

[49] *Ibid.*, Bk. II, Chap. 8:13.

[50] Shab. 33b.

[51] Abot 2:5.

[52] Tanh. Mishapatim, 2.

[53] Ta'an. 11a.

[54] *Ibid.* See also Elijahu R. Chap. 20.

[55] Ber. 32b.

[56] Hag. 22b.

[57] B.K. 91b.

[58] *First Apology of Justin*, Chap. 29.

[59] Lev. R. 34:3.

[60] See Franz Rosenthal, "A Judaeo-Arabic Work Under Sufic Influence," *H.U.C. Annual*, XV (1940), 433–484; see S. D. Goitein, "A Jewish Addict to Sufism," *J.Q.R.*, XLIV (1953), pp. 37–47.

[61] See the author's *Messianic Speculation in Israel*, pp. 50–57.

[62] Saadia, *The Book of Beliefs and Opinions*, p. 367.

[63] *Ibid.*, p. 393.

[64] *Ibid.*, p. 395.

[65] *Ibid.*, p. 387.

[66] Bahya, *Hovot Ha-Lebabot, Sha-'ar Ha-Perishut*, ed. A. Ziproni (1928), p. 244.

[67] *Ibid.*, pp. 250–255.

[68] Ber. 3a; see Rosh commentary *ad loc.*; *Tur Orah Hayim*, Chap. 1.

[69] Tur. 571:1.

[70] See the author's *Messianic Speculation in Israel*, Chaps. III, IV, and Asaf in *Zion* V, 117 and 124.

[71] *Sefer Hasidim*, ed. Jehuda Wistinetzki (1924), par. 984, p. 242.

[72] *Ibid.*, par. 986.

[73] *Ibid.*, par. 1006.

[74] *Ibid.*, par. 1661.

[75] *Ibid.*, par. 1556.

[76] Scholem, *op. cit.*, pp. 103–105.

[77] *Sha'are Teshubah*, Chaps. 1of.

[78] S. Schechter, *Studies in Judaism*, 2nd. ser. (1908), p. 242.

[79] 'Ab. Zar. 20b.

[80] *Sha'are Kedushah*, p. 17.

[81] Schechter, *op. cit.*, pp. 292–301.

[82] *Shibhe Ha-Ari*, ed. Koretz (1785), p. 32b.

[83] *Mesillat Yesharim*, Jewish Pub. Soc. (1936), trans. Mordecai M. Kaplan, p. 118.

[84] *Ibid.*, p. 124.

[85] *Ibid.*, p. 125.

[86] *Ibid.*, p. 129.

[87] *Ibid.*, p. 130.

[88] *Ibid.*, p. 133.

[89] *Ibid.*, p. 134.

[90] *Ibid.*, p. 162.

[91] *Ibid.*, p. 169.

[92] Shab. 30b.

[93] *Shibhe Ha-Besht*, ed. Berdichev (1815), p. 809.

[94] See Isaac Werfel, *Sefer Ha-Hasidut* (1947), p. 60a.

[95] *Ibid.*, p. 38a.

[96] *Ibid.*, p. 10b.

[97] *Ibid.*, p. 23a.

[98] *Mishneh Torah, De'ot*, 3:1.

[99] *Guide*, II, 39, p. 232.

[100] *Kuzari*, II, p. 113, trans. Hartwig Hirschfeld (1927).

[101] *Ibid.*, III, p. 22a.

[102] Ber. 5a.

[103] *Ibid.*, 5b.

[104] B.M. 85a.

[105] Maimonides, Mishneh Torah, *Hilch. Yesode Ha-Torah*, 5:10–11.

[106] Ber. 5b.
[107] Abot 6:4.
[108] Ex. R. 313.
[109] B.B. 116a.
[110] 'Erub. 41b.
[111] *Zohar, Terumah* II, p. 165a.
[112] Gen. R. 9:7. See also Yoma 69b.
[113] Sifre on Dt. 6:5.
[114] *Zohar*, ed. Soncino (1934), III, 80B, also III, 63a,b.
[115] San. 91a,b.
[116] Ber. 9:5.
[117] *Ibid.*, 43b; Tos. Ber. 7:4.
[118] Gen. R. 13:2.
[119] *Nature in Greek Poetry* (1939), pp. 2, 146, 154, 158, 47, 176, 191, 194.
[120] S. H. Butcher, *Some Aspects of the Greek Genius*, p. 250.
[121] *Ibid.*, p. 254.
[122] Ps. 8, 19, 29, 65, 104, 107. On a comparison between Ps. 104 and *The Hymn to the Aton*, see Moses Buttenwieser, The Psalms (1938), pp. 158–161: "Its dependence upon the Hymn to the Sun notwithstanding, Psalm 104 is poetically incomparably superior to it, being in fact a new creation which bears throughout the stamp of the distinct genius of Israel." It is noteworthy that this single Egyptian approximation to a great nature hymn comes from one who most closely approximated monotheism.
[123] Verses 35–68.
[124] J. Ḳid. 2:65d.
[125] 'Erub. 54a.

CHAPTER XII. THAT MEN ARE NOT EQUAL

[1] S. Davis, *Race-Relations in Ancient Egypt* (1952), p. 2.
[2] Isocrates, *Panegyricus*, 50.
[3] *Ibid.*, 149, 150; *To Philip*, 132, 139.
[4] *Iphigenia in Aulis*, 1400–1401.
[5] *Menexenus*, Steph. 245.
[6] Targum Jonathan on Gen. 2:7.
[7] *Mechilta*, III, 157.
[8] San. 44a.
[9] *Sifre*, ed. Friedmann, p. 134a.
[10] Yeb. 77a.
[11] Ber. 28a.
[12] Kid. 4:1.
[13] *Ibid.*, 75a.
[14] *Ibid.*, 71a.
[15] *Ibid.*, 72b.
[16] J. Peah VIII, 21b.
[17] Kid. 70b.
[18] *Ibid.*, 71a.
[19] *Ibid.*, 70b.
[20] *Ibid.*, 71b. See also on the taunting of King David, Ruth R. 8:1.
[21] J. San. 4:11.

[22] See Nahum N. Glazer, *Franz Rosenzweig: His Life and Thought* (1953), p. 301.

[23] Ex. R. 32:1; Tanḥuma Num. ed. Buber (1913), p. 76.

[24] Mid. Tanḥ. on that verse.

[25] 'Ab. Zar. 2b.

[26] See Canticles R. on vv. 1-4.

[27] Num. R. 3:2.

[28] Giṭ. 5:8.

[29] *Ibid.*, 61a.

[30] *Ibid.*, 5:5.

[31] Tos. B.K. 10:15.

[32] See Ivan Engnell, *Studies in Divine Kingship in the Ancient Near East* (1943), pp. 4f.

[33] See H. Frankfort, *Kingship and the Gods* (1948), p. 297.

[34] See E. A. Speiser, "Authority and Law in Mesopotomia," *Jour. Am. Orient. Soc.*, July–Sept., 1954, p. 8.

[35] Yaë Kichi Yabè, *Japan*, Dec. 1915. Quoted in Post Wheeler's *The Sacred Scriptures of the Japanese* (1952), Intro., p. xiii.

[36] Maimonides, *Sefer Ha-Miẓvot*, Positive Commandment 173.

[37] See the author's *Democratic Impulse in Jewish History* (1938), pp. 4f.

[38] *Ibid.*, p. 6.

[39] *Ibid.*, pp. 15–16.

[40] *Seder Eliyahu Raba*, XV, 3.

[41] Abot 4:4; Derech Ereẓ Zuṭa, Chap. I.

[42] Ḥul. 92a.

[43] Abot D'Rabbi Nathan, Chap. 16.

[44] Pes. 49b.

[45] Ket. 111b.

[46] Lev. R. 9:3.

CHAPTER XIII. THAT MEN ARE NOT FREE

[1] See *Catholic Encyclopedia*, "Predestination."

[2] John Calvin, *Instruction in Faith*, trans. Paul T. Fuhrmann (1949), pp. 36–37.

[3] Sura X, 99f.

[4] Sura XVI, 95.

[5] Sura II, 284.

[6] Mak. 10b.

[7] Abot 3.

[8] B.B. 16a.

[9] Nid. 16b; Ber. 33b.

[10] *Ḥobot Ha-Lebabot*, 3:8.

[11] *Hilch. Teshubah.*, Chaps. 5, 6.

[12] See *Hasagot Ha-Rabad* to Maimonides, *Hilch. Teshubah*, Chap. 5, end.

[13] *The Book of Beliefs and Opinions*, IV, 4, p. 188.

[14] Bk. 5:20.

[15] *Emunah Ramah*, ed. S. Weil (1919), pp. 96–97.

[16] *Milḥamot Adonai*, III, 4.

[17] L. K. Frank, *Cultural Determinism and Free Will* (1951), p. 26.
[18] Abot 6:2.

CHAPTER XIV. THAT MEN SHOULD NOT RESIST EVIL

[1] *The Book of Tao*, XXXVIII. See *The Wisdom of Lao-Tse*, trans. Lin Yutang (1949).
[2] *The Book of Tao*, XVI.
[3] *Ibid.*, XXIX.
[4] *Ibid.*, XVIII.
[5] *The Mask of Anarchy.*
[6] Ber. 58a.
[7] Encyclopedia of Religion and Ethics, XII, 675.
[8] *Politics* 1:8.
[9] *Bhagavad-gita*, trans. Swami Prabhavananda and Christopher Isherwood (1951), pp. 40, 44. See also Append. II.
[10] Koran 66:39.
[11] *Mechilta* II, 262.

CHAPTER XV. THAT DEATH IS BETTER THAN LIFE

[1] Sophocles, *Oedipus at Colonus*, 1225f.
[2] Tosef. Sab. 16:17.
[3] Otto J. Baab, *The Theology of the Old Testament* (1949), p. 200.
[4] San. 10:1.
[5] Ber. 5:2.
[6] Sotah 9:15.
[7] Ber. 1:5.
[8] Sotah 9:15.
[9] Shab. 39b.
[10] J. G. Frazer, *Adonis, Attis, Osiris* (1919), II, 5.
[11] Hag. 2:1.
[12] Abot 4:17.
[13] Albo, *Book of Roots*, IV, Chaps, 39–40.
[14] Solomon Zeitlin, *Introduction to the Second Book of the Maccabees* (1954), p. 55.
[15] W. F. Albright, *From the Stone Age to Christianity*, pp. 287–288.
[16] J. San. 10:1.
[17] San. 10:1.
[18] Élie Faure, *History of Art* (1921), I, 36–38.
[19] Book of Jubilees 22:16–17.
[20] E. A. Wallis Budge, *The Papyrus of Ani* (1913), p. 56. See also J. G. Frazer, *The Golden Bough*, VI, 15–16.
[21] W. K. C. Guthrie, *The Greeks and Their Gods* (1953), p. 115.
[22] Suk. 5a.
[23] *Enoch* 18:12–16.
[24] *Ibid.*, 27:1–5.
[25] Kohler, *Heaven and Hell* (1923), p. 122.
[26] 'Eduyyot 2:10.
[27] J. Bikkurim 2:1; J. San. 11:7; Sab. 89b.

[28] San. 90a,b.
[29] B.B. 16a.
[30] Ecclus. 41:3-4.
[31] *Ibid.*, 41:13.
[32] Eccles. R. 7:8; J. Ḥag. 2:1.
[33] Crescas, *Or Adonai*, III, Kelal 2 and 4.
[34] Albo, *op. cit.*, I, Chap. 29:31.
[35] *Ibid.*, I, 15. See also I, 26.
[36] Bevan, *Jerusalem Under the High Priests* (1948), pp. 83-84.
[37] R. W. Livingstone, *The Pageant of Greece* (1928), p. 23.
[38] Abot 1:3, attributed to Antigonus of Socho, 2 c. B.C.
[39] 'Ab. Zar. 19a.
[40] Ned. 62a; *Sifre*, Chap. 48, ed. Friedmann (1864), p. 84b.
[41] Abot 4:5.
[42] *Ibid.*, 1:13.
[43] *Sifre, ibid.*, Ned. 62a.
[44] *Comm. on Mishna, Sanhedrin*, Chap. 10, Mishneh Torah, *Hilch. Teshubah*
10:1b.
[45] Abot 4:2, attributed to Simeon b. Azzai (2 c.).
[46] Semaḥot 6:11. See Saul Lieberman, *Hellenism in Jewish Palestine*, pp.
164-5.
[47] Kelim 8.
[48] Pes. 50a; B.B. 10b.
[49] H. A. Fischel, "Martyr and Prophet," *J.Q.R.*, XXXVII, p. 375.
[50] *Against the Galileans*, Loeb Class. Lib. "Julian" Ill, p. 415.
[51] Koran, Sura XLV, 10-39.
[52] Ber. 17a.
[53] Mo. Ḳ. 27b.
[54] J. Sheḳ. 2:5; Gen. R. 82:10.

CHAPTER XVI. DIFFERENCES AND UNDERLYING UNITY

[1] *Judaism*, I, 285.

INDEX